●

Also written or co-written by Michael McLaughlin

The Silver Palate Cookbook

The Manhattan Chili Co. Southwest American Cookbook

The New American Kitchen

The Back of the Box Gourmet

The El Paso Chile Company's Texas Border Cookbook

Fifty-two Meat Loaves

food

for the

best of

times

cooking for the weekend

Michael McLaughlin

simon & schuster

new york london toronto sydney tokyo singapore

SIMON & SCHUSTER
Simon & Schuster Building
Rockefeller Center
1230 Avenue of the Americas
New York, New York 10020

Designed by Bonni Leon-Berman

Manufactured in the United States of America

1   3   5   7   9   10   8   6   4   2

Library of Congress Cataloging-in-Publication Data

McLaughlin, Michael.
Cooking for the weekend : food for the best of times / Michael McLaughlin.
p.   cm.
Includes index.
1. Cookery.   I. Title.
TX715.M47434   1993
641.5—dc20   92-38950
CIP

ISBN: 0-671-72578-5

For my parents
Jim and Shirley,
seven days a week

ACKNOWLEDGMENTS

Among the many tasters who happily volunteered as guinea pigs, knowing full well the kind of tense kitchen drama involved in bringing a menu testing to its conclusion, I would especially like to thank Pip and Dick Stromgren; Janet, Greg, and Jonathan Grenzke; Dave and Judy Radebaugh; John Boyajian and family; Arthur Schwartz and Bob Harned; Jasper White; Rose Levy Beranbaum; and Nicole Routhier.

Among colleagues and friends who graciously allowed me permission to use their recipes, or provided unknowing inspiration for my penchant for adaptation, I thank Jasper White, Patricia Wells, Susan Herrmann Loomis, Nicholas Malgieri, Adrienne Welch, Christopher Styler, Pamela Morgan, Florence Fabricant, Michele Scicolone, Gerry Cohen, Adrienne Dahncke, and Ricki Carroll.

At Simon & Schuster I have nothing but praise for both publisher Linda Cunningham and editor Toula Polygalaktos, who have shown remarkable empathy and support for a book not of their own choosing. For Kerri Conan, who did do the choosing, I have thanks and also regrets that we didn't get to finish this one together.

Without the continued support—moral, artistic, and financial—of Bob and Susan Lescher (and the limitless good cheer of Carolyn Larson), I could surely continue to write, but it wouldn't be half so rewarding.

Thanks also go to everyone at *Bon Appétit*, but especially to Barbara Fairchild, who keeps me thinking and working in menus; thanks to Johanne Killeen and George Germon for the green tomatoes, among other favors; major thanks to Francine (The Caterer) Maroukian, Nancy Hoffman, and Michael Honstein, who always take my calls, no matter what mood I'm in.

And to Lou, Lisa, Sally, and Amelia Ekus, very special thanks indeed, for the grill and the kitchen and for all those wonderful weekends.

contents

introduction 15

saturday lunches

summer 20
fall 36
winter 52
spring 67

company on saturday night

summer 84
fall 110
winter 132
spring 152

sunday breakfasts and brunches

summer 170
fall 183
winter 198
spring 214

later on sunday

summer 228
fall 248
winter 271
spring 283

tgif 301

cook's and gardener's sources 317

index 323

"Food for pleasure, and not just nourishment, is best cooked in one's own kitchen and eaten with the feet under one's own table."

—Nicholas Freeling,
The Kitchen Book (1970)

INTRODUCTION

Welcome to the weekend. *This* is living—an unencumbered two days of cooking, food, and friends. In the kitchen—the rec room of the 1990s—the weekend lets us make food for the fun of it. Freed from the frustrations of those hasty little end-of-the-workday suppers, we can fulfill all our long-simmered culinary fantasies.

Fifty-two times a year, as the seasons turn and as our hungers ebb and flow, the weekend clears a place for us in the crowded schedule of life. Permission is granted to self-indulge, to do the things we want to do for as long as we want to do them. Now is the time for slow-cooked stews and long-risen breads, sweet spontaneous snacks and loving gifts of food, put up in season for family and friends. In summer or in winter, at home in the sweltering city or playing it cool at the shore, for forty-eight hours or so (less time spent sleeping in, napping in a hammock, or daydreaming by the fire), we have all the time in the world to cook up fabulous food. For one meal or for many, for a few close friends or for a busy houseful of company, a weekend spent even partially in the kitchen is a weekend enjoyed to the fullest.

My weekends officially begin with Saturday lunch. I urge you to find time—in the midst of too much to do, errands to run, closets to clean, and gardens to weed—for a light, lively, and relatively simple lunch—a meal all the more welcome because it is so unexpected. Saturday lunches are informal food—tacos, calzones, overstuffed sand-wiches, and big bowls of thick, hot soup. Desserts are kept simple—fresh fruit, store-bought ice cream, and homemade cookies. Such menus are zesty and brief, leaving plenty of time to wash the car, head off to the movies, jog down to the beach, or slip out to finish the Christmas shopping. There's even time to head back to the kitchen, in case there's more good eating ahead.

Saturday night is the time for company. If ever one night of the week were traditionally dedicated to having a great time, it's Saturday. Sundown signals a mysterious, urgent beat, a compulsion to mix and mingle. Saturday menus are serious, multicourse affairs served to a modest crowd, and whether they take place on Midsummer Night's Eve around a smoking back-yard grill or in a candlelit dining room during the first blanketing snowfall of the year, zesty appetizers and elegant desserts, green salads and cheese boards, good wines, rich coffee, and relaxed conversation are the order of the day.

Sundays start slow. It takes a lot of time to read the Sunday papers from front to back, and no one wants to climb out of a big, soft bed until breakfast is on the table. Still, someone has to do the work, and a batch of sweet, warm sticky buns, a plate of blueberry flapjacks, a thick and steaming bowl of multigrain porridge, and stacks of hot, buttery toast make it all worthwhile. Such Sunday meals can be family breakfasts, Dad whipping up his special omelets, fuel for the rest of the day (the last half of the weekend!), or they can be dressy brunches, relaxed but elegant, invited company dining on chicken hash or caviar-stuffed potatoes, all of it celebrated to the popping sound of champagne corks and a little quiet Vivaldi, perhaps, on the CD player.

Later on Sunday the weekend becomes free-form. It's a fragile time, and biorhythm experts warn that the "Sunday blues" can sneak up on even the jolliest celebrant. Now is the time for sweet inspiration. A batch of fudge or warm granola cookies or a plate of maple-glazed cider donuts will lift everyone's spirits. On Super Bowl Sunday the menu is peanuts, chili dogs, and chocolate-dipped malted ice cream cones; while on Easter it's a roast leg of lamb with all the springtime trimmings. As the weekend meanders to its inevitable conclusion, the meals can also become smaller, cozier affairs, the last quiet islands of indulgence before Monday morning's reality intrudes. Bistro-style stuffed cabbage, a steaming sausage and polenta casserole, or homey meat loaf and potatoes will all nourish and fortify against the busy week ahead.

Life, of course, is not an AT&T commercial and my name is not Martha. I'm realistic enough to know that weekends, as often as not, are spent with cranky, teething babies or a briefcase full of extra work from the office, or merely curled up mindlessly in a chair, reading the latest Danielle Steel or Tom Clancy novel from cover to cover, fueled by little more than carry-out pizza and light beer. Everyone needs to plotz once in a while, and I would be the first to give my stamp of approval to such regularly scheduled dropping out.

Weekends, though, are what we make them, and when you want to make them special, this book will help. Along with Saturday lunches, Saturday night parties, Sunday breakfasts and brunches, and later-on-Sunday events of all kinds, you'll find my strategies for organizing and serving a weekend's worth of meals. "Guests," to me, means "volunteers," and with a renewed and lively interest in cooking, everyone is willing to chip in on some onerous kitchen task or other. There's plenty of do-ahead advice, too, in case you're a kitchen brigade of one. Since time in the kitchen also means time to cook up things never dreamed of during the week, there are plenty of kitchen projects sprinkled throughout the book. When tomatoes are abundant and in prime shape, make your own dried tomatoes (considerably cheaper than store-bought). Put up a batch of chicken stock, turn Concord grapes into delicious jelly, get the kids to help make a roaster full of crunchy granola, or steep lemon peel in good vodka for tomorrow morning's brunch. Since people always nibble, I've included suggestions on using leftovers wisely, and several longer sections give my advice on turning out the perfect green salad, composing a cheese board, making a great cup of coffee, or coping with a country ham—weekend know-how of the most practical kind. If your weekend starts at 5:00 P.M. Friday, there's even TGIF—a section of quick and stylish main courses that can help get you into the kitchen at the earliest possible moment. And should you need, the book concludes with a mail order section for ingredients and equipment, plus seeds for the home gardener, all chosen to help you have the best weekend possible.

As if we needed any more reason to celebrate two days off with plenty of time, good food, and stimulating company to enjoy, ask yourself: Why is a week seven days long? For years it has seemed to scientists to be merely a religious or a sociological determination, having little to do with any natural phenomenon. But Franz Halberg, the "father" of chronobiology, believes there are deep-seated natural cycles that compel us toward the seven-day week. "They are in our genes," Dr. Halberg has said, "and it is very big news." Very big—and very good—news indeed.

saturday lunches

summer spaghetti "alla carbonara"

arugula and watercress salad with

red wine vinaigrette

peaches and ice cream with blueberry-lime sauce

Summer weekends are the best weekends. I always kick off at least one high summer weekend with this Saturday lunch, a menu that takes advantage of corn, tomatoes, basil, and berries at their respective peaks of seasonal perfection.

strategy

With the prime ingredients already at hand, this menu goes together quickly, most of it just before it gets eaten. Clean the salad greens (15 cups greens, half arugula and half watercress) and then prepare the pasta. Toss the salad (dress it with olive oil and red wine vinegar, according to the directions for Basic Mixed Green Salad with Vinaigrette on page 23) and serve it with the pasta (but on separate plates), or present it afterward, with fresh goat's-milk or sheep's-milk cheese and more bread if you like. Any good bread will do, by the way, although focaccia (homemade, page 32, or purchased) is particularly apt. You should cook and chill the blueberry sauce in advance, but slice the peaches and garnish the dessert just before serving. Drink a cold, well-balanced Sauvignon Blanc or a lightly chilled Valpolicella.

●

summer spaghetti ''alla carbonara''

serves 6

This recipe breaks all the rules for the classic Italian dish of pasta, eggs, unsmoked belly bacon (*pancetta*), and cheese, hence the qualifier in the title. Still, it is delicious, quick, and a proper celebration of prime summertime ingredients. Choose one of the new super-sweet corn hybrids, so that the tender kernels will be cooked by the heat of the spaghetti. For a thoroughly different (also not authentic) but equally delicious plate of pasta, try this recipe with *pancetta* in place of the smoked bacon.

1 pound slab bacon, trimmed and cut into ¼-inch dice
1 pound dried semolina spaghetti, preferably imported
1 tablespoon salt
6 ears super-sweet corn, shucked
3 eggs
½ cup freshly grated Parmesan cheese, plus additional cheese to pass at the table
1 pound (about 5) ripe plum tomatoes, cored and cut into ¼-inch dice
½ cup finely julienned fresh basil, plus additional sprigs for garnish
Freshly ground black pepper

In a cold skillet set the bacon over medium heat and cook, stirring occasionally, until crisp and brown, about 10 minutes. With a slotted spoon, transfer the bacon to absorbent paper to drain.

Bring a large pot of water to a boil. Stir in the spaghetti and the salt and cook, stirring once or twice, until the pasta is just tender, 8 to 10 minutes.

Meanwhile, cut the kernels off each of the ears of corn, holding each ear over a large bowl. With the back of the knife, scrape the juices off each cob into the bowl with the kernels. Whisk in the eggs and ½ cup Parmesan. Stir in the tomatoes and basil.

Quickly drain the spaghetti. It is important that the pasta remain piping hot; it need not be completely free of cooking water. Add the hot pasta all at once to the bowl with the corn mixture and toss well. Add the bacon, season generously with black pepper, and toss again.

Divide the pasta among plates, garnish with sprigs of basil, and serve immediately, passing the remaining cheese at the table.

peaches and ice cream with blueberry-lime sauce

serves 6

If the peaches are thin-skinned, perfectly ripe, and free from spots, they won't need to be peeled.

3 cups fresh blueberries, picked over and rinsed
¼ cup sugar
¼ cup crème de cassis (black currant liqueur)
2 tablespoons fresh lime juice, strained
1 tablespoon arrowroot
8 medium peaches
2 pints (about) premium vanilla ice cream, softened
Thin lime slices and fresh mint sprigs, for garnish

In a small nonreactive saucepan combine the blueberries, sugar, crème de cassis, and lime juice. Cook over medium heat, stirring often, until most of the berries have burst and the mixture is juicy, about 7 minutes. Remove from the heat, stir in the arrowroot, and cool to room temperature. In a food processor, purée the blueberry sauce until smooth. Transfer to a container, cover, and refrigerate until cold, at least 5 hours. *The sauce can be prepared up to 3 days ahead.*

Over moderate heat bring a medium saucepan of water to a simmer. Cut a small, shallow "X" in the tip of each peach. Working in batches, lower the peaches into the simmering water with a slotted spoon. Turn the peaches in the water for 1 minute, then transfer them to a bowl of cold water.

Peel the peaches (the skins should pull off easily). Halve and pit them and cut each half into 4 slices. On dessert plates arrange the sliced peaches in a fan-shaped arc. Center a scoop of ice cream within the arc of peaches. Spoon the blueberry sauce over each scoop of ice cream, using about ⅓ cup per serving and allowing the sauce to run off the ice cream and across the peaches. Garnish each plate with lime slices and mint sprig, and serve immediately.

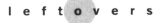

leftovers

Unused blueberry sauce is good over yogurt, fresh berries, or fruit-filled crêpes.

BASIC MIXED GREEN SALAD WITH VINAIGRETTE

Americans adore salads but are very bad at making them. I'm talking about green salads here, and I'm thinking of a wedge of pale green, bland, and crunchy iceberg smothered under a viscous technicolor ooze of bottled catalina, thousand island, or ranch (whatever that means) dressing. This is mostly fifties and sixties stuff, of course, what I grew up eating (don't call my mother—she knows how I feel). If you've found your way to the front of the line at a major salad bar recently, however, you'll know such practices persist across much of the country.

But tastes are changing. Acquired French and Italian finesse have led some of us to treat our salads with a little more respect, and the increasingly varied greens we're finding at the market are deserving of that TLC. While some of the more fragile, exotic, and expensive of baby European lettuces may not yet be offered for sale at the A&P, the days when durable iceberg was the only choice are long gone. Among the most reliable alternative sources for greens these days are farmers' markets, health food stores—hothouse-grown organic greens being a lively new industry—and the nearest home garden. (See my Cook's and Gardener's Sources for seed companies specializing in salad seeds.) A well-made salad of varied greens, deftly and lightly dressed with good oil and vinegar, served up with style, often as a course of its own, is a practice finally gaining popularity in weekend kitchens all over America.

There is good eating as well as a certain amount of showmanship in tossing such a salad (in other, quainter, times, making the salad, like carving the roast, was the special province of the patriarch and was performed at the head of the table under the awed gaze of family and guests; today everyone chips in). While there's a trick or two to arriving at the perfect salad, it's a surprisingly easy thing to pull off.

A credible salad can be composed starring a single green, or combining three to five greens of contrasting textures, tastes, and colors. It can be a lively mélange, such as the classic Provençal mixture of foraged and cultivated baby lettuces called *mesclun* (from the Niçoise *mesclumo*, or mélange). As with all produce shopping, it is wise to remain flexible and to purchase only those greens in excellent condition. Variety is always pleasing to the eye and the palate, but quality is ultimately more important.

Greens are perishable, quickly falling prey to extended storage in their original plastic wrappings. Ideally they should be consumed the day purchased (and purchased the day harvested), but reality often intrudes. To keep greens successfully, first separate the heads or bunches, discarding any tough or brown outer leaves. Soak and then rinse the greens thoroughly in cool water. Dry them completely (I recommend a rotary salad spinner, preferably one with a pull-string action; see Cook's and Gardener's Sources).

Wrap the moisture-free greens loosely in paper towels, tuck the towels into plastic bags, and *partially* close the bags. Store the bagged greens in the crisper section of the refrigerator for up to two days, if necessary. Pick through the greens for wilted leaves, remove any tough stems or ribs, and tear the greens into bite-sized pieces, if desired, just before dressing them.

Since we are talking simple green salads here, the list of ingredients for the dressing is necessarily brief. Excellent (imported) olive oil, either light or lusciously green and heavy (cook's choice), or a combination of olive and walnut oils; excellent (imported) red wine, balsamic, sherry, or white wine vinegars (or, on occasion, a berry- or an herb-flavored vinegar); coarse kosher or sea salt; and freshly ground black pepper are the four essentials.

Prepare 2 to 2½ cups of bite-sized greens for each diner. Gently mix the greens in a large bowl (one large enough to accommodate them while they are tossed about). Drizzle the greens generously with oil and toss thoroughly. (The oil protects the greens from the wilting effects of both salt and vinegar.) Season with salt (coarse salt dissolves more slowly and thus will take longer to wilt the greens) and toss again. Drizzle the greens lightly with about one-third as much vinegar as oil (if you have successfully coated the greens with oil you will see the vinegar standing in beads on the oiled leaves) and toss again. Taste and adjust the seasonings. Then add such options as a cup or two of fresh herb leaves, especially milder-flavored herbs like basil, dill, parsley, or mint. Or scatter crumbled blue or goat cheese or toasted walnuts or pecans over the greens. Finally grind fresh pepper generously over the salad and toss one last time. (Edible flowers, such as pansies and nasturtiums, are best sprinkled over the salad after it has been plated, to keep them intact and to ensure that they can be seen and appreciated.) Serve the salad more or less immediately. If you have successfully dried the greens and if you have dressed them skillfully, there will be no dressing remaining in the bottom of the bowl, but each bite will be perfectly balanced between the tastes of the greens, the oil, and the vinegar.

jasper white's lobster and corn chowder

old bay slaw (page 69)

cheddar-dill scones with honey mustard butter

shaker lemon pie

When lobster and sweet corn are at their most abundant and affordable, this New England shore dinner features one way to combine and enjoy both prime ingredients in one spectacular and easy dish.

strategy

Begin the dessert well in advance, since the sliced lemons must macerate with the sugar for a full 24 hours for the pie not to be bitter. I like a bracing lemon dessert after a seafood main course, but Berry Picker's Pie (page 107) or Strawberry-Rhubarb-Crumble (page 299) would make excellent substitutes. The slaw can be assembled a day in advance. The chowder can be started several hours ahead, but it must be completed and the scones must be baked at the last minute. Although the main course comes hot and fresh off the stove, this menu is worth serving outdoors, if only to help recreate the particular stretch of Maine coast that inspired the feast—some foods should be eaten under an open sky.

•

jasper white's lobster and corn chowder

serves 4

White, at his Boston restaurant Jasper's, serves up food that is at once gutsy and elegant, always celebrating the best ingredients New England has to offer. As he points out in the introduction to this recipe, printed in his book, *Jasper White's Cooking from New England* (HarperCollins), he utilizes "native butter and sugar corn, Vermont corncob-smoked bacon, the first new potatoes and onions of the year, Maine lobsters and unprocessed sweet cream from Guilford, Vermont." Even when made with slightly less impeccable ingredients, the dish is a wonder. Pour a chilled, not too dry Sauvignon Blanc or Samuel Adams beer.

Salt
4 small (1-pound) lobsters
3 quarts water
6 ears sweet corn, shucked
8 ounces smoky slab bacon with rind
8 fresh thyme sprigs
1 teaspoon whole black peppercorns
4 bay leaves
1 medium yellow onion, peeled
3 cups diced (¾-inch) yellow onions
½ stick (4 tablespoons) unsalted butter
1 pound (8 or 9) new red-skinned potatoes, cut into ⅓-inch-thick slices
1½ cups whipping cream
Freshly ground black pepper
Minced chives, for garnish

Bring a large pot of water (there should be enough to completely cover the lobsters when they are added) to a boil. Stir in 1 tablespoon salt. Add the lobsters and cook for exactly 3 minutes after the water returns to a boil. Drain. When the lobsters are cool enough to handle, break off the tails and claws.

Crack the claws and arms and carefully remove all the meat; do not discard the shells. Cut the tails in half lengthwise and remove the intestinal tracts. Cut the meat into bite-sized pieces. Refrigerate all the meat, covered.

In a large pan cover the remaining lobster shells and bodies with 3 quarts water. Bring to a simmer. Cut the corn from the cobs (there should be about 3½ cups) and reserve; add the cobs to the pan with the lobster bodies. Cut the rind from the bacon and add it to the pan. Pick the thyme leaves from the stems and reserve; add the stems to the pan with the lobster bodies. Add the peppercorns, bay leaves, and whole onion to the pan. Partially cover and simmer, stirring once or twice, for 1¼ hours. Strain the stock; there should be between 6 and 7 cups. *The recipe can be prepared to this point several hours in advance. Cool the stock to room temperature and refrigerate, covered.*

SATURDAY
LUNCHES
•
27

Cut the bacon into ¼-inch dice. In a large, deep pan over medium heat, cook the bacon, stirring once or twice, until crisp, about 10 minutes. Add the diced onions, thyme leaves, and butter; cook until the onions are just tender, about 6 minutes. Add the corn kernels, potatoes, and stock. Simmer about 20 minutes, until the potatoes are just tender. Add the cream and reserved lobster meat, season to taste with salt and fresh black pepper, and simmer 2 minutes more.

Ladle the chowder into soup plates, sprinkle with chives, and serve immediately.

•

cheddar-dill scones with honey mustard

butter

makes 12 scones

Moist, crumbly, dill-flecked scones, slathered with a piquant mustard butter, are a delicious accompaniment to the chowder. The mixture of grains—white and wheat flours plus cornmeal—recalls classic Boston brown bread and ties the scones beautifully to the New England main course.

2 eggs
⅓ cup plus 1 tablespoon buttermilk
⅓ cup finely minced fresh dill
1 cup whole-wheat flour
1 cup unbleached all-purpose flour
1 cup yellow cornmeal
2 tablespoons sugar
2 teaspoons baking powder
¾ teaspoon salt
1 teaspoon freshly ground black pepper
1¼ sticks (5 ounces) unsalted butter, well chilled and cut into small pieces
6 ounces (about 1½ cups) grated sharp Cheddar cheese
Honey Mustard Butter (recipe follows), softened

Position a rack in the upper third of the oven and preheat the oven to 375° F. Lightly butter two 9-inch pie pans.

In a medium bowl whisk together the eggs, buttermilk, and dill. In a large bowl stir together the whole-wheat and white flours and the cornmeal. Stir in the sugar, baking powder, salt, and pepper. With a pastry cutter, cut in the butter until the mixture resembles coarse meal. Stir in the egg mixture and the cheese; the dough will be stiff and crumbly. Knead it briefly in the bowl until the dough just holds together.

Divide the dough equally in half and transfer the pieces to the prepared pie pans. Pat the dough out into 8-inch rounds about 1 inch thick. With a pizza wheel or a long, sharp knife, score each round into 6 equal wedges.

Bake the scones about 25 minutes, or until the edges are crisp and golden and a tester inserted into the center of a scone comes out clean. Cool at least 5 minutes in the pan on a rack.

Break the scones apart along the score lines and serve hot or warm, accompanied by Honey Mustard Butter.

●

honey mustard butter

makes about 1 cup

1½ sticks (6 ounces) unsalted butter, softened
¼ cup honey mustard

In a small bowl cream the butter until fluffy, then beat in the mustard. Transfer the mustard butter to a crock, cover, and refrigerate for up to 3 days or freeze for up to 1 month. Soften to room temperature before using.

●

shaker lemon pie

makes one 9-inch pie, serving 6

This lemon-drop–flavored dessert illustrates Shaker frugality (even the bitter pith of the fruit is utilized) as well as the Shakers' astonishing ability to balance sweet and sour. I have adapted it from a recipe appearing in *We Make You Kindly Welcome*, published by The Shaker Village, Pleasant Hill, Kentucky. Two caveats: Don't adjust the rather daunting amount of sugar—it's perfect. And don't be nonplussed the first time you roll the pie's top crust over a filling that is more or less completely liquid— rest assured, it works. This dessert hardly needs embellishing, but it could well be served with a scoop of Häagen-Dazs blueberry sorbet/vanilla ice cream swirl.

2 large lemons
2 cups plus 2 teaspoons sugar
4 eggs
1 egg yolk
2 tablespoons whole-wheat flour
Pie crust (page 107), shaped into 2 disks and chilled

Using a very sharp knife, slice away and discard the solid bumps of pith at either end of the lemons. Cut the lemons in half lengthwise, then cut each half crosswise into paper-thin slices, removing and discarding the seeds as you go.

In a medium bowl combine the sliced lemons and 2 cups of the sugar and let stand at room temperature, covered, stirring once or twice, for 24 hours. The lemons will exude their juices and form a thick, sugary syrup.

Position a rack in the middle of the oven and preheat the oven to 450° F.

Whisk the eggs and egg yolk into the lemon mixture. On a work surface lightly sprinkled with half the whole-wheat flour, roll out one of the prepared pastry disks to form an even round about 12 inches in diameter; the crust will be thick. Transfer the dough to a 9-inch pie pan, preferably glass.

Turn the lemon mixture into the prepared pie shell, distributing the lemon slices evenly. Sprinkle the work surface with the remaining whole-wheat flour. Roll out the second pastry disk into a round about 12 inches in diameter. Lay the top crust over the lemon filling. Trim the crusts, leaving an overhang of ½ inch. Fold the lower crust over the upper, pinching it gently but firmly to seal. Crimp decoratively.

Bake the pie for 15 minutes. Lower the oven temperature to 375° F and bake another 20 minutes, until a knife inserted near the edge of the pie comes out clean. Sprinkle the remaining sugar evenly over the top of the pie. Cool completely on a rack before cutting and serving.

l e f t  v e r s

The scones can be heated, loosely wrapped in foil, in a 350° F oven, or they can be split and toasted under a broiler. The pie can be stored, well wrapped, in the refrigerator and served the next day.

focaccia sandwiches

pasta, chickpea, and broccoli salad with

sun-dried tomatoes

fresh figs with lemon mascarpone and

raspberry sauce

These meat-and-cheese-stuffed focaccia sandwiches are among the best ways I know to quell the hungry beast within. The casual Italian-style lunch menu also includes a fresh and colorful approach to the ever-popular pasta salad and concludes with an easy, summertime fruit dessert.

s t r a t e g y

The increasing availability of bakery focaccia means you may not have to make your own, but it's likely your fresh focaccia will be better than anything you can buy. It's also an easy bread to bake and it freezes well. The assorted meats, cheeses, and other sandwich fillings are mix-and-match—use what you can find and in the combinations you and your family like. Present the sandwiches already assembled or, on a very informal occasion, let eaters construct their own.

●

focaccia sandwiches

makes 6

Ham, roast beef, prosciutto, mortadella, pepperoni, salami, smoked turkey, Swiss cheese, Provolone—all are likely players in these overstuffed Italian hero sandwiches. Select at least two meats and one cheese, although more variety won't hurt a thing. Crisp lettuce, juicy tomatoes, thin-sliced onions, pickled hot peppers, and a drizzle of vinegar and oil are my favorite garnishes, but roasted sweet peppers, arugula, fresh basil leaves, tapenade, artichoke purée, mayonnaise, and mustard are also possibilities. Here's the general blueprint from which to proceed.

Focaccia (recipe follows)
⅓ cup red wine vinegar
⅓ cup olive oil
1½ pounds assorted sliced sandwich meats
12 ounces sliced cheese
½ cup sliced pickled jalapeños or hot cherry peppers
1 large beefsteak tomato, thinly sliced
6 medium romaine or other crisp lettuce leaves

With a serrated knife, trim the edges from the focaccia, cut it into 6 equal squares, and split each square in half horizontally. Lay the squares of focaccia cut side up on the work surface.

Drizzle the cut sides of the focaccia evenly with the vinegar and oil. Top the bottom pieces with meats and then the cheese, dividing evenly. Top the cheese with peppers to taste, a tomato slice, and a lettuce leaf. Set the sandwich tops in place, slice each one in half diagonally, and secure with a pick if desired. *The sandwiches can be assembled up to 1 hour in advance. Wrap with plastic and drape loosely with a dampened clean towel.*

●

focaccia

serves 6 to 8

The uncomplicated, pizza-crust–like Italian hearth bread called focaccia is a pleasure to make and to eat. Baked in a pan, crusty and thick, as it is here, it makes an excellent sandwich bread. It can be eaten as is, toasted or grilled, dipped into excellent olive oil (flavored or plain), and will mop a plate clean of tomato sauce, stew, roasting juices, or vinaigrette as well as any baguette ever baked. (For a thin, crisp variation of focaccia, see Garlic Pizza Crisps on page 41.)

2 cups lukewarm (105° to 115° F) water
1 package dry yeast
5 cups (about) unbleached all-purpose flour

1 tablespoon olive oil
1 tablespoon salt

In a large bowl whisk together the water and yeast and let stand 5 minutes. Whisk in 2 cups of the flour to form a thin batter. Cover and refrigerate 12 hours.

Brush a 9- by 13-inch baking pan with the oil. Whisk the salt into the batter. Stir in 2 to 2½ cups flour to form a soft and sticky dough. Generously flour the work surface, turn out the dough, and knead about 5 minutes, incorporating additional flour as required, until a soft, slightly sticky but elastic dough is formed. Flour the top of the dough and, with a rolling pin, roll it out into a rectangle about 9 by 13 inches. Transfer the dough to the prepared pan and pat and stretch it to fill the pan. Cover with a towel and let rise at room temperature until doubled in bulk, about 2 hours.

After the dough has doubled, position a rack in the upper third of the oven and preheat the oven to 400° F.

Remove the towel covering, set the pan on the rack, and bake the focaccia for 30 minutes. Remove the bread from the pan and bake it directly on the oven rack for 5 minutes more, until the focaccia is crisp and sounds hollow when thumped. Transfer to a rack and cool completely.

●

pasta, chickpea, and broccoli salad with sun-dried tomatoes

serves 6

Gimmicky pasta salads, fortunately, have fallen from favor. However, some—like this one—closely resemble an authentic hot Italian pasta dish and thus retain their integrity. If you can't locate *orecchiette*, an "ear"-shaped dried pasta, substitute bow ties (*farfalle*) or wagon wheels (*ruote*).

⅔ cup dried chickpeas, picked over and soaked 24 hours in cold water to cover (see Note)
Salt
5 cups small broccoli florets (from 1 large bunch)
12 ounces dried semolina *orecchiette* pasta, preferably imported
½ cup chopped oil-packed sun-dried tomatoes, homemade (page 46), or purchased (see Cook's and Gardener's Sources)
½ cup olive oil
3 tablespoons red wine vinegar
1 teaspoon freshly ground black pepper
¼ cup minced wide-leaf parsley

Drain the chickpeas. In a saucepan cover them with cold water and bring to a boil, skimming any scum that forms on the top. Lower the heat and simmer 20 minutes. Add 2 teaspoons salt and continue to simmer until the chickpeas are just tender, 15 to 20 minutes. Drain.

Bring a large pot of water to a boil. Add the broccoli florets and 1 tablespoon salt; cook, stirring once or twice, until just tender, about 4 minutes. With a slotted spoon remove the florets from the water and transfer immediately to a large bowl of ice water. When cool, drain thoroughly.

Meanwhile, raise the heat under the broccoli-cooking water, and when it returns to a boil, add the pasta. Cook, stirring occasionally, until just tender, 10 to 14 minutes. Drain immediately and cool.

In a large bowl toss together the chickpeas, broccoli, pasta, sun-dried tomatoes, olive oil, vinegar, pepper, and ½ teaspoon salt. Taste and adjust the seasoning. *The salad can be prepared to this point several hours in advance. Store covered in the refrigerator but allow it to return to room temperature before serving.*

Add the parsley and toss well just before serving.

NOTE   *I like the slow and homey kitchen business of sorting through dried beans and then soaking them in water overnight. The soaking leaches out some of the starches that cause intestinal gas, and I think the beans cook more quickly and evenly. In a pinch though, you may use the quick-soak method: In a heavy pan cover the beans with a generous amount of cold water. Set over medium heat and bring just to a boil, skimming any scum that forms on the surface. Remove from the heat and let stand at room temperature in the cooking water until cool, about 2 hours. Drain, add fresh cold water to cover generously, and proceed as if cooking soaked beans.*

●

fresh figs with lemon mascarpone and

raspberry sauce

serves 6

Mascarpone is an utterly rich and buttery Italian cream cheese. Available at some cheese stores or by mail order (see Cook's and Gardener's Sources), it's also easy to make at home (page 35). Because the imported cheese-shop version is often over the hill and because the fresh cheese is simply delicious, making a batch of your own won't seem an unreasonable project. When you have it, use it in Tiramisù (page 267) or in this fresh, pretty dessert.

RASPBERRY SAUCE

3 baskets (6 ounces each) fresh raspberries, plus additional berries for garnish, picked
    over, rinsed only if necessary
¾ cup granulated sugar
2 tablespoons fresh lemon juice, strained

6 ounces mascarpone, homemade (page 35) or purchased, at room temperature
3 tablespoons confectioners' sugar
2 tablespoons finely minced lemon zest
12 ripe fresh figs, such as black Mission

For the raspberry sauce In a food processor combine the raspberries, sugar, and lemon juice and process until smooth. Transfer the sauce to a covered storage container and refrigerate. *The sauce can be prepared 3 days ahead.*
To assemble In a small bowl stir together the mascarpone, confectioners' sugar, and lemon zest; do not overmix or the cheese will separate.

Quarter the figs as you would an apple. Arrange 8 quarters, cut sides up, in a circle on each of 6 dessert plates. Spoon a dollop of the mascarpone mixture in the center of each circle, dividing it evenly and using it all. Drizzle the figs and mascarpone with some of the raspberry sauce, using about ¼ cup sauce per serving. Scatter whole berries over each portion and serve immediately.

leftovers

Focaccia can be grilled, toasted, or sautéed (it makes wonderful croutons), brushed with Garlic Butter (page 243) or Savory Oil (page 232) or not, as you wish. The pasta salad can be kept for a second day, although the broccoli will discolor; you may wish to remove it and add fresh broccoli just before serving time. The raspberry sauce is delicious on pancakes, waffles, ice cream, yogurt, fresh berries, and on and on.

nick malgieri's mascarpone

makes about 1 pound

Because mascarpone, the super-rich Italian cream cheese, is so perishable and so essential to desserts, such as Tiramisù (page 267), you may want to make your own. It's a simple enough process, as outlined in the recipe below, which is from baking expert Nick Malgieri's book *Great Italian Desserts* (Little, Brown). For the recipe to work properly, the cream must not be ultra-pasteurized.

1 quart heavy cream, *not* ultra-pasteurized
1 tablespoon white wine vinegar or fresh lemon juice, strained

Choose a stainless-steel bowl with a lip that fits on the rim of a large saucepan so that the bottom does not touch the bottom of the pan. Add water to the pan and place the bowl in the pan so that the bowl touches the surface of the water but the lip still sits firmly on the rim of the pan. Remove the bowl, place the pan on medium heat, and bring the water to a boil.

Pour the cream into the bowl and set the bowl over the boiling water. Lower the heat under the pan to medium and warm the cream, stirring it occasionally and checking the temperature often with an instant-reading thermometer, until it reaches 190° F. Stir in the vinegar and continue to stir gently until the cream begins to curdle. Remove the pan from the heat, cover the bowl, and allow the curds to firm up for 10 minutes.

Line a strainer or colander with a piece of dampened butter muslin (see Cook's and Gardener's Sources) or several thicknesses of dampened cheesecloth. Set the strainer over a bowl and gently spoon the curds into the strainer. Let the mascarpone cool to room temperature, cover the strainer tightly with plastic wrap, and refrigerate for 24 hours to allow the cheese to finish draining and become firm.

Transfer the cheese from the strainer to a tightly covered container and refrigerate. The mascarpone should be used within 3 or 4 days.

smoked turkey, brussels sprouts, and potato salad

with honey-mustard dressing

rye bread

new crop apples

vermont colby cheese

With a nip of fall in the air, this menu of seasonal flavors becomes particularly welcome. A main-course salad is an agreeable way to feed a small crowd efficiently, and crisp, just-picked apples, good bread, and tangy, high-quality cheese are the perfect no-work accompaniments.

s t r a t e g y

The salad can be assembled ahead, although the Brussels sprouts should be added shortly before serving to prevent their discoloration by the dressing. Offer a basket of sliced, good-quality, deli-style rye bread (I like mine *with* caraway seeds) and set out a fruit-and-cheese board featuring the first local apples (always a revelation after months of last season's storage fruit) and an excellent Colby cheese, like that from the Crowley Cheese Factory (see Cook's and Gardener's Sources). If you would like a serious dessert, prepare Marmalade Gingerbread (page 149). Drink a Gewürztraminer, a crisp lager-style beer, or icy unfiltered apple cider. This is an especially successful portable meal—one you may want to take along on a leaf-watching expedition or for a tailgate picnic.

smoked turkey, brussels sprouts, and
potato salad with honey-mustard dressing

serves 6

You may add a tablespoon or two of minced fresh dill to the salad along with the parsley.

10 ounces small Brussels sprouts
Salt
1½ pounds new red-skinned potatoes, well scrubbed and quartered
⅓ cup coarse-grained mustard
⅓ cup cider vinegar
¼ cup honey
⅔ cup corn oil
1½ pounds smoked turkey breast, homemade (page 38) or purchased, cut into ¾-inch dice
½ cup diced red onion
½ cup minced wide-leaf parsley
Freshly ground black pepper
1 large head red leaf lettuce, leaves separated, rinsed, and spun dry

Trim the Brussels sprouts and cut a shallow "x" in the stem end of each. Over high heat bring a pot of water to a boil. Stir in 1 tablespoon salt, add the Brussels sprouts, and cook until just tender, about 8 minutes. Drain and transfer immediately to a large bowl of ice water. Cool completely, drain well, and halve the Brussels sprouts vertically.

In a large saucepan cover the potatoes with cold water. Stir in 1 tablespoon salt, set over high heat, and bring to a boil. Cook until just tender, about 8 minutes.

Meanwhile, in a medium bowl whisk together the mustard, vinegar, and honey and ½ teaspoon salt. Gradually whisk in the corn oil; the dressing will thicken.

Drain the potatoes and transfer them to a large bowl. Pour half the dressing over the hot potatoes and let stand, stirring once or twice, until cool.

Combine the Brussels sprouts, turkey, onion, remaining dressing, and parsley with the potatoes. Season generously with freshly ground pepper and toss again. Divide the lettuce leaves among the plates and spoon the salad onto the lettuce. Drizzle with any dressing remaining in the bowl and serve immediately.

l e f t  v e r s

The salad is not a successful leftover. Any remaining apples can be sautéed and combined with leftover Colby (grated) in an omelet. Serve with leftover deli rye, toasted and buttered, for a wonderful fall breakfast.

applewood-smoked turkey breast

makes one 5-pound breast

The simple electric water smokers now widely available (see Cook's and Gardener's Sources) work beautifully and will let you home-smoke any number of meats or seafood with a minimum of effort. It's a slow process but not a complicated one, which makes it ideal weekend work, and the results are moist, fresh-tasting, and far superior to all but the best smoked meats you can buy. Now that bone-in fresh turkey breasts are stocked in most supermarkets, this easy recipe has become a staple at my house. When smoked over a lighter wood like mesquite, the turkey breast can be served warm and juicy, straight from the smoker. When smoked over a stronger wood like apple or hickory, the meat is best eaten at room temperature in sandwiches, salads, or simply for weekend emergency nibbling.

4 applewood smoking chunks (see Cook's and Gardener's Sources)
1 cup Chicken Stock (page 90) or canned broth
⅓ cup genuine maple syrup (see Cook's and Gardener's Sources)
1 bone-in turkey breast (about 5 pounds), preferably fresh

Soak the wood chunks in water for at least 1 hour. In a small bowl stir together the chicken stock and maple syrup. In a shallow dish pour the stock mixture over the turkey breast and let stand, basting it occasionally, for 1 hour.

Drain the wood chunks and arrange them in the bottom of an electric water smoker according to the manufacturer's directions. Put the basin of hot water in place. Set the upper rack in place, then set the turkey breast on the rack and cover the smoker.

Smoke undisturbed for 2 hours. Baste the turkey breast with about one-third of the stock mixture, opening the smoker for no more time than is necessary, and smoke about 2 more hours, basting twice more. The smoking time will vary widely with the outdoor temperature and wind conditions, but the turkey breast is done when an instant-reading thermometer inserted into the breast at the thickest part, but not touching the bone, registers 165° F. Remove the turkey from the smoker and serve it hot, warm, or cold.

mixed green salad with

prosciutto-wrapped pears and bocconcini

white bean and pasta soup with sun-dried tomatoes

garlic pizza crisps

amaretto-and-wine-poached dried fruit compote

hazelnut biscotti

Soup satisfies, and none more so than the hearty bean-and-pasta potage that is the centerpiece of this autumn menu. Like most of the lunches in this book, this meal would also make an excellent supper.

strategy

Prepare 20 cups of the Basic Mixed Green Salad with Vinaigrette (page 23), then garnish each plate with the pears and *bocconcini,* as directed below. Serve it alongside the soup (which deserves to be ladled from a handsome tureen, if you have one, right at the table). The soup isn't technically demanding and can be partially completed a day ahead, leaving the cook free to concentrate on turning out freshly baked pizza crisps. Arrange the crisps standing up in a napkin-lined basket for greatest visual impact. The compote will keep a week or more under refrigeration (it's the ideal standby weekend dessert), and store-bought biscotti or any other crisp, fairly plain cookie can be substituted for the homemade version. Drink a lightly chilled Valpolicella.

●

green salad with prosciutto-wrapped pears
and bocconcini

serves 8

The mixed greens, dressed with olive oil and red wine vinegar, are garnished with small balls of fresh mozzarella (*bocconcini*) and wedges of ripe, juicy pear wrapped in rich pink prosciutto. Now that genuine prosciutto from Parma is once again available in this country, this would be an excellent way to sample that unique product. Ask that the meat be sliced slightly thicker than the typical "paper-thin" rendition.

2 juicy, ripe large pears, such as Bartlett
3 tablespoons fresh lemon juice, strained
16 *bocconcini,* available from specialty cheese shops (see Cook's and Gardener's Sources)
     or packed in water in some supermarkets—look for the Polly-O label
16 slices prosciutto, preferably imported
20 cups Basic Mixed Green Salad with Vinaigrette (page 23), prepared with at least 3 kinds
     of greens plus arugula

Peel the pears only if the skins are tough or spotty. Cut each pear into eighths and remove the core. Brush the pears with lemon juice. Drain the *bocconcini.*

Cut the slices of prosciutto in half lengthwise. Wrap each pear wedge and each *bocconcini* with a strip of prosciutto. Divide the dressed green salad among 8 plates. Garnish each plate with 2 wrapped pear wedges and 2 wrapped *bocconcini* and serve, passing a peppermill at the table.

●

white bean and pasta soup with
sun-dried tomatoes

serves 8

This thick and satisfying soup is, more or less, "pasta fazool"—*pasta e fagioli*— adapted slightly to the modern weekend pantry, in which there is usually a jar of oil-packed sun-dried tomatoes. With a salad and good bread, it's a complete meal; in smaller portions it can be served as a first course for a big Italian feast. If you have no fresh fennel, substitute an equal amount of diced celery.

¼ cup olive oil

3 cups diced yellow onions

1 cup diced fresh fennel

3 medium carrots, peeled and diced

6 garlic cloves, peeled and minced

1 teaspoon crushed dried red pepper

2 bay leaves

1½ cups (about 12 ounces) dried white beans, such as cannellini or Great Northern, picked over and soaked 24 hours in cold water to cover

10 cups canned chicken broth diluted with 1 cup water

6 ounces (about 3 cups) dried semolina pasta bow ties (*farfalle*), preferably imported

⅔ cup chopped oil-packed sun-dried tomatoes, homemade (page 46) or purchased (see Cook's and Gardener's Sources)

⅓ cup minced wide-leaf parsley

Salt

1 cup freshly grated Parmesan cheese, preferably imported

In a large soup pot heat the oil over medium heat. Add the onions, fennel, carrots, garlic, red pepper, and bay leaves; cook, covered, stirring once or twice, for 10 minutes.

Drain the beans. Add them and the diluted broth to the pan, raise the heat, and bring the soup to a boil. Lower the heat and simmer, partially covered, stirring occasionally, for 1¼ hours. *The soup can be prepared to this point 1 day ahead. Cool, cover, and refrigerate. Bring the soup back to a simmer, thinning it with water if necessary.*

Add the pasta bow ties and the chopped tomatoes and simmer, partially covered, until the beans and pasta are very tender and the soup is very thick, about 15 minutes. Stir in the parsley and season to taste with salt. Let the soup stand off the heat, covered, for 1 minute. Discard the bay leaves and serve, passing the grated cheese at the table.

●

garlic pizza crisps

serves 8

Flat and crackly, these dramatically oversized garlic-scented flatbreads are almost nothing but crust and are delicious with soups, salads, or cheese. The two long, slow risings, which take place overnight in the refrigerator, make for terrific-tasting bread that is easy on the cook's schedule. I like to use the flavored oil from the pumate (sun-dried tomato) jar (now available without the tomatoes, but with the flavor, bottled by Dean & DeLuca; see Cook's and Gardener's Sources, or use the oil from homemade dried tomatoes, page 46). The crisps can be baked on ordinary sheet pans, but for the best texture I recommend you bake them on bread-baking tiles or a pizza stone instead (see Cook's and Gardener's Sources). Note that you will then need to bake the crisps in two batches, unless you own two sets of baking tiles. The crisps are best eaten the same day they are baked.

1 package dry yeast
2 cups lukewarm (105° to 115° F) water
4½ cups (about) unbleached all-purpose flour
Salt
8 tablespoons olive oil, preferably flavored with sun-dried tomatoes
6 garlic cloves, peeled and thinly sliced
⅓ cup yellow cornmeal
2 tablespoons minced fresh rosemary
Coarse (kosher) salt
Freshly ground black pepper

In a mixing bowl whisk together the yeast and water; let stand 5 minutes. Whisk in 2 cups of the flour. Cover the bowl tightly with plastic wrap and refrigerate for 12 hours.

Whisk in 1 tablespoon salt, then stir in enough additional flour (about 2 cups) to make a soft, sticky dough. Turn the dough out onto a well-floured work surface and knead about 5 minutes, until it is smooth and elastic. Divide the dough into 4 pieces; form each piece into a ball. Place 1 tablespoon of the olive oil in each of 4 medium bowls. Place 1 dough ball in each bowl and turn to coat with oil. Cover each bowl tightly with plastic wrap and refrigerate overnight.

In a small bowl combine the remaining 4 tablespoons olive oil and the garlic; let stand 30 minutes.

Arrange bread-baking tiles or a pizza stone, if available, on an oven rack. Preheat the oven to 500° F. Evenly sprinkle two 11- by 17-inch baking sheets with the cornmeal.

On a floured surface roll one piece of dough as thin as possible into a 12- to 14-inch-long oval. Transfer the dough to one of the prepared pans. Repeat with a second ball of dough.

If using baking tiles, set the baking pan with the ovals of dough on the opened oven door. One at a time transfer the ovals to the heated bread tiles (just lift them onto the tiles—a little stretching or the occasional hole won't harm the finished bread).

With a pizza-cutting wheel or a long, sharp knife, score each oval once in half lengthwise. Brush each oval with some of the garlic oil and scatter one-quarter of the garlic over each oval of dough. Sprinkle with the rosemary and add coarse salt and fresh pepper to taste. Close the oven door and bake about 15 minutes, until crisp and golden brown. Cool on a rack. Repeat with the remaining 2 balls of dough.

If you are not using baking tiles, score the dough, brush it with oil, sprinkle it with garlic, rosemary, salt, and pepper and bake it right on the cornmeal-dusted pan. You may then bake all 4 pizza crisps at once, on the 2 baking sheets, reversing the position of the pans on the racks from upper to lower and from front to back at the halfway point. The breads will take about 20 minutes to bake.

To serve, crack the crisps in half along the score marks and arrange in a napkin-lined basket.

VARIATION Parmesan Planks: *Roll out and score the ovals of dough as directed above. Brush them with plain or pumate (sun-dried tomato—flavored) olive oil, season them with fresh black pepper, then sprinkle evenly with ¾ cup grated Parmesan cheese. Bake and cool as the recipe directs.*

•

amaretto-and-wine-poached
dried fruit compote

serves 8

Mixed dried fruits, in a luscious amaretto-wine syrup, will stand by in the refrigerator until needed, as an ideal emergency weekend dessert. Although this is good when prepared with ordinary supermarket fruit, better-quality apricots, peaches, and prunes—not to mention dried cherries—will come from a gourmet shop or by mail. The fruits are added to the poaching syrup in order, from chewiest to tenderest; adjust the order given below according to the fruit you buy.

4¾ cups (about 1½ bottles) medium-dry white wine, such as Sauvignon Blanc
¾ cup amaretto liqueur
½ cup sugar
8 ounces each dried peaches, dried apricots, and prunes
4 ounces dried tart or sweet cherries (see Cook's and Gardener's Sources)
Whipping cream, for garnish

In a large nonreactive saucepan over medium heat, combine the wine, liqueur, and sugar. Bring to a simmer, stirring to dissolve the sugar.

Add the peaches and when the liquid returns to a simmer, partially cover the pan. Cook 10 minutes. Add the apricots and prunes. When the liquid returns to a simmer, partially cover the pan and cook 5 minutes. Add the cherries, stirring gently to avoid breaking up the fruit. When the liquid returns to a simmer, partially cover the pan and cook another 5 minutes, until all the fruit is just plump and tender.

Transfer the compote to a heatproof container and cool to room temperature. Cover and refrigerate. *The fruit can be prepared up to 10 days in advance.*

Serve slightly chilled, drizzled with a tablespoon or two of whipping cream, if desired.

VARIATION Cognac-and-Wine-Poached Dried Fruit Compote: *Substitute an equal quantity of Cognac or brandy for the amaretto and increase the sugar by 3 tablespoons.*

●

hazelnut biscotti

makes 2 ½ dozen

Biscotti, in Italy, has come to mean any cookie, but to me the word is best applied to these crisp, twice-baked, hazelnut-studded treats. Biscotti are an ideal weekend cookie—they are fun to make and they keep well, stored airtight, for several weeks, just getting harder and better all the while. The biscotti are delicious with an early morning cup of *caffè latte* or cappuccino, as well as with a midnight glass of milk. They are popularly enjoyed after a meal, dipped into a glass of *vin santo* (sweet wine), a practice that I find does little for either the biscotti or the wine. If you have no Frangelico, these can be made with amaretto.

12 ounces (about 2½ cups) unblanched whole hazelnuts (see Cook's and Gardener's Sources)
1¾ cups sugar
4 cups unbleached all-purpose flour
3 tablespoons unsweetened cocoa powder
2 teaspoons baking powder
½ teaspoon salt
6 eggs
3 tablespoons Frangelico (Italian hazelnut liqueur)
2 tablespoons hazelnut oil (see Cook's and Gardener's Sources)

Position racks in the upper and lower thirds of the oven and preheat the oven to 350° F. Butter 2 large baking sheets (do not use black bakeware).

In a shallow pan (like a cake tin) just large enough to hold them in a single layer, roast the hazelnuts, stirring once or twice, for 15 minutes, until the skins begin to loosen. Wrap the hot hazelnuts in a kitchen towel and let steam for 1 minute. Vigorously rub the towel-wrapped hazelnuts to remove the peels. Shake the nuts in a colander to separate them from the peels. Cool completely.

In a food processor combine half the roasted hazelnuts and the sugar and process until the nuts are finely chopped. On a cutting board coarsely chop the remaining hazelnuts.

In a large bowl thoroughly combine the sugar mixture, coarsely chopped nuts, flour, cocoa, baking powder, and salt. In a medium bowl thoroughly whisk the eggs. Whisk in the Frangelico and the oil.

Stir the egg mixture into the flour mixture. It will be dry and crumbly, but continue to mix, and even to knead the dough in the bowl with your hands until all the flour is incorporated; the dough will be damp and crumbly.

Divide the dough in half. On the prepared baking sheets form each half into a rectangular log 3 inches wide and 1 inch thick. (The logs will be about 14 inches long—arrange them diagonally across the baking sheets if necessary.)

Bake the logs for 40 minutes, exchanging the position of the baking sheets from top to bottom and from front to back at the halfway point. The logs are done when a knife inserted into the middle of each comes out clean. Cool on the baking sheets on a rack for 10 minutes.

Using a long metal spatula, slide one log onto the work surface. With a serrated knife and using a gentle sawing motion, cut the log crosswise into ½-inch slices. Repeat with the remaining log. Return the slices to the baking sheets, setting them upright and spacing them well apart.

Return the baking sheets to the oven and bake the biscotti 20 minutes, exchanging the position of the sheets from top to bottom and from front to back at the halfway point. The biscotti will be crisp and dry but should be browned only on the bottoms.

Cool completely on a rack. Store in an airtight container at room temperature.

l e f t  v e r s

Leftover soup will become very thick; thin it with water before reheating gently just until steaming. The fruit compote and the biscotti keep well for many days, and so can hardly be called leftovers. A little fruit compote makes a nice topping for a bowl of yogurt or hot porridge (page 188).

michele scicolone's marinated dried tomatoes

makes about 4 cups

If the price of your last jar of imported sun-dried tomatoes sent you into sticker shock, it's time to look for another way to acquire these moist, delicious morsels. When your garden produces a bumper crop of plum tomatoes (preferably from an Italian seed strain, see Cook's and Gardener's Sources), or if you find them for a rock-bottom price at the height of the season, stock up and produce your own *pumate* (what they're called in Italy), using this recipe adapted from Michele Scicolone's *The Antipasto Table* (Morrow). Although the process takes some hours, it requires little active supervision. Make a large jar of these for yourself, and then turn out several smaller jars as gifts for friends. Michele quite rightly notes that the marinating oil is delicious as a dip for focaccia (page 32).

24 fresh large plum tomatoes
Salt
Freshly ground black pepper
¼ cup (about) balsamic vinegar
¼ cup minced fresh basil
2 garlic cloves, peeled and sliced
Extra-virgin olive oil

Preheat the oven to 250° F. Cut the tomatoes in half lengthwise. With a grapefruit spoon, scoop out any white membrane and the seeds and juice.

Place the tomato halves, cut side up, on a large baking sheet. Sprinkle them lightly with salt and pepper. Spoon ¼ teaspoon balsamic vinegar into each tomato.

Bake the tomatoes for 3 hours, until most of the vinegar is absorbed and the tomatoes are only slightly moist.

Turn the tomatoes over and bake for 1 hour. Turn again and bake for 1 to 2 hours, until the tomatoes are wrinkled and leathery. Cool the tomatoes in the pan on a rack.

Layer the tomatoes, basil, and garlic in a sterilized 1-quart jar. Add enough oil to cover the tomatoes completely. Cover tightly and refrigerate at least 1 week before using. Add more oil as needed to keep the tomatoes submerged at all times. They will keep well for up to 3 months.

california club sandwiches

chopped romaine and spinach salad

with caesar dressing

caramel oranges in tequila liqueur

This lunch menu has a California theme with a Mexican influence, inspired by the inclusion of a Caesar-type salad (created by Tijuana restaurateur Caesar Cardini) and celebrated vigorously there and across the border in San Diego.

s t r a t e g y

This is a simple enough menu, although, with the exceptions of the salad dressing, cleaning the greens, and some of the dessert steps, most of it occurs more or less at the last minute. If you would like a cookie with the simple fruit dessert, consider the Orange-Cornmeal Butter Cookies on page 97 or the Mexican Chocolate Shortbreads on page 245. Drink an amber Mexican beer like Dos Equis or pour a lightly chilled white Zinfandel.

For a completely different approach to enjoying the same ingredients, combine the Caesar greens and dressing with the smoked turkey, avocado, bacon, and tomato of the sandwiches to create a main-course salad. Serve it with whole-wheat toast or make fresh whole-wheat croutons.

●

california club sandwiches

makes 4

This is a fanciful sandwich, not authentic, but with a California flair, blending south-of-the-border influences with that California classic, the Cobb salad. Please note that the crusts are trimmed from the bread. This makes it less awkward to eat the sandwiches and at the same time reveals the many layers of goodness within. If this strikes you, as it once did me, as prissy and wasteful, consider: All those mayonnaise-anointed crusts, bits of bacon and tomato, and shards of turkey that litter the cutting board rightfully belong to the cook—your reward for making and serving a California club.

1 recipe Lemony Mayonnaise (page 292), prepared using lime juice and zest instead of lemon
2 pickled jalapeños, stemmed and minced
1 pound thinly sliced smoked turkey breast, homemade (page 38) or purchased
12 thin slices whole-wheat sandwich bread, lightly toasted
1 buttery-ripe, black-skinned avocado, pitted, peeled, and cut into 16 thin wedges
12 strips of bacon, cooked crisp and halved crosswise
8 thin tomato slices
8 crisp lettuce leaves, such as romaine

In a small bowl stir together the mayonnaise and pickled jalapeños.

Divide the turkey into 8 equal portions. Spread 1 piece of toast with about 1 tablespoon mayonnaise. Arrange 1 portion of turkey on the toast and top with 2 avocado wedges and 3 pieces of bacon. Set a tomato slice on the bacon and lay a lettuce leaf on top. Spread 1 tablespoon of mayonnaise on each side of another piece of toast. Set the toast on the lettuce. Cover with another portion of turkey and top with 2 more avocado wedges and 3 more bacon pieces. Set a tomato slice and a lettuce leaf on the bacon. Spread 1 side of a piece of toast with about 1 tablespoon mayonnaise and set in on the lettuce, mayonnaise side down.

Repeat with the remaining ingredients to make 3 more sandwiches. Flatten each sandwich slightly with your palm, and secure with sandwich picks if desired. With a long, sharp knife, trim the crusts and cut each sandwich diagonally in half. Serve immediately.

chopped romaine and spinach salad with

caesar dressing

serves 4

It takes a sturdy green like romaine to stand up to my creamy and assertive Caesar dressing. Spinach adds bold, dark green color and additional flavor; watercress can be substituted.

8 cups coarsely chopped inner romaine lettuce leaves (from 1 large head), rinsed and spun dry
4 cups coarsely chopped spinach leaves, rinsed and spun dry
1¼ cups (about) Caesar Dressing (recipe follows)
Freshly ground black pepper

In a large bowl combine the romaine and spinach. Add 1 cup of the Caesar dressing and toss thoroughly. Add additional dressing if desired, season generously with fresh black pepper, and toss again. Serve immediately.

caesar dressing

makes 2½ cups

This recipe yields about twice as much dressing as you'll need for the salad. The extra is useful as a dip for crudités or poached shrimp and excellent as the dressing on a chicken salad. It also allows you to toss a sirloin on the grill and have a crisp Caesar salad ready by the time the steak is medium-rare—an accomplishment that can earn you the reputation of a weekend culinary wizard.

⅓ cup fresh lemon juice, strained
¼ cup grated Parmesan cheese
1 egg, at room temperature
1 egg yolk, at room temperature
4 oil-packed anchovy fillets, chopped
1 medium garlic clove, peeled

1 tablespoon Worcestershire sauce
1 tablespoon Dijon-style mustard
1 teaspoon freshly ground black pepper
½ teaspoon salt
1 cup corn oil
1 cup olive oil

In a food processor combine the lemon juice, Parmesan cheese, egg, egg yolk, anchovy fillets, garlic, Worcestershire, mustard, pepper, and salt; process until smooth. With the machine running, pour in the oils through the feed tube in a quick, steady stream. The dressing will thicken slightly and become creamy. *The dressing can be prepared up to 3 days ahead. Transfer to a container, cover, and refrigerate; return to room temperature before use.*

●

caramel oranges in tequila liqueur

serves 4

Monte Teca is a honey-textured, tequila-based Mexican liqueur in which I detect notes of vanilla, caramel, and, possibly, citrus. I use it to marinate sliced oranges, which, after chilling, are drizzled with a crackling cage of caramel. During subsequent refrigeration, the caramel partially dissolves, mixing with the tequila liqueur and the juice of the oranges to produce a delicious syrup—a dramatic and easy dessert.

4 large oranges
½ cup Monte Teca
1 cup sugar
¼ cup water

Cut a slice off the top and bottom of 1 orange to reveal the flesh inside. Set the orange on one flat end and, cutting downward and following the curve of the fruit, slice away the orange peel and white pith. Repeat with the remaining oranges. Cut the oranges crosswise into 4 or 5 thick slices each.

Lay the orange slices in a shallow nonreactive dish. Pour the Monte Teca over them, cover, and marinate in the refrigerator for 2 hours.

In a small heavy saucepan over medium-high heat, stir together the sugar and water. Bring it to a boil and then let it cook without further stirring until it turns a rich amber, 7 to 8 minutes.

Meanwhile, arrange the orange slices in an overlapping row or circle on 4 dessert plates. Spoon the juices from the dish over the oranges.

Immediately remove the caramel from the heat and dip the bottom of the pan once or twice in cold water to stop the cooking. Spoon the hot caramel over the oranges, using it all and coating them heavily. (The contact between the hot caramel and cold fruit may produce some sizzling.)

Refrigerate the dessert plates, uncovered, for about 1 hour, until the caramel has partially dissolved and has mixed with the marinating juices. Serve cold.

gerry cohen's horseradish mustard

makes 3 cups

Gerry Cohen is a man of firm opinions, one of the firmest being that this potent sweet-hot mustard is absolutely delicious. While cooking up a batch of your own in the face of the overwhelming selection of prepared mustards in even the most rudimentary of gourmet food shops may seem like a fool's hobby, if you like mustard and horseradish as much as Gerry and I do, this pungent condiment is well worth the effort. The recipe can be multiplied upwards directly and a small jar of mustard makes a nice addition to a holiday gift basket of food.

1 cup white wine vinegar
1 cup Coleman's powdered mustard
2 tablespoons mustard seed
½ teaspoon crushed dried red pepper
2 eggs
¾ cup sugar
¼ cup prepared horseradish, drained
¼ cup minced yellow onions
2 tablespoons fresh lemon juice, strained
2 garlic cloves, crushed through a press
½ teaspoon salt
¼ teaspoon ground cloves
¼ teaspoon cayenne pepper

In a small, nonreactive bowl, slowly whisk the vinegar into the mustard powder. Stir in the mustard seed and red pepper, cover, and let stand at room temperature for 12 hours.

In the top of a double boiler whisk together the mustard mixture and the eggs. Whisk in the sugar, horseradish, onion, lemon juice, garlic, salt, and cloves. Set over simmering water and cook, stirring frequently, until thick, about 50 minutes. Immediately remove the mustard from the double boiler and cool to room temperature. Cover and refrigerate for at least 24 hours, to allow the flavors to mellow, before using. The mustard will keep two weeks.

ham, pear, and watercress sandwiches

with horseradish mayonnaise

tangy mashed potato salad

tarragon mustard slaw

apple, cranberry, and sour cream cake with

black walnuts

As winter deepens, this lunch is welcome, celebrating such seasonal flavors as smoky ham, beets, dill, horseradish, pears, and apples in a casual but satisfying menu.

s t r a t e g y

Both the slaw and the mashed potato salad can be prepared a day in advance, although I prefer the potato salad when it has never been refrigerated. If you do fix the potato salad ahead, set aside the onion and add it just before serving. The sandwiches, as always, require some last-minute assembly. The cake is best when served still warm from the oven. Since there is a lot of mayonnaise and sour cream in this menu, you may wish to use the low- or nonfat store-bought versions of both. Drink a not-too-bitter dark beer or a chilled Gewürztraminer with this meal.

ham, pear, and watercress sandwiches
with horseradish mayonnaise

makes 4

A favorite sandwich of mine with the familiar tastes of ham, Swiss cheese, and pumpernickel paired with some surprising partners—pears, horseradish, and watercress.

⅓ cup mayonnaise
¼ cup prepared horseradish
8 slices pumpernickel or black bread, lightly toasted on one side only
1 pound Black Forest or other good-quality ham, thinly sliced
4 thin slices (about 4 ounces) aged Swiss cheese
½ ripe, juicy pear, cored and cut into 12 thin slices
½ medium bunch watercress, tough stems removed, rinsed, and spun dry

In a small bowl whisk together the mayonnaise and horseradish.

Lay 4 slices of pumpernickel, untoasted sides up, on the work surface. Spread the bread with half the mayonnaise mixture, dividing it evenly. Arrange the ham over the mayonnaise, dividing it evenly. Arrange the cheese over the ham, the pear slices over the cheese, and the watercress over pear. Spread the remaining mayonnaise mixture on the untoasted sides of the remaining slices of bread. Top the sandwiches with the bread, mayonnaise side down. Cut the sandwiches in half on the diagonal and secure with sandwich picks if desired. *The sandwiches can be assembled about 1 hour in advance and held, wrapped in plastic and draped with a dampened clean towel, at room temperature.*

●

tangy mashed potato salad

serves 4

If cold mashed potatoes sounds like a gruesome leftover, you haven't tasted them mixed with a tart yogurt, mayonnaise, and dill dressing. Be sure to leave plenty of lumps.

2 pounds (about 8 medium) red-skinned potatoes, scrubbed and quartered
Salt
1 cup plain yogurt
1 cup mayonnaise
3 tablespoons minced fresh dill
2 tablespoons red wine vinegar
1 teaspoon freshly ground black pepper
⅓ cup finely diced red onions

In a medium saucepan cover the potatoes with cold water. Stir in 1 tablespoon salt, set over medium heat, and bring to a boil. Lower the heat slightly and simmer, stirring once or twice, until the potatoes are very tender, about 12 minutes. Drain and cool slightly. In a large bowl coarsely mash the potatoes, leaving some lumps. Cool to room temperature.

In a medium bowl whisk together the yogurt, mayonnaise, dill, vinegar, pepper, and ½ teaspoon salt. Pour the dressing over the potatoes and toss thoroughly. *The salad can be prepared to this point 1 day ahead. Cover and refrigerate, but return it to room temperature before serving.*

Stir the onions into the salad and adjust the seasoning before serving.

tarragon mustard slaw

serves 6

Use white, red, or Napa cabbage in this simple slaw. If you have fresh tarragon, by all means add it, but the dried herb produces excellent results.

3 medium beets with stems
¾ cup plain yogurt
¾ cup mayonnaise
¼ cup Dijon-style mustard, preferably tarragon-flavored
1½ tablespoons minced shallot
1½ tablespoons minced fresh tarragon, or 1½ teaspoons dried tarragon, crumbled
1½ teaspoons sugar
¾ teaspoon salt
½ teaspoon freshly ground black pepper
8 cups finely shredded cabbage
6 cup-shaped Boston lettuce leaves, left whole

Preheat the oven to 400° F.

Trim the beet stems to about ½ inch. Wrap the beets tightly in a packet of foil and bake until very tender, about 1 hour. Cool completely. *The beets can be baked up to 2 days ahead.* Peel and dice the beets.

In a medium bowl whisk together the yogurt, mayonnaise, mustard, shallot, tarragon, sugar, salt, and pepper.

In a large bowl toss together the dressing and cabbage. Cover and refrigerate at least 1 hour. *The slaw can be prepared up to 1 day ahead.* Toss again and adjust the seasoning. Place a lettuce leaf on each serving plate and divide the slaw among the leaves. Top the slaw with the diced beets just before serving.

●

apple, cranberry, and sour cream cake
with black walnuts

serves 6 to 8

This easy little cake whips together in minutes. While it is useful as the dessert after an informal meal like this one, it's just as good at brunch or with nothing more than a cup of coffee, whenever the mood for something sweet strikes.

1 cup unbleached all-purpose flour
½ cup whole-wheat flour
2 teaspoons baking powder
1 teaspoon baking soda
½ teaspoon salt
½ cup dried cranberries (see Cook's and Gardener's Sources) or raisins
½ cup black walnuts (see Cook's and Gardener's Sources) or regular walnuts
¾ stick (6 tablespoons) unsalted butter, softened
¾ cup plus 2 teaspoons sugar
1 egg
½ cup sour cream
1 teaspoon Vanilla Rum (page 66) or vanilla extract
1 large apple, preferably McIntosh, peeled, cored, and cut into 20 thin slices
¼ teaspoon ground cinnamon
Unsweetened whipped cream, for garnish

Position a rack in the middle of the oven and preheat the oven to 350° F. Butter a 9-inch cake pan.

In a medium bowl stir together the flours, baking powder, soda, and salt. Stir in the cranberries and walnuts.

In a large bowl cream the butter and ¾ cup of the sugar. Whisk in the egg, sour cream, and vanilla rum. Stir in the dry ingredients; do not overmix. Spoon the batter into the prepared pan and spread it evenly to the edges. Press the apple slices, core side down, into the batter in a flower petal pattern. In a small bowl stir together the remaining 2 teaspoons sugar with the cinnamon and sprinkle evenly over the cake.

Bake 40 to 45 minutes, until the cake is puffed and browned and a tester inserted in the middle comes out clean. Cool slightly on a rack; serve warm with whipped cream, if desired.

leftovers

Both the slaw and the potato salad will be acceptably edible the next day but no longer than that. The cake, though best warm, makes great snacking even when cold, accompanied by a glass of icy milk.

spicy sausage, pepper, and black bean calzones

romaine spears with garlic vinaigrette

caramel oranges in tequila liqueur

(page 50)

Calzones—those half-moon–shaped packets of pizza dough filled with melting cheeses and other good things—make splendid lunchtime eating. This is good-natured fare, the kind we're allowed to pick up with our hands, food that is fun to make and to devour with gusto.

s t r a t e g y

Note that the calzone dough can be prepared up to 48 hours in advance. Shaping and filling the dough packets is almost as entertaining as eating them, although it may take a few runs through the recipe before your output looks as slick as that of a professional *pizzaiola*. Relax. Even misshapen calzones *taste* good. Serve them on the hot side of warm, but not straight from the oven. Cut each calzone in half crosswise to reveal its intriguing innards and arrange them on the same plate as the salad. Drink beer with this fiery, flavorful menu.

spicy sausage, pepper, and

black bean calzones

makes 6

If you have a pizza stone or a set of bread-baking tiles (see Cook's and Gardener's Sources), this would be a good time to employ them. However, unless you have a very large oven as well as a very large pizza stone or a double set of baking tiles, you will have to bake the calzones in two batches. I think the crisp crust that results is worth that fuss, but you may prefer instead to bake the calzones all at the same time on two cornmeal-sprinkled baking sheets—the crusts will be *almost* as crisp. Although I like the flavor and extra fire provided by the poblano chiles, Italian frying peppers or even sweet red or green peppers can be substituted.

DOUGH

1 package dry yeast

1¾ cups lukewarm (105° to 115° F) water

2½ teaspoons salt

¾ cup whole-wheat flour

3½ cups unbleached all-purpose flour

6 teaspoons olive oil

FILLING

¾ cup dried black beans, picked over and soaked 24 hours in cold water to cover

2 teaspoons salt

4 tablespoons olive oil

12 ounces andouille (see Cook's and Gardener's Sources) or other spicy pork or pork and
    beef sausage, cut into ½-inch dice

1 medium-large onion, peeled and thinly sliced

6 medium poblano chiles (see Cook's and Gardener's Sources), stemmed, cored, and cut
    into ⅛-inch-wide strips

1 cup (about 8 ounces) ricotta cheese

⅓ cup yellow cornmeal, for the baking sheets

12 ounces jalapeño Monterey Jack cheese, grated

For the dough In a mixing bowl whisk together the yeast and water; let stand 5 minutes. Whisk in the salt and the whole-wheat flour. Stir in enough of the all-purpose flour to form a soft, sticky dough. Turn the dough out onto a generously floured work surface and knead about 5 minutes, until it is smooth and elastic, adding more flour as needed.

Divide the dough into 6 equal pieces. On the floured work surface form each piece into a ball. Place 1 teaspoon oil in each of 6 small bowls. Place 1 dough ball in each bowl and turn to coat with oil. Cover each bowl tightly with plastic wrap and refrigerate between 24 and 48 hours.

For the filling Drain the beans. In a medium saucepan cover them by 3 inches with fresh cold water and set over medium heat. Bring to a boil, then lower the heat and simmer, uncovered, for 20 minutes. Stir in the salt and continue to simmer until the beans are just tender, about 25 minutes more. Drain and cool.

In a large skillet warm 2 tablespoons of the olive oil over medium heat. Add the sausage and cook, stirring occasionally, until crisp and brown, 10 to 12 minutes. With a slotted spoon transfer the sausage to paper towels to drain.

Pour off all but 2 tablespoons of the fat in the skillet. Return the skillet to medium heat, add the onion and chiles, and cook, covered, stirring once or twice, for 5 minutes. Uncover, raise the heat slightly, and cook, stirring often, until the vegetables are tender and lightly browned, 5 to 7 minutes. Remove from the skillet and cool.

In a strainer set over a bowl, let the ricotta drain for 30 minutes. If you are not using pizza stones or bread-baking tiles, sprinkle two 11- by 17-inch baking sheets evenly with the cornmeal. Position racks in the upper and lower thirds of the oven. If using pizza stones or bread-baking tiles, set them on the racks. Preheat the oven to 500° F.

Lightly flour the work surface. Roll a ball of dough out into an 8-inch round. Spread one-sixth of the ricotta over half the dough, leaving a ½-inch border. Top the ricotta with one-sixth each of the beans, the sausage, and the onion mixture. Top with one-sixth of the grated cheese. Stretch and fold the other half of the dough over the filling to enclose it and form a half-round. Crimp the edges firmly to seal; brush the top of the calzone with some of the remaining olive oil. Repeat with the remaining dough and filling.

Using a long, wide spatula, transfer the calzones to the prepared baking sheets and set them in the oven. If you are using the stones or tiles, transfer the calzones directly to them. Bake the calzones 20 to 25 minutes, until the bottoms are crisp, the tops lightly browned, and the cheeses bubbling. If using baking sheets, exchange their position in the oven from top to bottom and from front to back at the halfway point. Cool slightly on a rack; serve warm.

●

romaine spears with garlic vinaigrette

serves 6

Crisp, pale-green-to-yellow inner romaine leaves make an attractively spiky-looking and tasty salad. Substitute another crisp green (limestone or Bibb would be a good choice) if you wish.

3 tablespoons balsamic vinegar
1 egg yolk, at room temperature
1 teaspoon Dijon-style mustard
1 garlic clove, peeled
½ teaspoon salt
½ teaspoon freshly ground black pepper
⅔ cup olive oil
Tender inner leaves of 3 large heads romaine, rinsed and spun dry

In a small bowl whisk together the vinegar, egg yolk, and mustard. Force the garlic through a press into the bowl. Whisk in the salt and pepper. Continue to whisk while slowly dribbling in the olive oil; the dressing will thicken. Adjust the seasoning.

Arrange the romaine leaves on serving plates. Drizzle with the dressing and serve immediately.

leftovers

The calzones are good cold, or they can be reheated, unwrapped, in a hot oven for an informal lunch or midnight snack, accompanied by a cold beer or a glass of red wine.

braised chile beef tacos with corn and olives

salad of black-eyed peas with cilantro-orange dressing

fresh limeade plus!

texas legend ice cream sundaes

More zesty finger food, this time with a clear-cut Tex-Mex influence. These tacos are filled with tender, braised beef, instead of ordinary ground meat, and along with the unexpected accompaniments, are part of a deeply flavorful and satisfying casual meal.

s t r a t e g y

It requires a rather lengthy cooking process to turn chewy stewing beef into a tender, tasty taco filling, but the marination and subsequent braising are spread out over several days and can be done well in advance. In fact, the filling freezes well and can be prepared on one weekend for serving at another. For simplicity's sake I have called for store-bought taco shells, but if you prefer to fry your own, you have my blessing—the tacos will be even better. The salad is quick—I don't find that black-eyed peas need any soaking—and will be at its best when freshly made. The ice cream topping will last in the refrigerator (if well hidden) for up to one week. Squeezing all those limes for the tequila-spiked fresh limeade takes (1) large limes at room temperature, (2) an efficient citrus-juicing device, and (3) a thirsty volunteer with a strong arm.

●

braised chile beef tacos with corn and olives

serves 6 to 8

This recipe comes from Michael Honstein, a friend in Tucson who frequently features it at weekend lunch parties around the pool in his back yard. Use a good-quality preblended chili powder (the kind with the cumin, garlic, and so on already in it).

¼ cup chili powder
6 garlic cloves, peeled and crushed through a garlic press
5 tablespoons fresh lime juice, strained
6 tablespoons olive oil
1 tablespoon ground cumin, preferably from toasted seeds (see Note)
2½ pounds boneless stewing beef, cut into 1½-inch cubes
1 can (28 ounces) Italian plum tomatoes, crushed with the fingers and drained
2 cups canned beef broth
1 bottle (12 ounces) dark beer
3 cups finely chopped yellow onions
2 fresh jalapeños, stemmed and minced
1 package (10 ounces) frozen corn, thawed and drained
25 pimiento-stuffed green olives, sliced
Salt
Freshly ground black pepper
12 jumbo or 18 regular-size prepared taco shells
12 ounces Cheddar cheese, shredded
½ head romaine lettuce, rinsed, spun dry, and finely shredded
3 medium tomatoes, stemmed, seeded, and diced
Bottled red and green hot salsas and sour cream, for serving

In a small food processor or blender, purée the chili powder, garlic, lime juice, half of the olive oil, and the cumin. In a large nonreactive bowl, combine the purée and the stewing beef and mix well. Refrigerate, covered, stirring once or twice, for 24 hours.

Position a rack in the lower third of the oven and preheat the oven to 350° F. In a heavy 4½- to 5-quart ovenproof pot combine the marinated beef and its juices, the tomatoes, broth, and beer. Set over high heat and bring just to a boil. Cover and place in the oven to bake for 45 minutes, stirring once or twice. Uncover and continue baking until the beef is just tender, about 40 more minutes. Cool. Shred the beef and return it to the braising liquid. Cover and refrigerate overnight.

In a large, deep skillet over low heat, warm the remaining 3 tablespoons olive oil. Add the onions and jalapeños, cover, and cook, stirring once or twice, until the onions are tender, about 15 minutes. Remove any hardened fat from the surface of the braised beef. Strain the beef braising liquid into the skillet. Bring to a boil, lower the heat slightly, and simmer briskly, uncovered, for 30 minutes. Add the shredded beef and simmer until very thick, about 15 minutes. Stir in the corn and olives and adjust the seasoning. *The filling can be prepared to this point well in advance of serving. Cover and refrigerate for up to 3 days or freeze up to 1 month. Defrost thoroughly before proceeding.*

Simmer the filling until heated through, about 5 minutes. To serve, fill each taco shell halfway with the meat mixture, then top with cheese, lettuce, and tomatoes. Serve immediately, passing the salsas and sour cream separately.

NOTE *Toasted cumin has a rich, mellow, nutty flavor that is distinctive and delicious. To toast the seeds, spread about ½ cup (a lesser quantity is likely to scorch—the whole toasted seeds keep well in a covered jar) in a small, heavy dry skillet over low heat. Cook, stirring often, until the seeds are fragrant and brown, 7 to 10 minutes. Remove the seeds from the skillet immediately and cool. Grind in a spice mill or with a mortar and pestle just before using.*

●

salad of black-eyed peas with cilantro-

orange dressing

serves 8

Sometimes I find very large black-eyed peas at my neighborhood health food store— they make the salad even better than the smaller supermarket peas do.

3 cups dried black-eyed peas, picked over and rinsed thoroughly
Salt
⅔ cup fresh orange juice, strained
3 tablespoons red wine vinegar
⅔ cup sliced green onions
½ cup finely chopped cilantro
½ cup olive oil
Freshly ground black pepper

In a large saucepan generously cover the black-eyed peas with water. Stir in 1 tablespoon salt, set over medium heat, and bring to a boil. Lower the heat slightly and simmer until just tender, about 25 minutes. Drain immediately.

In a mixing bowl combine the hot black-eyed peas, orange juice, and vinegar and cool to room temperature, tossing gently once or twice.

Stir in the green onions, cilantro, and olive oil. Season generously with freshly ground pepper, and salt if needed. *The salad can be prepared up to 4 hours in advance. Refrigerate only if necessary, returning the salad to room temperature before serving.*

●

fresh limeade plus!

serves 6 to 8

Plus tequila, that is—making this an especially potent grown-up thirst quencher. Serve it well chilled (to avoid diluting your hard-squeezed lime juice) in tall ice-packed glasses.

4 cups freshly squeezed lime juice (about 32 limes), strained
3 cups water
2½ cups sugar
1 cup gold tequila

Whisk together the lime juice, water, sugar, and tequila until the sugar is dissolved. Chill at least 5 hours, until very cold. Serve over ice.

●

texas legend ice cream sundaes

serves 6 to 8

German's Sweet Chocolate Cake—that towering confection of buttermilk-chocolate layers, sandwiched with an abundant and gooey coconut-pecan filling—is a Texas institution. Possibly it was even invented in Texas; in fact, many a Texas family legend claims it as the creation of its matriarch. The truth is shrouded, as are many legends, by the past, but the dessert lives on, here reinterpreted as an ice cream sundae—cakeless, but cooling after two or three fiery tacos.

1½ cups pecans

1 can (3½ ounces or 1⅓ cups) sweetened flaked coconut

1 cup whipping cream

¾ cup packed light brown sugar

¾ stick (6 tablespoons) unsalted butter

⅓ cup bourbon

¼ cup light corn syrup

1 tablespoon Vanilla Rum (page 66) or vanilla extract

1 tablespoon fresh lemon juice, strained

2 pints each premium vanilla and chocolate ice cream, softened

Position a rack in the middle of the oven and preheat the oven to 375° F.

Spread the pecans in a layer in a metal pan (like a cake tin) and bake, stirring them once or twice, until they are crisp and lightly toasted, about 15 minutes. Cool and coarsely chop.

Raise the oven temperature to 400° F. Spread the coconut in a layer in a metal pan (like a cake tin) and bake, stirring often, until crisp and golden, about 15 minutes. Cool.

In a heavy medium saucepan over moderate heat, combine the cream, sugar, butter, bourbon, and corn syrup. Bring to a boil, stirring often. Adjust the heat and simmer briskly, stirring occasionally, for 15 minutes, until the sauce has thickened. Remove from the heat and cool slightly; stir in the vanilla rum and lemon juice. *The dessert can be prepared to this point a week ahead. Store the pecans and coconut, tightly covered, at room temperature. Cool the sauce to room temperature, cover, and refrigerate. Reheat just until warm in a heavy saucepan, stirring often, before proceeding.*

Stir the pecans and 1 cup of the coconut into the sauce. Divide the ice cream among dessert bowls, placing a scoop of vanilla and a scoop of chocolate in each. Spoon the sauce over the ice cream, sprinkle each serving with some of the remaining coconut, and serve immediately.

l e f t o v e r s

Any remaining taco filling can be reheated to make tacos for another meal, or folded into flour tortillas and deep-fried to make chimichangas (serve them with sour cream, salsa, and shredded lettuce), or heated and spooned onto a toasted hamburger bun to make a Tex-Mex sloppy joe. The bean salad can be enjoyed on another day but will need fresh cilantro and a boost of orange juice and vinegar. The ice cream topping will keep in the refrigerator after the pecans and coconut are added but will lose some of its crunch. Try it warmed and spooned over waffles or pancakes. (It can even be used as a cake filling.)

vanilla rum

makes 4 ounces

Inspired by a precious, carefully hoarded, but eventually exhausted bottle of vanilla extract presented to me as a gift from some Caribbean island or other, this is my homemade substitute. Whether the souvenir was actually rum-based or not no longer matters—*this* is now my house vanilla extract and can be used in any recipe that calls for vanilla with spectacular results. At holiday time I make extra bottles for inclusion in gift baskets and cook's and baker's Christmas stockings. The vanilla beans will flavor the rum for at least two batches; so when the bottle runs low, don't hesitate to top it up with additional rum, starting over with fresh vanilla beans only when the first two finally seem to be losing potency.

2 whole vanilla beans
½ cup amber (*añejo*) rum

Split the vanilla beans lengthwise, then cut each half in half crosswise. In a small jar with a lid or a sealable bottle, combine the vanilla bean pieces and rum. Let stand, shaking the jar occasionally, for 2 weeks. Use the mixture in place of regular vanilla extract.

crab cake sandwiches

old bay slaw

raspberry—key-lime squares

With spring in the air, eating quickly but well before getting on with enjoyment of the season is a priority, especially with a carefree Saturday stretching ahead. These sandwiches are speedy indeed but far from ordinary when they're extravagantly stuffed with plump crabmeat, as featured in this Southern coastal menu.

s t r a t e g y

   Picking over crabmeat is not a pretty job and certainly not one for amateurs. Getting out every crunchy bit of shell and cartilage without unduly breaking up the luscious lumps of crabmeat is essential to the full enjoyment of the crab cakes, so select your kitchen volunteer carefully—or just do the job yourself. The slaw can be prepared a day ahead, if necessary, as can the easy dessert. Evoke the coast and serve this meal on paper plates, outside, seated at a bare table under the best big old tree you can find. Drink beer, sweetened iced tea, or Dr Pepper.

●

crab cake sandwiches

makes 4

Purists will enjoy these on toasted, buttered buns, free of mayonnaise or other garniture, but I like a little dressing and I love a thin slice of ripe tomato and a leaf of crisp lettuce.

5 tablespoons unsalted butter
¼ cup finely diced yellow onions
¼ cup finely diced celery
1 pound fresh jumbo lump crabmeat, picked over
½ cup finely crushed saltine crackers
1 egg
1 tablespoon Dijon-style mustard
1 tablespoon fresh lemon juice, strained
Freshly ground black pepper
4 good-quality round sandwich buns, split and toasted
Lemony Mayonnaise (page 292), Green Goddess Mayonnaise (page 289), or Green Aioli (page 77)
Thin tomato slices and crisp lettuce leaves (optional)

In a small skillet over low heat, melt 2 tablespoons of the butter. Add the onions and celery and cook, covered, stirring once or twice, for 8 minutes. The vegetables should retain some of their crispness. Cool to room temperature.

In a medium bowl gently toss the crabmeat, sautéed vegetables, and cracker crumbs. In a small bowl whisk together the egg, mustard, and lemon juice. Pour the mixture over the crabmeat, season generously with fresh pepper, and stir until just combined. Form the crab mixture into 4 thick patties. Transfer to a plate and refrigerate the crab cakes for 1 hour.

In a large skillet melt the remaining 3 tablespoons butter over medium-high heat. When it is foaming, carefully add the crab cakes and cook, turning once, until crisp and brown, about 4 minutes per side.

Place each crab cake on a toasted bun, top with mayonnaise, and tomato and lettuce if desired. Serve immediately.

VARIATION *Try the crab cakes plain for brunch, accompanied by crisp bacon, scrambled eggs, fried tomatoes, and buttermilk biscuits.*

●

old bay slaw

serves 4

The creamy dressing for this shore dinner's coleslaw is spiked with Old Bay Seasoning, a crab-boil spice mixture available in fish stores and some gourmet shops (see Cook's and Gardener's Sources). Other brands of seafood seasoning can be substituted.

¾ cup plain yogurt
¾ cup mayonnaise
1 tablespoon fresh lemon juice, strained
1 tablespoon Dijon-style mustard
4 teaspoons sugar
2 teaspoons Old Bay Seasoning
½ teaspoon freshly ground black pepper
6 cups finely shredded green cabbage (1-pound head)
½ cup finely diced red onion
Salt
Radicchio leaves, for garnish

In a bowl whisk together the yogurt, mayonnaise, lemon juice, mustard, sugar, seasoning, and pepper. In a medium bowl combine the cabbage, onion, and dressing. Season with salt to taste and adjust the other seasonings. Refrigerate at least 1 hour. *The recipe can be prepared up to 1 day ahead. Reserve the onion and add it just before serving.*

Toss the slaw, adjust the seasoning, and serve, garnished with radicchio leaves.

VARIATION Shrimp Slaw: *For a main-course salad serving 4, add 1½ pounds shelled and deveined medium shrimp that have been poached for 4 minutes in boiling salted water.*

●

raspberry key-lime squares

makes about 20

It is hard to actually improve upon classic lemon squares, but it is possible to improvise a little for a change of pace. This particular riff (based on a recipe from

Minute Maid) turned out to be delicious. Bottled Key lime juice is available from a number of mail-order companies (see Cook's and Gardener's Sources).

2 sticks (8 ounces) unsalted butter, softened

½ cup unsifted confectioners' sugar, plus 2 tablespoons for garnish

2⅓ cups unbleached all-purpose flour

4 eggs

1 egg yolk

2 cups granulated sugar

⅓ cup Key lime juice

1 teaspoon baking powder

1 cup (about 11 ounces) raspberry preserves

Position a rack in the middle of the oven and preheat the oven to 350° F. Butter a 9-by 13-inch metal baking pan.

In a large bowl cream the butter and ½ cup confectioners' sugar until light and fluffy. Add 2 cups of the flour and stir until a soft dough forms. Pat the dough evenly into the prepared pan and bake 15 minutes. (The dough should not brown except at the edges.) Cool in the pan on a rack for 5 minutes.

Meanwhile, in a large bowl whisk the eggs and egg yolk until foamy. Whisk in the granulated sugar, then the Key lime juice, the remaining ⅓ cup flour, and the baking powder.

Spread the raspberry preserves over the warm crust evenly, leaving a ¼-inch border. Pour the egg mixture evenly over the preserves. Return the pan to the oven and bake 30 to 35 minutes, until the topping is puffed, lightly browned, and just set.

Sprinkle the top evenly with the remaining 2 tablespoons confectioners' sugar and cool completely on a rack. *The squares can be baked 1 day ahead. Wrap well and store at room temperature.*

Cut around the pan ¼ inch in from the edge (this crust may be too crisp and brown to serve). Lift out the crust portion and discard (or nibble it yourself if it is not too brown). Using a pizza wheel or a sharp knife, cut the remainder into 20 squares or bars. Carefully remove with a pancake-type turner and arrange in a single layer on one or two plates. Cover loosely with plastic wrap and store at room temperature. If necessary, sift additional confectioners' sugar over the squares just before serving.

l e f t o v e r s

Any remaining Raspberry Key-Lime Squares can be stored in a single layer in an airtight container at room temperature for up to 3 days.

antipasto platter, al forno—style

risotto with asparagus, porcini, and basil

mixed greens with red wine vinaigrette

fresh figs with lemon mascarpone and raspberry sauce (page 34)

or

christopher styler's tiramisù (page 267)

Like most pastas, most risotti are not traditionally considered by Italians as suitable main courses. In this country though the long-simmered dish of Arborio rice with added savory elements is quickly becoming a rich, comfortable, and even stylish entrée (also like pasta), as illustrated by this easy spring menu.

s t r a t e g y

Risotto requires steady stirring, which is essential for the even cooking of the plump grains. Because this main course is a one-dish affair, such more-or-less constant attention seems to me a fair exchange for all the good eating that results. The various colorful elements of the antipasto can be prepared ahead, leaving only arranging the platter for the last minute, something that can be accomplished by a volunteer or by the chef between stirs. Make 15 cups of Basic Mixed Green Salad (page 23), including plenty of arugula, and dress it with olive oil and red wine or balsamic vinegar. Either of the suggested desserts also can be completed substantially in advance and only need to be portioned, arranged, and garnished. Offer plenty of good bread and pour a light Chianti or a Pinot Noir from the American Northwest.

•

antipasto platter, al forno—style

serves 6

Johanne Killeen and George Germon's Al Forno, in Providence, Rhode Island, is one of my favorite places to dine out. One necessity on every visit is an order of antipasto. Served up on a prosciutto-covered white platter the size of a modest manhole cover, Al Forno's antipasto includes savory mounds of five or six intriguing edibles. The authentic specifics can be cooked up from Johanne and George's *Cucina Simpatica* (HarperCollins); a reasonable approximation also can be created using recipes found elsewhere in the book you are holding. The one constant, says Johanne, is the prosciutto, preferably the prosciutto di Parma recently reintroduced to this country after a long absence. This appetizer is an assemblage, one that easily can be expanded or reduced to feed any number of hungry people.

12 thin slices imported prosciutto
½ cup White Bean Salad (page 93)
½ cup Greek Garlic Sauce (page 93)
6 *bocconcini* (fresh mozzarella balls, available in some supermarkets, or see Cook's and Gardener's Sources)
6 oil-packed sun-dried tomato halves, homemade (page 46) or purchased (see Cook's and Gardener's Sources), julienned
⅓ cup Red Pepper Spread (page 125)
6 thin slices baguette, lightly toasted
½ cup Black Olives with Orange and Basil (recipe follows)
3 tablespoons olive oil
Freshly ground black pepper

Select a large serving platter. Lay the prosciutto in a more-or-less single layer in the center of the platter. Arrange the bean salad in a mound on the open border around the edge of the platter (if there is one) or place it directly on the prosciutto. Do the same with the garlic sauce and the *bocconcini*. Top the *bocconcini* with the julienned sun-dried tomatoes. Dollop the red pepper spread on the slices of toasted baguette and arrange the resulting crostini on the platter. Scatter the black olives randomly around the platter. Drizzle the olive oil evenly over all, season with fresh pepper, and serve immediately.

black olives with orange and basil

As a component of the antipasto platter above or as an appetizer on their own, these orange-marinated black olives are easy and delicious.

8 ounces brine-cured imported black olives, preferably Gaeta (see Cook's and Gardener's Sources), rinsed and drained
2 tablespoons olive oil
2 tablespoons fresh orange juice, strained
1 tablespoon minced fresh orange zest
¼ teaspoon crushed dried red pepper
2 tablespoons minced fresh basil

In a medium bowl combine the olives, olive oil, orange juice, orange zest, and crushed red pepper. Cover and let stand at room temperature for 1 hour. *The olives can be prepared to this point 1 day ahead and refrigerated. Return to room temperature before proceeding.*

Add the basil and stir well.

risotto with asparagus, porcini, and basil

serves 6

Stock-simmered Arborio rice, subtly flavored with wild mushrooms and fresh basil, is a savory vehicle for tender asparagus. This recipe makes modest (but rich) portions, suitable for lunch, following the substantial antipasto.

1 pound medium asparagus, trimmed and peeled (see Note)
Salt
½ ounce dried porcini mushrooms (see Cook's and Gardener's Sources)
1 cup dry white wine
6 cups Chicken Stock (page 90) or 5 cups canned chicken broth diluted with 1 cup water
¾ stick (6 tablespoons) unsalted butter
1 cup finely diced yellow onions

2 garlic cloves, peeled and minced

1½ cups (about 10 ounces) Arborio rice (see Cook's and Gardener's Sources)

1 cup (about 4 ounces) grated Parmesan cheese

⅓ cup minced fresh basil, plus basil sprigs for garnish

Cut the asparagus diagonally into 1-inch pieces. Bring a pot of water to a boil. Stir in 1 tablespoon salt, add the asparagus, and cook until barely tender, about 3 minutes. Drain and transfer immediately to a bowl of ice water. Cool completely and drain well.

In a strainer under cold running water, rinse the porcini. In a small nonreactive saucepan bring the wine to a boil. In a heatproof bowl pour the wine over the porcini. Cover and let stand until cool. With a slotted spoon remove the porcini; mince and reserve. Carefully pour the wine into another container, leaving any sandy residue behind in the bowl. *The recipe can be completed to this point several hours in advance. Wrap the asparagus and store at room temperature; refrigerate the wine.*

In a medium saucepan combine the wine and the stock. Cover and bring just to a simmer over low heat.

Meanwhile, in a heavy 4-quart saucepan over low heat, melt the butter. Add the onion, porcini, and garlic; cook, stirring once or twice, for 8 minutes. Add the rice and stir to coat the grains with butter. Stir in 1 cup hot stock. Bring to a simmer and cook, stirring often, until the rice has absorbed most of the stock, about 7 minutes. Continue to cook the risotto, adding hot stock ½ cup at a time and stirring often (although not constantly), until the grains are tender but still slightly firm to the bite, about 35 minutes.

Stir in the asparagus and cook 2 minutes, until heated through. Remove from the heat, stir in ⅓ cup of the Parmesan and the basil, and let stand, covered, for 1 minute. The completed risotto should be somewhat runny. Serve immediately, garnished with basil sprigs if desired, and accompanied by the remaining Parmesan and a peppermill.

NOTE *Pencil-thin asparagus may look properly infantile (a necessary quality in a spring vegetable), but medium asparagus are usually more affordable and have more flavor. Bending the stalks until they snap and then discarding the bottoms is wasteful. Instead, cut off the woody ends and then, using a swivel-bladed vegetable peeler, pare the stalks about halfway up, or to where the peel becomes tender.*

 l e f t o v e r s

Various unused components of the antipasto platter can be refrigerated, to become parts of other appetizer combinations or merely enjoyed as emergency nibbles. Leftover risotto (this recipe anyway) isn't very successful—nor is it very likely.

lillet with a twist of orange

salted almonds

poached monkfish and green bean salad with

green aioli and potato croutons

coeurs à la crème with mango sauce and strawberries

For one of the blessed moments when the children are elsewhere, and civilized adults can gather to talk about something other than mutant turtles and toilet training, this menu might well be the meal of choice. Light, sophisticated, even pretty, it's a quiet spring oasis in the hustle of regular life.

s t r a t e g y

Although the monkfish can be poached a day ahead, it will actually have the best texture and flavor if never refrigerated, which means that optimum advance cooking time is somewhere around two hours. The crisp potato croutons should be sautéed at the last minute. Arrange the plates, dress the salads, and scatter the hot potatoes over them just before serving.

The dessert, on the other hand, must be made a day ahead (or started even further in advance, if you're making your own *fromage blanc*) in order to drain and firm up. The mango sauce, too, will keep well for several days under refrigeration. Start your grown-up's lunch with the orange-scented vermouth called Lillet, served well chilled with a twist of orange peel, and drink a citrusy Sauvignon Blanc with the main course.

•

poached monkfish and green bean salad
with green aioli and potato croutons

serves 4

Monkfish (also called lotte and anglerfish) is a huge, ugly creature, that is sold, fortunately, in simple meaty fillets that resemble pork tenderloins and give no indication of the size and form of the beast from which they have been cut. Monkfish has a texture that reminds some people of lobster, and some claim it even has a lobsterlike flavor. (I think it tastes like monkfish.) Ask the fishmonger to remove the tough membrane that covers the fillets as well as the strip of soft, grainy flesh that runs alongside the main fillet.

1 pound (about 3 medium) boiling potatoes, peeled and cut into ½-inch dice
Salt
12 ounces green beans, trimmed
5 cups water
3 cups dry white wine
2 garlic cloves, peeled and slightly crushed
Zest of 1 large lemon, removed in strips with a vegetable peeler
Stems from 1 bunch parsley
12 black peppercorns
2 bay leaves
2 thick (2 inches) monkfish fillets (about 2½ pounds), tough membrane and grainy side strip
    removed
3 tablespoons olive oil
Freshly ground black pepper
Green Aioli (recipe follows)

In a saucepan cover the potatoes with cold water. Stir in 1 tablespoon salt, set over medium heat, and bring to a boil. Lower the heat slightly and simmer until the potatoes are just tender, about 7 minutes. With a slotted spoon, remove the potatoes and drain well. Bring the water back to a boil. Add the green beans and cook until just tender, about 5 minutes. Drain and transfer immediately to a bowl of ice water. Cool completely and drain well. *The recipe can be prepared to this point 1 day ahead. Wrap the vegetables separately and refrigerate.*

In a deep nonreactive skillet just large enough to hold the fish fillets in a single layer, combine the water, wine, garlic cloves, lemon zest, parsley stems, peppercorns, bay leaves, and 1 tablespoon salt. Set over medium heat, bring to a simmer, and cook, partially covered, for 10 minutes. Add the monkfish and adjust the temperature so that the liquid barely simmers. Cook, partially covered, until the fish fillets are just tender at their thickest point, 12 to 15 minutes. Remove from the heat and cool to room temperature in the skillet. *The fish can be prepared to this point 2 hours ahead and kept at room temperature, or may be refrigerated in the poaching liquid for up to 24 hours. Return the fillets to room temperature before proceeding.*

Remove the fish from the poaching liquid and pat dry. Cut the fillets crosswise into 1½-inch-thick disks. Arrange the green beans and the fish on serving plates.

Heat the olive oil in a heavy skillet over medium-high heat. When it is very hot, almost smoking, add the potato cubes and cook, stirring and tossing, until they are crisp and brown, about 10 minutes. Season to taste with a sprinkle of salt and pepper.

Nap the monkfish and green beans generously with the aioli. Scatter the hot potato cubes over the salads and serve immediately.

●

green aioli

makes about 1 ½ cups

Aioli—garlic mayonnaise—gets a touch of pale green color and a bit of added flavor from the addition of a fistful of parsley.

¾ cup chopped wide-leaf parsley
2 egg yolks, at room temperature
3 tablespoons fresh lemon juice, strained
½ teaspoon salt
¼ teaspoon freshly ground black pepper
½ cup corn oil
¾ cup olive oil
3 cloves garlic, peeled

In a food processor combine the parsley, egg yolks, lemon juice, salt, and pepper. Process until smooth. With the machine running, dribble the oils into the processor through the feed tube in a quick, steady stream; the dressing will thicken. Force the garlic through a press into the aioli; adjust the seasoning. *The aioli can be prepared up to 24 hours in advance. Transfer to a container, cover, and refrigerate. Bring the mayonnaise to room temperature before serving.*

●

coeurs à la crème
with mango sauce and strawberries

serves 4

Heart-shaped puddings of light and creamy fresh cheese, delicately sweetened, are served in a puddle of honeyed mango sauce and garnished with a few perfect strawberries. The *coeur* molds are pierced with holes to allow the whey to drain out, firming the puddings as they chill, and are available in plastic or ceramic (see Cook's and Gardener's Sources). Other fruit sauces—Blackberry (page 96), Raspberry (page 34), or Blueberry-Lime (page 22)—can be substituted for or used in tandem with the mango sauce. If you wish to make your own *fromage blanc*, the recipe is on page 80.

1 pound *fromage blanc,* at room temperature
½ cup plus 1 tablespoon superfine sugar
¼ cup whipping cream
4 egg whites, whipped to stiff peaks
Mango Sauce (recipe follows)
12 small, pretty, fresh strawberries

Cut four 6-inch squares of butter muslin (see Cook's and Gardener's Sources) or doubled cheesecloth. Dampen the squares in cold water. Line each of four 2½- to 3-inch heart-shaped *coeur à la crème* molds with a square of muslin.

Force the *fromage blanc* through a fine sieve into a bowl. Stir in the sugar and whipping cream, then fold in the egg whites. Spoon the mixture into the prepared molds, mounding it if necessary and using it all. Fold the overhanging muslin to enclose the cheese mixture. Set the molds on a rack set on a jelly-roll pan and refrigerate, loosely draped with plastic wrap, for at least 24 hours. *The* coeurs *can be prepared up to 2 days ahead.*

Fold back the muslin that encloses the *coeurs.* Set a dessert plate atop each *coeur* and invert the mold and the plate together. Lift off the mold; peel away and discard the muslin. *The* coeurs *can be unmolded several hours before serving. Drape loosely with plastic wrap and refrigerate on the dessert plates. Blot up any excess liquid on the plates with a paper towel before proceeding.*

Spoon the mango sauce partially around each *coeur,* dividing it evenly and using it all. Garnish each plate with a strawberry and serve immediately.

●

mango sauce

makes about 1 cup

1 very ripe large (about 1 pound) mango
3 tablespoons fresh orange juice, strained
3 tablespoons honey
2 tablespoons fresh lemon juice, strained

Cut the mango away from its large pit in sections. Scrape the flesh from the mango peel into a food processor. Add the orange juice, honey, and lemon juice and process until smooth. Adjust the sweet-tart balance and process again. Refrigerate the purée until serving time. *The recipe can be prepared up to 3 days ahead.*

l e f t  v e r s

If there are leftover salad ingredients, combine chunked fish, sliced green beans, and some of the aioli to make a single serving of delicious fish salad to enjoy at another meal. There will be leftover aioli to use as a dip or sauce for crudités, poached or deep-fried seafood, roast chicken, or on sandwiches such as turkey or tuna. The *coeurs à la crème* will keep for a day or so. The mango sauce will also keep a day or two and is delicious over ice cream, waffles, and grilled or broiled pineapple.

the new england cheesemaking company's
fromage blanc

---

m a k e s   a b o u t   1 ½   p o u n d s

Fromage blanc is a delicate, fresh cream cheese, available in both imported and domestic versions. Making your own at home is an easy and interesting kitchen project, and the results will not only be fresher than what you can buy but will also be free from preservatives and stabilizing gums. *Fromage blanc* can be used wherever cream cheese is called for, and it is essential in making *coeurs à la crème* (page 78). Spread it on a bagel, sweeten it with honey and dollop it on pancakes or waffles, or spoon it over a bowl of prime summer berries. The cheese can be salted or not, as you wish, and the addition of garlic, herbs, or pepper will turn it into a savory appetizer. The starter required to begin the curdling process can be ordered by mail (see Cook's and Gardener's Sources) and stored in the freezer. The same culture and the formula below can also be used to make *chèvre frais* (fresh goat's cheese) from goat's milk purchased at a health food store.

3½ quarts whole or skim milk
1 package *fromage blanc* or *fromagina* starter
1 teaspoon salt

In a 4-quart saucepan over medium heat, warm the milk until an instant-reading thermometer registers 175° F. Transfer the milk to a large bowl and set the bowl in the sink. Fill the sink with enough cold water to come three-quarters of the way up the sides of the bowl, add a tray or two of ice cubes to the water, and cool the milk, stirring it once or twice, until the thermometer registers between 72° and 86° F.

Whisk in the packet of starter. Drain the sink of water and let the milk mixture stand in the bowl loosely covered at room temperature for 12 hours. The milk will thicken and form soft custardlike curds.

Line a colander or a large sieve with dampened butter muslin (see Cook's and Gardener's Sources) or several thicknesses of dampened cheesecloth. Ladle the curd into the colander and let it drain in the sink or over a bowl for about 4 hours (longer for a drier, firmer cheese or shorter for a softer, moister cheese).

Transfer the cheese to a container, stir in the salt, and refrigerate, covered. The cheese will keep up to 1 week.

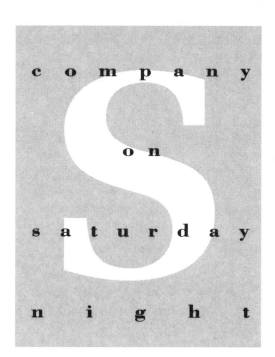

company on saturday night

chilled yellow tomato soup with black olive cream

grilled honey-thyme magret of duck with peaches

lentil, grain, and mushroom salad with basil

mixed green salad with peppered cheese

raspberry brownies

If duck is always cold-weather food in your kitchen, then you've missed the pleasures of it hot and juicy from the grill on a balmy summer's night. When all around you are barbecuing beef, consider the following menu for a distinctive and delicious change of pace.

s t r a t e g y

To keep your cool, prepare both the soup and the grain salad a day ahead. Present the entrée on a handsome platter (peaches cut side up in the center, sliced *magret* fanned around them), garnished with sprigs of fresh thyme. Prepare 16 cups of Basic Mixed Green Salad (page 23), using plenty of arugula and dressing it with olive oil and red wine vinegar. Garnish each salad with a one-ounce slice of tangy sheep's or goat's milk cheese, generously sprinkled with freshly ground black pepper.

•

chilled yellow tomato soup with black olive cream

Tomatoes now grow in a veritable rainbow of colors, but once, when they were a newly discovered Western Hemisphere rarity, tomatoes were only yellow, hence the Italian word *pomodoro*, or golden apple, by which they were first known. If you find yellow plum-type tomatoes—at the farmer's market or planted in your own garden or that of a tomato-growing friend—grab them for this cool, rich soup. (For yellow tomato seeds, see Cook's and Gardener's Sources.) If you can't find yellow tomatoes, use red, and the soup, although less unusual, will still taste delicious. Either way, it is served with a dramatic and delicious drizzle of black-olive–infused cream.

SOUP

5 tablespoons unsalted butjter
2 large leeks (white part only), well cleaned and chopped (about 3 cups)
1 tablespoon finely minced fresh thyme or 1 teaspoon dried
2 bay leaves
2 pounds plum tomatoes, preferably yellow, trimmed and chunked
3½ cups Chicken Stock (page 90) or canned broth
2 teaspoons sugar
1 tablespoon salt
1 teaspoon freshly ground black pepper

BLACK OLIVE CREAM

⅓ cup black olive purée (olivada) or tapenade (see Cook's and Gardener's Sources)
¼ cup whipping cream

2 red plum tomatoes, trimmed and diced, for garnish

For the soup In a 4-quart nonreactive pot over low heat, melt the butter. Add the leeks, thyme, and bay leaves; cook, covered, for 20 minutes, stirring once or twice. Stir in the tomatoes, stock, sugar, salt, and pepper. Bring to a simmer, then cook, uncovered, stirring once or twice, for 25 minutes, until the tomatoes are very tender and the soup has thickened. Cool slightly, remove the bay leaves, and force the soup through the medium blade of a food mill (or purée in a food processor). Transfer to a bowl, cover, and refrigerate until cold, at least 5 hours. *The soup can be prepared to this point up to 2 days ahead.*

For the black olive cream In a small bowl whisk together the black olive purée and the cream.

To assemble Taste the soup and adjust the seasoning. Ladle into chilled bowls and drizzle the purée over each serving. Sprinkle with diced red tomatoes if desired and serve immediately.

●

grilled honey-thyme magret of duck

with peaches

serves 8

Boldly oversized, the boneless breast steaks, or *magret*, of the special hybrid Moullard duck are available by mail order from New Jersey–based D'Artagnan, supplier of much of Manhattan's (and the country's) domestically produced foie gras.

4 *magret,* about 3 pounds total (see Cook's and Gardener's Sources)
3 tablespoons minced fresh thyme, plus additional thyme sprigs for garnish
2 tablespoons red wine vinegar
2 tablespoons olive oil
2 tablespoons honey
2 garlic cloves, peeled
1½ teaspoons freshly ground black pepper
2 cups aromatic fruitwood smoking chips, preferably peach (see Cook's and Gardener's
    Sources)
Coarse (kosher) salt
4 ripe but firm medium peaches or nectarines, halved and pitted
2 tablespoons vegetable oil

Trim the *magret,* removing the skin and any surface fat. In a blender or small food processor combine the thyme, vinegar, olive oil, honey, garlic, and pepper; process until smooth. In a shallow dish pour this mixture over the *magret.* Cover and marinate at room temperature, turning once or twice, for 2 hours.

Soak the wood chips in water for 30 minutes. Prepare a charcoal fire and allow it to burn until the coals are evenly white, or preheat a gas grill to medium-high. Drain the chips and scatter them over the coals or the grill stones. When the chips are smoking, position the grill rack about 6 inches above the heat source. Lay the *magret* on the rack, cover, and cook, turning once or twice, until the duck is done to your liking, about 10 minutes for medium rare, 12 to 14 minutes for medium. Transfer to a cutting board, sprinkle with coarse salt, and keep warm.

If using a gas grill, turn the heat to high. Brush the peaches lightly with the vegetable oil. Lay them, cut side down, on the grill rack over the hottest part of the fire if using charcoal and cover the grill. Cook, rotating them once to create an attractive pattern of grill marks on the cut sides, until hot and tender, about 2 minutes. Transfer to a plate.

Carve the *magret* across the grain and at a slight angle into thin slices. Spoon any juices from the cutting board over the sliced *magret* and serve immediately, accompanied by the peaches.

●

lentil, grain, and mushroom salad

with basil

serves 8

Nutty, moist, and crunchy, this cool salad is an excellent foil to the rich and smoky duck meat. Look for wheat berries at the health food store. Wehani, a long-grain brown rice with a uniquely sweet flavor and reddish color, is also available in health food stores and in some specialty food markets; ordinary brown rice can be substituted.

1 cup wheat berries, soaked 24 hours in cold water to cover
Salt
½ cup pearl barley, rinsed and drained
¼ cup Wehani rice, rinsed and drained
1 cup brown lentils, picked over .
1½ cups packed fresh basil leaves, plus additional basil sprigs for garnish
1 cup (about) olive oil
⅓ cup sherry vinegar
1 teaspoon freshly ground black pepper
8 ounces cremini (brown) or cultivated white mushrooms, wiped clean, trimmed, and thinly
    sliced

Drain the wheat berries. Bring a medium saucepan of water to a boil. Stir in the wheat berries and 2 teaspoons salt. Lower the heat and simmer, partially covered, for 20 minutes. Stir in the barley and rice; cook another 30 minutes, until the grains are just tender. Drain and cool.

Bring a medium saucepan of water to a boil. Stir in the lentils and 1½ teaspoons salt. Lower the heat and simmer, partially covered, until the lentils are just tender, about 20 minutes. Drain. In a bowl, combine the grains and the lentils.

In a food processor combine the basil leaves, 3/4 cup of the olive oil, the vinegar, 1½ teaspoons salt, and the pepper. Purée until smooth. Pour the dressing over the grains and lentils and toss. *The salad can be prepared to this point 1 day ahead. Cover and refrigerate, but let the salad return to room temperature before proceeding.*

Add the mushrooms to the salad and toss well. Adjust the seasoning and add more oil if the salad seems dry. Garnish with basil sprigs if desired. Serve at room temperature.

●

raspberry brownies

makes 16

Delicate cocoa brownies, spangled with juicy fresh berries and drizzled with dark chocolate, are an informal yet sophisticated conclusion to this summertime menu. Serve them with strong iced cappuccino (page 171).

BROWNIES

2 sticks (8 ounces) unsalted butter, softened

1¼ cups granulated sugar

½ cup firmly packed light brown sugar

4 large eggs

½ cup unsweetened cocoa powder

1 tablespoon framboise eau-de-vie (clear raspberry brandy) or Grand Marnier

1 teaspoon Vanilla Rum (page 66) or vanilla extract

¼ teaspoon salt

1¼ cups unbleached all-purpose flour

1 basket (6 ounces) fresh raspberries, picked over, rinsed only if necessary

GLAZE

4 ounces bittersweet chocolate, chopped

2 tablespoons framboise eau-de-vie or Grand Marnier

2 teaspoons hot water

Confectioners' sugar

For the brownies   Position a rack in the middle of the oven and preheat the oven to 325° F. Butter a 9- by 13-inch metal baking pan.

In a large bowl cream together the butter and both sugars until fluffy. Whisk in the eggs, one at a time, beating well after each addition. Stir in the cocoa, framboise, vanilla rum, and salt. Fold in the flour; do not overmix. Pour the batter into the prepared pan. Sprinkle the raspberries evenly over the surface of the batter. Bake until a tester inserted into the center of the brownies comes out clean, about 30 minutes. Cool completely in the pan on a rack.

For the glaze In the top of a double boiler combine the chocolate, framboise, and water. Set over barely simmering water and stir until smooth. Cool slightly.

To assemble Cut the brownies into 2- by 3-inch bars. Sift confectioners' sugar lightly over the brownies, then dip a fork into the glaze and drizzle it decoratively over the tops. Let stand until the glaze sets, about 30 minutes. *The brownies can be decorated about 4 hours before serving. Cover loosely and store at room temperature.*

l e f t o v e r s

A cup of cold tomato soup and a sandwich of duck breast, arugula, and olive purée on crusty bread makes an excellent lunch the next day. Or serve the cold duck breast over any remaining grain salad for a quick meal. Leftover brownies (rarely a problem) can be wrapped well, stored at room temperature, and enjoyed at will.

chicken stock

makes about 3 quarts

Lack of time is surely the reason more cooks don't make chicken stock, for the technique is simplicity itself. Dedicate a short chunk of a weekend every now and then to this easy, reassuring process and store the rich result in the freezer, where you'll find endless uses for it. This is a double-strength stock, begun with leftover chicken poaching water (preferably) or even canned chicken broth.

⅓ cup (about) olive oil
4 pounds chicken wings, necks, and backs, patted dry
2 cups chopped yellow onions
2 cups chopped leeks (white part only), well cleaned
1 cup chopped carrots
1 small parsnip, peeled and finely diced
3 quarts chicken poaching water, or canned chicken broth, or a combination
1 cup dry white wine
Stems from 1 bunch wide-leaf parsley
2 teaspoons salt
6 fresh thyme sprigs, or 1 teaspoon dried thyme, crumbled
12 whole black peppercorns
3 bay leaves

In a deep, heavy stockpot warm half the oil over medium-high heat. Working in batches, add the chicken parts and cook, turning occasionally and adding additional oil if necessary, until lightly browned, about 10 minutes. Transfer the browned chicken parts to a bowl and reserve.

Add the onions, leeks, carrots, and parsnip to the stockpot and cook, covered, over medium heat, stirring occasionally, until the vegetables are tender and lightly colored, about 15 minutes. Return the browned chicken to the pot. Add the chicken poaching water and wine. Add water if necessary to cover the ingredients by 2 inches. Bring to a simmer and cook, uncovered, skimming the scum that forms on the top, for 15 minutes.

Stir in the parsley stems, salt, thyme, peppercorns, and bay leaves. Partially cover the stockpot and simmer, stirring once or twice, for 2 hours. Remove from the heat and cool to room temperature.

Pour the stock through a strainer set over a large bowl, pressing as much liquid out of the solids as possible with a spatula or the back of a spoon.

Cover the stock and refrigerate until cold, at least 5 hours. Remove any hardened surface fat. *The stock can be transferred to smaller containers and refrigerated up to 3 days or frozen up to 6 months.*

fish stock

Fish stock is even easier and quicker to make than chicken stock. For best flavor it is simmered only 30 minutes, and it is absolutely preferable to the usual suggested substitution—bottled clam juice. The fish frames (ordered from the fishmonger) should come from mild, nonoily fish such as cod, sole, or flounder and should be free from any bloody gills or viscera. If fresh fennel is unavailable, substitute an equal quantity of chopped celery.

¼ cup oil
1 cup chopped yellow onions
1 cup chopped well-cleaned leeks (white part only)
1 cup chopped fresh fennel, leafy green tops included
½ cup chopped carrot
5 pounds fish frames
2 cups white vermouth
3 quarts (about) water
2 teaspoons salt
Stems from 1 bunch wide-leaf parsley
3 fresh thyme sprigs
12 whole black peppercorns
1 medium lemon, thinly sliced

In a deep, heavy stockpot warm the oil over medium heat. Add the onions, leek, fennel, and carrot; cook, covered, for 15 minutes, stirring once or twice.

Add the fish frames and vermouth and then enough water to just cover the solids. Bring to a simmer, skimming the scum that forms on the surface. Stir in the salt, parsley stems, thyme, peppercorns, and lemon. Simmer, partially covered, for 30 minutes. Cool to room temperature. Pour the stock through a strainer set over a large bowl. Let the stock drain for 30 minutes but do not press on the solids or the stock will become cloudy.

Measure the stock. If there is more than 2½ quarts, transfer the stock to a pan, set it over medium heat, and simmer gently, uncovered, until it is reduced to 2½ quarts. Cool to room temperature, cover, and refrigerate until cold, about 5 hours. Remove any hardened surface fat. *The stock can be refrigerated, covered, up to 3 days or frozen up to 3 months.*

white beans with greek garlic sauce and mixed green salad

grilled lemon-herb rabbit on a bed of artichoke, red pepper, and black olive pasta

vanilla-rose ice cream with blackberry sauce

orange-cornmeal butter cookies

Greece seems a country of perpetual summer, a joyous place of easy laughter, plentiful wine, and robust food—which is precisely the mood I try to create when friends gather in my American back yard for a summertime meal, the good times helped along considerably by this Greek-inspired grill menu.

s t r a t e g y

All the various elements of both the starter and the dessert (including the cookies) can be completed well in advance, leaving the cook free to concentrate on the last-minute requirements of the grilled rabbit and the pasta. Since one operation takes place on the grill and the other on the stove, a volunteer will come in handy. Pour a chilled dry rosé like Bandol, or a slightly cool lighter red wine, such as a Pinot Noir from Oregon or Washington state.

•

white beans with greek garlic sauce and

mixed green salad

serves 6

This lusty starter—a mixed plate of herbed white bean salad, creamy garlic sauce, baked beets, and tart greens—is adapted from one served at Periyali, an elegant little Greek restaurant in lower Manhattan. Steve Tzolis, one of Periyali's owners, has said that this unusual bread-and-almond–thickened version of the ubiquitous (and potent) Greek garlic sauce *skordalia* comes from Crete.

GREEK GARLIC SAUCE

1 medium red-skinned potato (about 8 ounces), peeled and quartered
Salt
4 cups cubed white bread, from a day-old baguette or a long Italian loaf
4 cups cold water
1 cup (about 4½ ounces) blanched whole almonds
6 garlic cloves, peeled and any green shoots removed
1¼ cups olive oil
⅓ cup fresh lemon juice, strained
1 teaspoon freshly ground black pepper

WHITE BEAN SALAD

1 pound large dried white kidney (cannellini) beans, picked over and soaked 24 hours in
    cold water to cover
2 tablespoons finely minced fresh oregano
2 tablespoons fresh lemon juice, strained
¾ teaspoon freshly ground black pepper
½ cup olive oil
½ cup finely minced wide-leaf parsley

12 cups Basic Mixed Green Salad with Vinaigrette (page 23)
3 medium beets, baked (page 55), peeled, and sliced

For the garlic sauce In a small saucepan cover the potato with cold water. Stir in 2 teaspoons salt, set over medium heat, and bring to a simmer. Cook until tender, about 15 minutes. Drain and cool. In a bowl combine the stale bread cubes with 4 cups cold water. Let stand until the bread is softened, about 5 minutes. With your hands, squeeze out any excess water from the bread.

In a food processor fitted with the steel blade, combine the almonds, garlic, and potato; process until fairly smooth. Add half the bread and process; then add half the oil and process. Repeat with the remaining bread and oil. Add the lemon juice, 1 teaspoon salt, and the pepper; process until smooth. *The garlic sauce can be prepared 2 days ahead. Cover and refrigerate; return to room temperature before using.* Just before serving adjust the seasoning.

For the bean salad Drain the beans and put them in a heavy pot. Cover them with fresh cold water and set over medium heat. Bring to a boil, skimming any scum from the surface, and cook, uncovered, for 20 minutes. Stir in 2 teaspoons salt and continue to cook until the beans are just tender, about 20 minutes. Drain and transfer to a medium bowl. To the hot beans add the oregano, lemon juice, 1 teaspoon salt, the pepper, and olive oil; toss. Cool to room temperature. *The salad can be prepared to this point 1 day ahead. Cover and refrigerate; return to room temperature.* Just before serving, stir in the parsley and adjust the seasoning.

To assemble Spoon a generous dollop of garlic sauce onto each salad plate. Spoon the bean salad around and over the sauce. Arrange the green salad beside the bean salad, then arrange the sliced beets over the green salad. Serve immediately, passing the peppermill.

●

grilled lemon-herb rabbit on a bed of artichoke, red pepper, and black olive pasta

serves 6

A simple herb-and-lemon marinade is one typical and effective Greek flavor maker, adding zesty savor to everything from whole fish and leg of lamb to vegetables of all sorts. When used on grilled rabbit, the marinade also ensures that the meat remains tender and moist. The crisp, smoky, herb-and-lemon-infused rabbit is served on a bed of creamy pasta that is colorful with artichoke hearts, roasted sweet peppers, and black olives.

PASTA

2 large, meaty sweet red peppers, preferably Dutch
Salt
1 lemon, thinly sliced
8 medium-large artichokes, stem ends trimmed slightly
12 ounces dried semolina pasta bow ties (*farfalle*), preferably imported

GRILLED RABBIT

3 tablespoons fresh lemon juice, strained

2 tablespoons minced fresh rosemary

2 tablespoons minced fresh thyme

3 garlic cloves, peeled and minced

¾ teaspoon freshly ground black pepper

⅓ cup olive oil

2 rabbits (about 6 pounds total), preferably fresh, each cut into 6 serving pieces

2 cups aromatic wood smoking chips, such as mesquite or grapevine (see Cook's and Gardener's Sources)

3 tablespoons unsalted butter

3 garlic cloves, peeled and minced

1 cup Chicken Stock (page 90) or canned broth

½ cup whipping cream

½ cup grated Parmesan cheese

½ cup Niçoise olives, rinsed and drained

⅓ cup finely chopped wide-leaf parsley

For the pasta Over the open flame of a gas burner or under a preheated broiler, roast the peppers, turning them as needed, until the skins are charred and black. Place the peppers in a closed paper bag or on a plate under a bowl and let stand until cool. Rub away the burnt skin, remove the stems and cores, and cut the pepper flesh into thin strips.

Bring a large pot of water to a boil. Stir in 1 tablespoon salt and the sliced lemon. When the water returns to a boil, add the artichokes and cook uncovered, stirring occasionally, until they are tender, about 25 minutes. Drain and cool to room temperature.

Pull away the artichoke leaves (discard them or get out the Hellmann's and nibble as you go) and scoop out the chokes. *The recipe can be prepared to this point 1 day ahead. Leave the artichoke hearts whole. Wrap them and the roasted pepper strips separately.*

Bring a large pot of water to a boil. Stir in 1 tablespoon salt, add the pasta, and cook, stirring once or twice, until just tender, about 10 minutes. Drain.

For the rabbit In a small food processor or blender combine the lemon juice, rosemary, thyme, garlic, and pepper; process until smooth. With the machine running, add the oil in a slow, steady stream. In a shallow nonreactive pan or bowl, pour the marinade over the rabbit. Cover and let stand at room temperature, turning the pieces once or twice, for 2 hours. Soak the wood chips in water for 30 minutes.

Prepare a charcoal fire and let the coals burn down until they are evenly gray, or preheat a gas grill to medium-high. Drain the wood chips and scatter them over the coals or grill stones. When the wood chips are smoking, position the rack about 6 inches above the heat source. Lay the rabbit pieces on the grill rack and cook, covered, basting with any remaining marinade and turning once, until the rabbit is crisply brown and cooked through but still juicy, 12 to 15 minutes. Remove from the heat and transfer to a platter; keep warm.

To assemble Slice the artichoke hearts. In a large skillet over low heat, melt the butter. Add the garlic and cook, stirring once or twice, for 3 minutes. Add the stock and cream. Raise the heat, bring the mixture to a boil, and boil hard for 1 minute. Stir in the artichoke hearts, roasted pepper strips, and ½ teaspoon salt. Simmer briskly for 1 minute. Stir in the pasta and cook over high heat, stirring and tossing often, until the sauce is almost absorbed by the pasta, 2 to 3 minutes. Stir in the Parmesan, olives, and parsley and season generously with fresh black pepper. Divide pasta among plates, top with pieces of grilled rabbit, and serve immediately.

●

vanilla-rose ice cream with

blackberry sauce

serves 6

Rose flower water adds an elusive, rather mysterious, and altogether tantalizing quality to this rich vanilla ice cream. By contrast, the blackberry sauce is vibrantly intense. If you have access to pesticide-free roses, garnish each serving with a perfect blossom.

ICE CREAM

4 egg yolks
¾ cup sugar
2 cups whipping cream
2 cups half-and-half
2 teaspoons Vanilla Rum (page 66) or vanilla extract
1 teaspoon rose flower water (see Cook's and Gardener's Sources)

BLACKBERRY SAUCE

3 baskets (6 ounces each) fresh blackberries, picked over, rinsed only if necessary
¾ cup sugar
2 tablespoons fresh lemon juice, strained

Fresh unsprayed roses, for garnish

For the ice cream In a large mixing bowl whisk together the egg yolks and sugar until thick and yellow.

In a large, heavy saucepan combine the whipping cream and half-and-half. Set over medium heat and bring just to a boil. Gradually whisk the hot cream into the egg yolk mixture. Return the mixture to the saucepan, set over low heat, and cook, stirring often, until the mixture thickly coats the back of a spoon, about 4 minutes. Remove from the heat and immediately transfer to a bowl. Cool to room temperature and stir in the vanilla rum and rose flower water. Cover and refrigerate until very cold, preferably overnight.

Transfer the chilled mixture to the canister of an ice cream maker and churn according to the manufacturer's instructions. Store the ice cream, covered, in the freezer. *The ice cream can be prepared up to 3 days ahead.*

For the blackberry sauce In a food processor combine the blackberries, sugar, and lemon juice; process until smooth (the seeds will remain). Transfer to a bowl, cover, and refrigerate until cold. *The sauce can be prepared up to 3 days ahead.*

Before serving, soften the ice cream in the refrigerator if necessary for easier scooping. Generously spoon the sauce into shallow dessert bowls. Scoop the ice cream onto the sauce, garnish with roses if desired, and serve immediately.

●

orange-cornmeal butter cookies

makes about 1 ½ dozen

A simple variation on a favorite recipe in *The New American Kitchen.* You may use white or yellow cornmeal, or even polenta meal if you wish.

9 tablespoons unsalted butter, softened
⅓ cup sugar
2 tablespoons finely minced fresh orange zest
1 egg yolk
½ teaspoon Vanilla Rum (page 66) or vanilla extract
¼ cup cornmeal
Pinch of salt
1 cup unbleached all-purpose flour

In a medium bowl cream together the butter, sugar, and orange zest. Whisk in the egg yolk and vanilla rum. Stir in the cornmeal and salt. Add the flour and stir until just combined.

Turn the dough out onto a piece of waxed paper. Top with a second piece of waxed paper and flatten to about ⅓ inch thick. Chill until firm, preferably overnight. *The dough can be prepared up to 3 days in advance and may be frozen up to 1 month. Soften the frozen dough in the refrigerator for 30 minutes before proceeding.*

Position racks in the upper and lower thirds of the oven and preheat the oven to 375° F. Lightly butter 2 baking sheets. With a round cutter (2 to 2½ inches in diameter), cut out the cookies; transfer them to the prepared sheets, spacing them well apart.

Bake the cookies 12 to 15 minutes, exchanging the position of the sheets on the racks from top to bottom and from front to back at the halfway point, until the cookies are golden and the edges and bottoms are lightly browned. Transfer carefully to paper towels and cool completely.

The cookies can be baked 2 days ahead. Store in an airtight container at room temperature.

l e f t o v e r s

Any remaining garlic sauce can be served with toasted pita scoops and raw vegetables as an appetizer like hummus, and it's wonderful dolloped onto grilled fish, chicken, or vegetables (particularly zucchini and eggplant!). Leftover white bean salad can be turned into a main course by the addition of flaked canned tuna. Similarly, uneaten grilled rabbit can be diced or sliced and combined with salad greens and a vinaigrette to make a delicious lunch or supper salad. The ice cream, blackberry sauce, and cookies will provide impromptu sweet treats for another day or two. Leftover blackberry sauce is wonderful over fresh whole berries and plain yogurt for breakfast.

GRILL CRAZY!

Grilling, probably the oldest form of cookery, is now also the freshest, rediscovered and transformed into something stylishly rustic, healthful, and delicious. Long gone (along with fire-roasted chunks of saber-toothed tiger) are the days of undersized, lightweight K-Mart hibachis, waiting forlornly on porches and balconies for a single summer's output of starter fluid-scented, barbecue-sauce–drenched, charred-on-the-outside, raw-on-the-inside chicken, beef, or whatever.

Now prime ingredients—game, seafood, sausages, veal, pork, vegetables, even fruit—subtly marinated or vividly sauced, turned on the grill until crisp and brown outside, succulent within, perfumed with fragrant woods and their own vaporized juices, have banished memories of scorched wienies and burgers forever. Cooking outdoors is at last known to be an acquired skill, not a genetically encoded male instinct, and more and more open-air chefs man (and woman) their grills with the same virtuosity that Ray Charles demonstrates on the piano.

Experience is the key to successful grilling (savvy sizzlers can even perform wonders on those skimpy bargain hibachis), but the performance edge supplied by the right equipment can't be denied.

When you shop for a grill, the fuel source is the first and the most important choice to be made. Restaurants known for their grilling sometimes cook over fragrant, open wood fires, which produce delicious food but are slow to start and tricky to maintain, and are better suited to a restaurant's long dinner hour than a speedy family meal. Lump charcoal, produced from chunks of wood without the addition of chemicals or other additives, can be difficult to find, but it burns long, hot, and evenly, imparts no flavor to the food, and can be relit and used another day. Ordinary briquettes contain some wood charcoal but also include such additives as coal, petroleum products, or binding glues. Sensitive palates can detect the flavors of these substances on food so grilled, although a fire of premium briquettes (*not* the self-starting variety) that has been lit by means other than charcoal lighter fluid (the major culprit in most grilling crimes) can yield good results. Chimney-type convection starters or electric starters are always preferable to lighter fluid, which, in addition to its culinary drawbacks, can be dangerous. Many cooks (including this one) avoid charcoal altogether, preferring to grill over a propane gas fire. Such grills quickly reach the proper temperature, have adjustable thermostatic controls (some can provide cooking surfaces at two different temperatures, useful when grilling several different foods), and can be combined with fragrant wood chips to produce smoky authenticity, if desired. Friends with sensitive palates say propane leaves a flavor; I detect none.

The next critical decision is size—namely, that of the grill's cooking surface. Generally, bigger is better, since while a large grill can accommodate a small amount of food, the reverse is not true. Food that is crowded onto an undersized grill will not cook or crisp evenly; the alternative—working in batches—means either cold food for some guests, or a long and sweaty evening over the coals for the grillmaster. Since grilling is one of the most pleasant ways of cooking for a crowd, it makes sense to plan for that eventuality. A 600-square-inch cooking surface will comfortably hold food for eight; surfaces up to 1,000 square inches are not uncommon.

The remaining choices are less crucial. Portability can help you move the grill out of the rain; a cover means the fragrant smoke of wood chips can more fully flavor food being grilled and may even let you adapt your grill for use as a home smoker; additional work space in the form of side shelves can make basting and plating easier (and can also offer you a spot to set your wineglass); side burners for everything from melting butter to boiling up a pot of corn on the cob are also options that can help you turn a relatively simple and rustic outdoor meal into a grand and complex feast. There is still a macho aura about grilling, and while it is possible to find a grill the size of a small automobile, with a sticker price to match, there is no direct correlation between the cost or complexity of the cooking unit and the quality of the food it produces: Experience is more important than expense.

The inexperienced usually grill too hot, apply sweetened sauces too early in the process, and fail to extinguish flare-ups of open flame promptly.

The ability to know when the grill is at the correct temperature often comes only with considerable experience. (The standard advice of holding one's hand near the grill until the pain reaches a certain level is another sound reason for choosing a thermostatic propane grill.) For most foods, charcoal should be burned down to an even, ashy gray-white with no flame visible. Wood should be an even and smoldering red-gray. The burners on propane burners should be set at medium-high and preheated for 10 minutes. The grill rack should be no less than 6 inches above the heat (for thicker, slower-cooking items—such as a butterflied leg of lamb—the grill should be higher). Turn the food once or twice and move it to a cooler spot on the grill if it appears to be browning too fast.

Sweet sauces like traditional American barbecue sauce, which burn quickly, should be applied near the end of the cooking period, or the food should be cooked over lower heat for a longer time (spread charcoal apart to form a cooler central "well"; turn propane down to medium-low). Baste lightly but often to build up a rich glaze, and serve any remaining sauce at the table.

Flare-ups of open flame are caused by fats dripping onto the heated part of the grill. Removing any external fat from the food before cooking can reduce flare-ups, but some are unavoidable, especially if you are basting the foods with an oil-based marinade. Keep a plastic plant spritzer bottle of water at hand and extinguish any flare-up immediately. Open flame burns rather than cooks food and will quickly ruin an otherwise delicious meal.

One final refinement. If you cook over charcoal or propane but like the smoky flavor of a real wood fire, consider using some of the many grilling and smoking wood chips available. Soaked in water, drained, and scattered over the coals or firestones, the chips quickly produce a light but distinct seasoning smoke. Hickory, pecan, and other nut woods are stronger and particularly appropriate with robust foods like beef, lamb, or pork; mesquite smoke is more delicate and can be used with almost anything, though it's particularly good with fish, chicken, or vegetables; maple, as well as chips of fruit-woods such as peach and cherry, produce a distinctly sweet-flavored smoke that is especially good with shellfish, pork, and chicken.

confetti deviled eggs

basil buttermilk fried chicken

curried corn, roasted sweet pepper, and zucchini salad

new potato salad with bacon and mustard seeds

berry picker's pie à la mode

or

raspberry brownies (page 88)

Francine the Caterer once sent me a postcard captioned "Herbs and Spices of Ohio," which was illustrated with drawings of a salt shaker, a pepper shaker, and a packet of artificial sweetener. Ohio, as well as the rest of the country, may once have shied away from strong seasonings, but times—fortunately—have changed, as this zesty picnic, full of modern American spice and fire, illustrates.

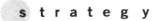 **s t r a t e g y**

The eggs can be boiled and the corn and potato salads prepared up to a day in advance, but the eggs should be filled and the chicken fried shortly before serving time.

●

confetti deviled eggs

makes 20 stuffed egg halves

Even folks who normally keep a close watch on their egg intake have been known to throw caution to the winds when confronted by a picnic platter of stuffed eggs, especially this variation, which is spiked with sun-dried tomatoes, jalapeños, green onions, and olives.

10 extra-large eggs, at room temperature (see Note)
Salt
⅓ cup mayonnaise
1 teaspoon Dijon-style mustard
¼ cup finely diced oil-packed sun-dried tomatoes, homemade (page 46) or purchased (see
 Cook's and Gardener's Sources)
3 tablespoons finely diced pickled jalapeños (about 2 medium)
3 green onions, trimmed and thinly sliced
6 imported brine-cured black olives, such as Kalamata, pitted and finely diced

With a pin, prick each egg at the wide end to a depth of about ¼ inch. Bring a pot of lightly salted water to a boil. Gently lower the eggs into the water and cook, turning them occasionally and maintaining the water at a simmer, for 13 minutes. Drain immediately and, one at a time, tap gently to crack the shells of the eggs all over with the back of a spoon. Transfer them to a bowl of cold water and let stand until cool. Shell the eggs under running water. *The eggs can be boiled up to 1 day ahead. In a bowl cover the shelled eggs with cold water and refrigerate. Drain and pat dry before proceeding.*

Halve the eggs lengthwise. Remove the yolks and in a small bowl mash them with the mayonnaise and mustard until smooth. Stir in the sun-dried tomatoes, jalapēnos, green onions, and olives.

Transfer the yolk mixture to a pastry bag fitted with a large star tip. Pipe the yolk mixture into the hollows of the egg whites, mounding it. Transfer to a plate. Refrigerate if necessary, loosely covered, until serving.

NOTE *For easiest peeling, hard-cooked eggs must be neither too fresh nor too old. Although a certain amount of guesswork is required, generally speaking, if the eggs have been purchased within 3 days from a busy supermarket with a good turnover of product, you will have good results—particularly if the eggs are peeled under running water as directed above.*

●

basil buttermilk fried chicken

serves 8

The dried herb infuses the chicken with its subtle flavor, but garnish the platter with sprigs of fresh basil for summery green color.

2 cups buttermilk
3 tablespoons dried basil, crumbled
2 teaspoons hot pepper sauce
2 chickens (3½ pounds each), cut into serving pieces
2 cups unbleached all-purpose flour
2 teaspoons salt
2 teaspoons freshly ground black pepper
2 pounds (about) solid vegetable shortening, for frying
Fresh basil sprigs, for garnish

In a large nonreactive bowl, whisk together the buttermilk, 1 tablespoon of the dried basil, and the hot pepper sauce. Add the chicken pieces, turn to coat, and marinate, covered, at room temperature, stirring once or twice, for 2 hours.

In a wide, deep plate (like a pie plate), combine the flour, the remaining 2 tablespoons dried basil, the salt, and the pepper. One at a time, lift the chicken pieces from the marinade, letting most of the excess drip back into the bowl. Dredge the chicken pieces in the seasoned flour. Transfer the chicken to a rack and let stand for 30 minutes to firm the coating.

In 2 large skillets over medium-high heat, melt enough shortening to come ½ inch up the sides. Heat the shortening until very hot (almost smoking), then carefully add the chicken pieces skin side down. Cook, uncovered, for 12 minutes. Turn the chicken and cook another 12 to 15 minutes, until done.

Drain the chicken on paper towels. Arrange the chicken on a platter, garnish with fresh basil sprigs, and serve hot, warm, or cool.

curried corn, roasted sweet pepper, and

zucchini salad

serves 8

Even during corn season I use canned or frozen kernels to make corn salads, saving prime ears of the sweet, just-picked stuff for buttering up at another meal. If lighting the grill seems preferable to heating up the broiler (and the kitchen), the peppers and zucchini can be browned over charcoal for extra flavor.

2 large sweet red peppers, preferably Dutch
5 large zucchini, scrubbed, trimmed, and quartered lengthwise (about 1⅔ pounds total)
7 tablespoons vegetable oil
2 tablespoons curry powder (see Note)
2 garlic cloves, peeled and slightly crushed
⅓ cup mayonnaise
⅓ cup plain yogurt
2 tablespoons honey
1 tablespoon fresh lemon juice, strained
1½ teaspoons salt
¼ teaspoon freshly ground black pepper
4 cups well-drained canned or thawed frozen corn kernels
½ cup diced sweet red onions

Over the open flame of a gas burner, under a preheated broiler, or on a charcoal grill, roast the peppers, turning them often, until the skins are charred. Transfer the peppers to a paper bag or a bowl covered with a plate and let stand until cool. Rub away the burned peel and wipe the peppers with paper towels. Stem and core the peppers, then cut the flesh into 2-inch strips.

Brush the zucchini quarters with 3 tablespoons of the vegetable oil. Over a charcoal grill or on a baking sheet under a preheated broiler, lightly brown the zucchini, turning the pieces occasionally, until just tender, about 8 minutes. Cool and cut into bite-sized pieces.

In a small saucepan over medium-low heat, combine the remaining 4 tablespoons vegetable oil, the curry powder, and the garlic. Cook, stirring often, until fragrant, about 5 minutes. Remove from the heat and cool to room temperature; discard the garlic.

In a small bowl whisk together the curry-oil mixture, mayonnaise, yogurt, honey, lemon juice, salt, and pepper. In a large bowl toss together the pepper strips, zucchini pieces, corn kernels, diced onions, and dressing. Adjust the seasoning. *The salad can be completed up to 1 day in advance. Cover and refrigerate, but return it to room temperature before serving.*

NOTE *Curry powders, like chili powders, vary widely, and you should sample several to find a favorite. As with chili powders, price is a good indicator of quality. Lawrence Curry (see Cook's and Gardener's Sources), with its deep, rounded flavor, is my house brand. To bring out all its complex subtleties, a curry powder should be cooked briefly in oil.*

●

new potato salad with bacon and

mustard seeds

serves 8

Hearty, crunchy, and slightly smoky, this salad is a useful addition to many a summer menu. Robust Spanish sherry vinegar is delicious here, but substitute red wine or balsamic vinegar if you prefer.

½ cup sherry vinegar
2 tablespoons yellow mustard seeds
8 ounces slab bacon, rind trimmed; cut into ¼-inch dice
3½ pounds (about 30) new red-skinned potatoes, scrubbed, trimmed, and quartered
Salt
⅔ cup olive oil
½ cup chopped wide-leaf parsley
2 teaspoons freshly ground black pepper

In a small bowl combine the vinegar and mustard seeds; let stand, stirring once or twice, for 1 hour.

In a cold skillet set the bacon over medium heat and cook, stirring occasionally, until crisp and brown, 8 to 10 minutes. With a slotted spoon transfer the bacon to paper towels to drain.

In a saucepan cover the potatoes with cold water. Stir in 1 tablespoon salt, set over medium-high heat, and bring to a boil. Lower the heat slightly and cook until the potatoes are just tender, about 8 minutes after the water boils. Drain immediately and transfer to a large bowl.

Stir ½ teaspoon salt into the vinegar mixture and pour it evenly over the hot potatoes. Toss gently; cool to room temperature.

Add the bacon, olive oil, parsley, and pepper to the salad and toss gently. Adjust the seasoning. *The salad can be prepared up to 1 day in advance. Cover and refrigerate, but return it to room temperature before serving.*

berry picker's pie à la mode

makes one 10-inch pie, serving 8

If your summertime fantasies include a jolly berry-picking expedition complete with blue skies, silver pails brimming over with sweet-tart berries bursting with juice, lips and fingers stained purple from those greedily eaten on the spot rather than harvested for later—be warned. Picking berries is sweaty, thorny work. Take my lazy man's advice and pick your berries at a roadside stand or at the produce store (also pick up a pint or two of vanilla ice cream) and enjoy the blue skies and fresh air lying coolly and comfortably on your back on the lawn, with a warm slice of pie à la mode close at hand.

CRUST

2½ cups unbleached all-purpose flour
½ teaspoon salt
¾ stick (6 tablespoons) unsalted butter, well chilled and cut into small pieces
½ cup solid vegetable shortening, well chilled and cut into small pieces
½ cup ice water
6 tablespoons whole-wheat flour (see Note)

BERRY FILLING

5 tablespoons regular tapioca
8 cups mixed blackberries, raspberries, and blueberries, picked over, rinsed only if necessary, and drained well
1½ cups sugar

GLAZE

1 egg, beaten
1 tablespoon sugar

Premium vanilla ice cream, slightly softened, for serving

For the crust In a large bowl or food processor combine the all-purpose flour and salt. Cut in the butter and shortening until the mixture resembles coarse meal. Add the water, 1 tablespoon at a time, until a soft dough forms. Sprinkle the work surface with 2 tablespoons of the whole-wheat flour. Turn the dough out onto the floured surface and divide it in half. Form each piece into a thick disk and wrap each disk well in plastic. Refrigerate at least 45 minutes. *The crust can be prepared to this point up to 1 day ahead.*
For the filling In a blender or small food processor grind the tapioca to a powder.

In a large mixing bowl gently combine the berries, sugar, and tapioca. Let stand 30 minutes.

To assemble   Position a rack in the middle of the oven and set a baking sheet on the rack. Preheat the oven to 400° F.

On a work surface lightly sprinkled with 2 tablespoons whole-wheat flour, roll out one of the pastry disks to a 14-inch round. Transfer the dough to a 10-inch pie pan. Spoon the berry filling and any accumulated juices into the pie shell, forming a slight mound in the center. On a work surface lightly dusted with the remaining 2 tablespoons whole-wheat flour, roll out the second pastry disk to a 12-inch round. Lay the top crust over the berries. Trim the crusts, leaving an overhang of ½ inch. Fold the lower crust over the upper, pinching it gently but firmly to seal. Crimp decoratively and cut 3 or 4 vent slits in the upper crust.

Set the pie on the heated baking sheet and bake 40 minutes. Brush the crust with the beaten egg, sprinkle evenly with the sugar, and bake for another 10 to 15 minutes, until the juices bubble up through the slits in the crust and the pie is a rich, golden brown. Cool completely before cutting. Serve with ice cream.

NOTE   *The whole-wheat flour used to roll out the pastry adds extra texture and color to the crust. Unbleached all-purpose flour can be substituted.*

l e f t o v e r s

Cold chicken and the corn and potato salads will make a great brown bag lunch the next day. Cold berry pie makes an unorthodox (but delicious) breakfast.

kitchen-counter blackberry corn-muffin cake

makes one 10-inch cake, serving 8 to 10

A cake sitting ready on the kitchen counter for hungry folks to slice away at will leave the weekend cook's time free for other tasks. Here is such a cake, equally good made with blueberries. The addition of cornmeal produces a handsomely golden and muffin-crumbly cake, perfect at brunch (omit the glaze), for snacking on the run, or as a plated dessert. Though not always easy to find, a bundt pan coated with a white (rather than a brown or black) nonstick finish will produce a lighter-colored, more tender-crusted cake.

CAKE

2 cups unbleached all-purpose flour

1 cup yellow cornmeal

2 teaspoons baking powder

¼ teaspoon salt

1½ sticks (6 ounces) unsalted butter, softened

2 tablespoons finely minced orange zest

1½ cups sugar

3 eggs

1½ cups buttermilk

2½ cups blackberries, picked over, rinsed only if necessary

GLAZE

3 tablespoons unsalted butter

3 tablespoons sugar

⅓ cup orange marmalade

1½ tablespoons whipping cream

Fresh blackberries, for garnish

For the cake   Butter a 10- to 12-cup nonstick bundt or ring pan. Flour the pan and tap out the excess. Preheat the oven to 375° F.

In a medium bowl thoroughly combine the dry ingredients. In a large bowl cream together the butter, orange zest, and sugar until light and fluffy. Beat the eggs, one at a time, into the butter mixture. Alternately add the dry ingredients and the buttermilk to the butter mixture in batches, beginning and ending with the dry ingredients. Fold in the blackberries. Spoon the batter into the prepared pan.

Bake the cake about 50 minutes, until it is puffed and golden (the top will crack) and pulled slightly away from the sides of the pan. A tester inserted into the cake should come out clean. Cool the cake in the pan on a rack for 10 minutes. Invert onto a rack and cool to room temperature.

For the glaze   In a small, heavy saucepan over low heat, stir together the butter, sugar, marmalade, and cream until smooth. Raise the heat slightly and bring the glaze to a boil. Lower the heat slightly and simmer briskly, stirring often, until thick, 5 to 7 minutes. Cool to room temperature.

Spoon the glaze slowly and evenly over the cake, allowing it to run down the sides. Transfer the cake to a plate and garnish with blackberries if desired.

deep-fried ravioli with red pepper mayonnaise

greek garlic sauce (page 93) with toasted pita triangles

mixed imported olives

salad with beets, cucumbers, feta, and dill

moussaka with zucchini, eggplant, and potatoes

parmesan planks (page 43)

amaretto-and-wine-poached dried fruit compote (page 43)

orange-cornmeal butter cookies (page 97)

On one of the first cool evenings of fall, when the urge to entertain on a larger scale and the craving to cook somewhere other than outdoors on the grill strikes, turn to this lusty, Mediterranean-inspired buffet.

s t r a t e g y

A do-ahead main-dish casserole and a do-ahead dessert make the cook's job of feeding twelve much simpler. (Note that you will need to double the recipes for the fruit compote and for the cookies.) The only bit of complicated last-minute cookery for this buffet is the deep-fried ravioli, and they take mere minutes. For the other appetizers, the garlic sauce can be prepared a day or two ahead, and the olives come from a gourmet or cheese shop. Buy an assortment of olives and tumble them together in a single bowl; drizzle with olive oil if you like and sprinkle with parsley.

If you're a bread baker, turn out a batch—or two—of the Parmesan Planks. (Or just toast additional store-bought pitas.) For authenticity, pour a cool white retsina—if you like that resinous Greek wine—or, if fall puts thoughts of red wine in your head, drink an Italian Barbera or the new, Chianti-like Sangiovese varietal produced by California's Atlas Vineyards.

●

deep-fried ravioli with red pepper mayonnaise

serves 12

Store-bought "fresh" ravioli, sealed in refrigerated plastic cartons, may not be sublime pasta, but they do deep-fry into crisply addictive little morsels, especially when dipped into a ruddy roasted pepper and sun-dried tomato mayonnaise.

Red Pepper Spread (page 125)
½ cup mayonnaise
2 tablespoons fresh lemon juice, strained
Salt
Freshly ground black pepper
1 carton (9 ounces) prepared cheese ravioli
1 carton (9 ounces) prepared meat ravioli
Corn oil for deep frying

In a small bowl, whisk together the red pepper spread, mayonnaise, and lemon juice. Season to taste with salt and pepper. *The mayonnaise can be prepared up to 2 days ahead. Cover and refrigerate, but let it return to room temperature before serving.*

Carefully separate any ravioli that are stuck together and discard any that are torn or whose filling is visible. In a deep fryer or deep, heavy pot fitted with a deep-fry thermometer, heat about 4 inches oil to 375° F. (The fryer or pot should be no more than half full of oil.) Working in batches, add the ravioli to the hot oil and fry, stirring once or twice, until crisp and golden, about 1 minute. With a slotted spoon, transfer the ravioli to paper towels to drain.

When all the ravioli are fried, serve them immediately, accompanied by the mayonnaise for dipping.

●

salad with beets, cucumbers, feta, and
dill

<u>serves 12</u>

Use a wide variety of sturdy greens to provide support for the hearty garnishings of baked beets, cucumbers, and crumbled feta.

12 cups bite-sized pieces of assorted greens, such as romaine, watercress, and arugula, rinsed and spun dry
Dill Dressing (recipe follows)
2 pounds (about 6 medium) beets, baked (page 55), peeled, and sliced
1 hothouse cucumber, rinsed and sliced into thin ovals
1½ cups (about 7 ounces) coarsely crumbled drained feta cheese, at room temperature

Just before serving, in a large bowl toss together the greens and two-thirds of the dressing. Mound the greens on a platter and top them with the beets and cucumber. Scatter the feta over the entire salad, drizzle the remaining dressing over all, and serve immediately.

●

dill dressing

<u>makes about 1¼ cups</u>

To preserve the fresh, lively flavor of the dill, make this dressing just before you use it.

3 tablespoons red wine vinegar
1 egg yolk, at room temperature
1 tablespoon Dijon-style mustard
½ teaspoon salt

½ teaspoon freshly ground black pepper
Pinch of sugar
⅔ cup olive oil
¼ cup finely minced fresh dill

In a small bowl whisk together the vinegar, egg yolk, mustard, salt, pepper, and sugar. Continue to whisk while slowly dribbling in the olive oil; the dressing will thicken. Stir in the dill and adjust the seasoning.

moussaka with zucchini, eggplant, and potatoes

serves 12

Who created this rich amalgam of spiced lamb sauce and eggplant baked under a savory crust of cheese and béchamel? The credit goes unawarded—the dish is centuries old and a Greek classic—but the winners are those who serve it and those who happily are served. The moussaka cuts into firm pieces that are easily transferred from serving dish to plate, and there's another advantage as well: Because it slices best when cold, the moussaka can be fully baked a day in advance and sliced, and then need only be reheated just before serving.

LAMB SAUCE

3 tablespoons olive oil
2 cups finely diced yellow onions
8 garlic cloves, peeled and minced
1½ pounds very lean lamb, finely ground
4 teaspoons dried oregano, crumbled
2 teaspoons dried thyme, crumbled
1½ teaspoons ground cinnamon
1½ teaspoons ground cumin, preferably from toasted seeds (page 63)
1½ teaspoons crushed dried red pepper
1 teaspoon ground ginger
1 teaspoon freshly grated nutmeg
2 bay leaves
1 can (28 ounces) Italian-style plum tomatoes, with their juices, crushed with the fingers
¾ cup dry red wine
1 tablespoon salt

Salt
3 medium eggplants (about 2½ pounds total), trimmed, halved lengthwise, and sliced crosswise ½ inch thick
4 large zucchini (about 2 pounds total), well scrubbed, trimmed, and sliced diagonally ⅓ inch thick
4 large red-skinned potatoes (about 2 pounds total), peeled and sliced ⅓ inch thick
½ cup (about) olive oil
5 eggs
Parslied Garlic Béchamel (recipe follows) at room temperature
⅔ cup grated Parmesan cheese

For the lamb sauce   In a heavy, 4½- to 5-quart pot warm the olive oil over low heat. Add the onions and garlic and cook, covered, stirring once or twice, until the onions are tender, about 15 minutes. Add the lamb, raise the heat to medium, and cook, stirring and crumbling the meat, for 5 minutes. Stir in the oregano, thyme, cinnamon, cumin, crushed pepper, ginger, nutmeg, and bay leaves; cook, stirring, for 5 minutes. Add the tomatoes, wine, and salt and bring to a boil. Turn the heat to low, cover, and cook, stirring once or twice, for 30 minutes. Uncover and continue to cook, stirring occasionally, until the lamb sauce is very thick, about 1½ hours. Remove the bay leaves. *The sauce can be prepared 3 days ahead. Cool to room temperature, cover, and refrigerate. Return to room temperature before proceeding.*

To assemble   In several colanders or working in batches, heavily salt the eggplant and zucchini and let the slices stand, tossing once or twice, for 1 hour until they have exuded their juices. Pat the vegetables dry.

In a medium saucepan, cover the potatoes with cold water. Stir in 1 tablespoon salt, set over medium heat, and bring to a boil. Lower the heat and simmer the potatoes until just tender, 4 to 5 minutes. Drain and rinse thoroughly with cold water.

In a large skillet heat 3 tablespoons of the olive oil over medium-high heat. Working in batches, cook the eggplant and zucchini slices, turning them once, until they are lightly browned, 3 to 4 minutes per side. Add more oil sparingly to the skillet only if needed to prevent sticking. With a slotted spoon transfer the browned vegetables to paper towels to drain.

Position a rack in the middle of the oven and preheat the oven to 350° F.

Separate 3 of the eggs. Whisk the egg whites and stir them into the lamb sauce. Whisk the egg yolks and remaining 2 whole eggs together in a small bowl. Stir the eggs into the béchamel.

In a 12- by 17-inch (18-cup) rectangular baking dish about 2½ inches deep, arrange half of the eggplant, zucchini, and potatoes in a roughly even layer. Sprinkle the vegetables with 3 tablespoons of the Parmesan. Spread the lamb sauce evenly over the vegetables. Arrange the remaining eggplant, zucchini, and potatoes over the lamb sauce and sprinkle with 3 more tablespoons of the Parmesan. Cover with the béchamel and gently shake the baking dish to eliminate any spaces between layers. Sprinkle the remaining 4 to 5 tablespoons Parmesan over the béchamel. Bake the moussaka until the top is puffed and golden brown and the center is set, about 1 hour. Let rest on a rack for 10 minutes before serving, or cool completely, cover, and refrigerate until firm, preferably overnight. *The dish can be prepared 1 day ahead.*

To serve, preheat the oven to 400° F. Cut the cold moussaka into 12 serving pieces. Cover the dish with foil and bake until the moussaka is hot and steaming, about 30 minutes.

parslied garlic béchamel

makes about 5 ½ cups

5 tablespoons unsalted butter
3 garlic cloves, peeled and minced
5 tablespoons unbleached all-purpose flour
5 cups milk
1½ teaspoons salt
1 teaspoon freshly ground black pepper
¼ teaspoon freshly grated nutmeg
1¼ cups grated Parmesan cheese
½ cup minced wide-leaf parsley

In a medium, heavy saucepan over low heat, melt the butter. Add the garlic and cook without browning, stirring often, for 4 minutes. Whisk in the flour and cook, stirring often, without allowing the flour to brown, for 5 minutes. Off the heat, gradually whisk in the milk. Stir in the salt, pepper, and nutmeg. Return the pan to the burner, raise the heat to medium, and bring the sauce to a boil, stirring constantly. Lower the heat slightly and simmer, partially covered, stirring often, until very thick, about 20 minutes. Remove the sauce from the heat, stir in the Parmesan, and transfer to a bowl. When the sauce is cool, stir in the parsley. *The béchamel can be prepared 1 day ahead. Press plastic wrap onto the surface of the cooled sauce and refrigerate.*

l e f t o v e r s

Leftover red pepper mayonnaise is good wherever mayonnaise is good. Try it on a smoked turkey and provolone sandwich or as a dip for cold shrimp. The moussaka reheats well in either a conventional or a microwave oven.

shrimp, leek, and dill spread (page 289)

endive with toasted hazelnuts and roquefort

country ham, sweet potato, and green onion beignets

dijon ragout of chicken and vegetables

white rice

gingered pear and cranberry trifle

This party for twelve follows an unusual menu plan—a long appetizer hour is followed by a simple one-dish entrée. It is a meal well suited to serious socializing, perhaps for guests who are strangers but who will find they have much in common if given the chance to get acquainted.

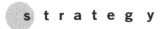 s t r a t e g y

There are three serious, rather solid appetizers in this menu, so a generous wine-and-conversation period of at least an hour is in order. Following that, the entrée is light, colorful, and simple to serve, accompanied by little more than white rice and good bread. The long cocktail hour means the cook can parade out the appetizers one at a time for maximum impact (and minimum kitchen gridlock). The dilled shrimp spread can be completed several days in advance; the endive appetizer should be assembled shortly before serving but the hazelnut-and-Roquefort topping can be mixed a day ahead; the beignets must be deep-fried at the last minute, but the sweet potato mixture also can be prepared a day ahead.

During the course of serving up these savory morsels, the cook can also make the white rice (for this menu use three cups uncooked rice and follow package directions) and complete the final steps of the mustardy chicken, carrot, and Brussels sprouts stew. Dessert consists of a made-in-advance cake, custard, and poached-fruit confection that needs only a last-minute garnishing.

●

endive with toasted hazelnuts and roquefort

makes 36

An oldie but a goodie, this classic combination always pleases. The final brushing with sherry vinaigrette is optional, but it adds a boost of flavor and an attractive gloss.

1 cup (about 4 ounces) skinned toasted hazelnuts (page 44)
4 ounces imported Roquefort or best-quality domestic blue cheese
6 Belgian endives
2 tablespoons sherry vinegar
1½ teaspoons Dijon-style mustard
Pinch of salt
Freshly ground black pepper
⅓ cup olive oil

Coarsely chop the hazelnuts. In a bowl thoroughly mix together the hazelnuts and Roquefort. *The nut mixture can be prepared 1 day ahead; refrigerate, covered, but return the mixture to room temperature before proceeding.*

Core the endives and separate into leaves. Select the 36 largest leaves, reserving the rest of the endive for another use. Mound the nut mixture on the ends of the endive leaves, using it all. Arrange the endive leaves on a serving platter.

In a small bowl whisk together the sherry vinegar, mustard, and salt and a grinding of pepper. Whisk in the oil. With a pastry brush, paint the exposed top surfaces of each endive leaf generously with the vinaigrette. Grind fresh pepper evenly over the filled, dressed endive leaves and serve immediately.

country ham, sweet potato, and green onion beignets

makes 48

Deep-fried sweet-potato fritters, full of smoky ham and green onions, make satisfying cocktail fare. The beignets are best served warm, not piping hot, passed in a napkin-lined basket, and either sprinkled with grated Parmesan cheese or accompanied by honey mustard as a dipping sauce.

2 pounds (about 4 large) sweet potatoes
4 ounces fat-free baked ham, preferably smoked country ham (pages 165–66), cut into
⅛-inch dice
4 green onions, trimmed and thinly sliced
3 eggs
⅓ cup unbleached all-purpose flour
½ teaspoon salt
½ teaspoon freshly ground black pepper
¼ teaspoon freshly grated nutmeg
Corn oil, for deep frying
Grated Parmesan cheese or honey mustard, for serving

Position a rack in the middle of the oven and preheat the oven to 400° F.

Prick each sweet potato several times with a fork and bake the sweet potatoes until they are very tender, about 1 hour. Cool, peel, and mash the sweet potatoes; there should be 2 cups.

In a bowl stir together the sweet potato, ham, green onions, eggs, flour, salt, pepper, and nutmeg. Refrigerate, covered, overnight.

In a deep fryer or in a deep, heavy pot fitted with a deep-fry thermometer, heat about 4 inches of the oil to 375° F. (The fryer or pot should be no more than half full of oil.) Measure out a level tablespoon of the batter (use a deep, rounded tablespoon rather than a shallow oval one for best results) and scrape the dough into the hot fat, forming a roughly sphere-shaped beignet. Repeat with the remaining batter, working in batches to avoid crowding the pan. Cook the beignets about 4 minutes, turning them in the oil frequently, until they are richly browned and crisp. With a slotted spoon, remove the beignets from the oil and drain on paper towels. Serve warm, sprinkled with the cheese or accompanied by a ramekin of honey mustard as a dipping sauce.

dijon ragout of chicken and vegetables

serves 12

This creamy stew of chicken and colorful vegetables is tender and satisfying, but the addition of plenty of good mustard and herbs adds sparkle. It's excellent buffet fare, since it doesn't require a knife, but you'll want to offer plenty of white rice and crusty bread for absorbing all of the luscious sauce.

2½ pounds carrots

3 baskets (10 ounces each) small Brussels sprouts

Salt

4 pounds skinless, boneless chicken breasts

5 cups Chicken Stock (page 90) or canned broth

1 cup dry white wine

¾ stick (6 tablespoons) unsalted butter

4 leeks (white part only), well cleaned and finely chopped (about 4 cups)

1½ cups finely diced yellow onions

⅓ cup unbleached all-purpose flour

6 egg yolks

½ cup Dijon-style mustard

1 cup half-and-half

½ cup minced wide-leaf parsley

3 tablespoons minced fresh chives

3 tablespoons minced fresh tarragon

Freshly ground black pepper

Peel the carrots. Slice 2 pounds of the carrots into thin ovals; finely chop those remaining. Trim the Brussels sprouts and cut a shallow X in the stem end of each. Bring a large pot of water to a boil. Stir in 1 tablespoon salt, add the sliced carrots, and cook until just tender, about 8 minutes. With a slotted spoon transfer the carrots to a large bowl of ice water. Return the water to a boil. Add the Brussels sprouts and cook until just tender, about 8 minutes. With a slotted spoon transfer the Brussels sprouts to a second large bowl of ice water. When the vegetables are cool, drain well.

Arrange the chicken breasts in a single layer in a large, deep skillet and cover with the stock and wine. Set over medium heat and bring slowly to a simmer, turning the breasts once or twice. Simmer until just cooked through, about 5 minutes. Remove the skillet from the heat and cool the chicken to room temperature in the poaching liquid. Drain and pat dry. Transfer the chicken to a cutting board. Strain and reserve the poaching liquid. Trim any fat and cartilage from the chicken and cut the meat into 1-inch cubes. *The recipe can be prepared to this point 1 day ahead. Wrap the vegetables and chicken separately and cover the poaching liquid. Refrigerate all ingredients.*

In a large, heavy saucepan over medium heat, melt the butter. Add the leeks, the onions, and the chopped carrots; cook, covered, stirring once or twice, until the vegetables are tender, about 15 minutes. Stir in the flour and cook, stirring constantly, for 3 minutes. Off the heat, whisk in the chicken poaching liquid. Set the pan over medium heat and bring the mixture to a boil, stirring often. Lower the heat, partially cover the pan, and simmer for 40 minutes. Strain the sauce, discarding the solids.

Position a rack in the middle of the oven and preheat the oven to 375° F. In a 4-quart ovenproof serving dish, combine the carrots, Brussels sprouts, and chicken. Cover and bake just until hot, about 20 minutes.

In a medium pan bring the sauce to a simmer. In a medium bowl whisk the egg yolks, then whisk in the mustard and half-and-half. Slowly whisk the hot sauce into the egg mixture. Return the mixture to the pan, set it over low heat, and cook without boiling, stirring often, until the sauce thickens, about 5 minutes. Stir in the parsley, chives, and tarragon and season to taste with salt and pepper. Pour the sauce over the vegetables and chicken, stir to combine, and serve immediately.

●

gingered pear and cranberry trifle

serves 12

The cake-fruit-and-pudding confection known as trifle is a perfect buffet dessert for a crowd. Elaborate-looking, easy to assemble (you may use a good-quality purchased pound cake), and utterly satisfying, it can be prepared up to a day in advance, leaving the cook free to deal with more urgent matters. Traditional trifle is rather boozy, this one less so, but you may choose to increase the amount of pear poaching syrup drizzled over the cake by one-third cup, and omit the brandy altogether.

POACHED PEARS

5 cups water
¾ cup sugar
Colored peel from 1 lemon, removed in strips with a vegetable peeler
3 tablespoons fresh lemon juice
1 chunk (2-inch) of fresh ginger, peeled and coarsely chopped
4 large, ripe but firm Bartlett pears, peeled, cored, and halved

CUSTARD SAUCE

12 egg yolks
1¼ cups sugar
¼ cup cornstarch
6 cups milk

FINAL ASSEMBLY

2 loaves (16 ounces each) pound cake
1½ cups prepared whole-berry cranberry sauce
½ cup strained pear poaching liquid
½ cup *eau-de-vie de poire* (unsweetened pear brandy)

TO SERVE

1½ cups whipping cream, well chilled
3 tablespoons slivered, unblanched almonds

For the poached pears In a medium, nonreactive pan combine the water, sugar, lemon peel, lemon juice, and ginger. Set over medium heat and bring to a boil, stirring to dissolve the sugar. Adjust the heat and briskly simmer the liquid, uncovered, for 5 minutes. Add the pears and cook, turning them once or twice, until they are just tender when pierced at their thickest with a sharp knife, about 5 minutes after the syrup returns to a simmer. With a slotted spoon transfer the pears to a bowl. Pour the hot syrup (including the ginger and lemon peel) over them. Cool to room temperature, cover, and refrigerate for at least 24 hours. *(The pears can be prepared up to 2 days ahead.)*

For the custard sauce In a large bowl whisk the egg yolks. Whisk in the sugar and cornstarch. In a heavy pan over moderate heat bring the milk just to a boil.

Slowly whisk the hot milk into the egg mixture. Return this custard mixture to the pan and set over low heat. Cook, stirring constantly, until the custard just reaches a simmer and is very thick, about 5 minutes. Remove from the heat immediately and transfer to a heatproof bowl. Cool slightly. (The custard should not be piping hot, but neither should it begin to firm or set.)

To assemble Cut the loaves of pound cake in half horizontally. Spread the cut side of the bottom half of each loaf with half the cranberry sauce. Reassemble the cakes. Cut the cakes in half lengthwise, then cut the cakes crosswise into ½-inch pieces (thus ending up with a lot of ½-inch by 1-inch by 2-inch "sandwiches" of cake and cranberry sauce). In a 20-cup serving dish about 2½ inches deep arrange the cake pieces, cut faces angled upward, in a single, slightly overlapping layer.

With a slotted spoon remove the poached pears from their syrup and cut them into ½-inch chunks. Scatter the pears evenly over the cake pieces. Stir together the pear poaching liquid and pear brandy. Drizzle evenly over the pears and cake pieces. Ladle the custard over the pears and cake pieces, gently shaking the dish to distribute the custard evenly. Cool completely to room temperature, cover, and refrigerate at least 12 hours and up to 24 hours.

To serve Whip the cream until stiff peaks form. Using a pastry bag fitted with a large star tip, pipe an open crosshatch pattern of whipped cream over the top of the trifle. Pipe rosettes of whipped cream in the gaps in the crosshatching. Sprinkle the almonds evenly over the trifle and serve immediately.

leftovers

The ragout can be used another day, reheated gently just until warmed through and eaten as is or used as a chunky pasta sauce.

steamed chocolate-walnut pudding

serves 6 to 8

Substitute this impressively tall, opulently moist, and chocolaty pudding for almost any dessert in any menu in the book. A dish that requires a long period of steaming may seem most appropriate for a fall or winter weekend (it *will* help counteract the drying effects of a houseful of active radiators), but because the pudding can be completed in advance and rewarmed, or simply served at room temperature, it can actually be enjoyed year round. You will need a six- to seven-cup cylindrical pudding mold with a hollow central core and a clamp-on lid, ideally of stainless steel (see Cook's and Gardener's Sources). Serve slices of the pudding warm with a rich vanilla custard sauce (crème anglaise) or at room temperature with raspberry sauce.

1¼ cups sifted unbleached all-purpose flour (measure by sifting it into dry-measure cups, then sweeping the tops level)
2 teaspoons baking powder
½ teaspoon baking soda
3 ounces unsweetened chocolate
½ stick (4 tablespoons) unsalted butter
1 cup packed light brown sugar
2 eggs
⅓ cup buttermilk
2 teaspoons Vanilla Rum (page 66) or vanilla extract
1 teaspoon instant espresso powder
½ teaspoon salt
1 cup (about 4 ounces) coarsely chopped walnuts or pecans
Raspberry Sauce (page 34) or Crème Anglaise (page 268), for serving

Set a metal rack in the bottom of a large soup pot or stockpot. The pot should be tall enough so that its lid fits tightly with the covered pudding mold sitting on the rack. Test it to be sure.

Add enough water to the pot to come halfway up the sides of the pudding mold when it is sitting on the rack. Bring the water to a boil, then lower the heat and keep the water hot while you make the pudding.

With a pastry brush lightly butter the inside of the pudding mold, paying special attention to any ornamental crevices and depressions on the bottom. Butter the inside of the lid.

In a medium bowl thoroughly mix the flour, baking powder, and soda.

In a medium saucepan over low heat, melt together the chocolate, butter, and brown sugar. Remove from the heat, transfer immediately to a large bowl, and cool 10 minutes.

Whisk the eggs, one at a time, into the chocolate mixture; then whisk in the buttermilk, vanilla rum, instant espresso, and salt. Stir in the walnuts.

Sift the dry ingredients into the chocolate mixture and stir until just combined. Spoon the batter into the prepared mold and smooth the top with the back of a spoon. Clamp the lid in place.

Return the water in the pot to a full boil, set the pudding mold on the rack, and cover the pot. Adjust the heat so that the water maintains a steady, gentle simmer for 1½ hours. Keep a kettle of hot water on the stove and replace the water in the pot should the level drop.

Remove the mold from the water. Remove the lid and let the pudding stand in the mold on a rack for 15 minutes. Invert the mold onto a plate; the pudding will drop out. Cool to room temperature, cover, and refrigerate until firm. *The pudding can be prepared up to 2 days ahead.*

Cut the pudding into thin slices (this is easier to do while it is cold). Let the pudding warm to room temperature and serve it with raspberry sauce; or warm the slices, covered with foil, in a 300° F oven for about 10 minutes and serve the pudding with crème anglaise.

florence fabricant's crostini with two spreads

roast pork loin with madeira mushroom gravy

patricia wells's provençal baked tomatoes

mashed sweets

pecan butter-rum tart

This is a deeply flavored autumn dinner party for six, featuring sure-fire crowd pleasers like roast pork and mashed sweet potatoes and concluding with a sweet and sophisticated twist on pecan pie.

s t r a t e g y

For casual service, present the crostini on a cutting board with the two spreads in small crocks. Or, slightly more formal, the crostini can be spread, half and half, with the red pepper and chicken liver mixtures and passed. The homey nature of the main dishes makes this meal a natural to serve family-style, passing the bowls and platters around the table. There aren't a lot of do-ahead options with this feast, but neither is it food that is technically demanding to prepare. Serve a Pinot Noir from California, Oregon, or Washington state.

florence fabricant's crostini with two spreads

serves 6

Crostini—crisp little toasts spread with a savory mixture—are delicious but often not very attractive. Florence Fabricant has deliciously solved that problem by adding a second bright-red spread of roasted sweet pepper and sun-dried tomato, giving the dish added color *and* flavor. This is my version of her recipe. Note that the pepper spread can be made in advance, but the chicken liver spread will be at its best prepared no more than two hours before serving and never refrigerated. This recipe is easily doubled, if there's a crowd on the way.

RED PEPPER SPREAD

1 large sweet red pepper, preferably Dutch
10 oil-packed sun-dried tomato halves, homemade (page 46) or purchased (see Cook's and Gardener's Sources)
2 tablespoons olive oil from the sun-dried tomato jar or pumate oil (see Cook's and Gardener's Sources)
¼ teaspoon salt
Pinch of crushed dried red pepper

CHICKEN LIVER SPREAD

2 tablespoons olive oil from the sun-dried tomato jar or pumate oil
⅓ cup finely diced yellow onion
2 garlic cloves, sliced
8 ounces chicken livers, trimmed and patted dry
1½ teaspoons small (nonpareil) capers, drained
2 teaspoons anchovy paste
Pinch of salt
Freshly ground black pepper

24 diagonally cut, thin slices of baguette, lightly toasted

For the red pepper spread Over the open flame of a gas burner or under a preheated broiler, roast the pepper, turning it often, until the peel is blackened. Transfer the pepper to a paper bag or a bowl covered with a plate and let stand until cool. Rub away the charred skin and stem and core the pepper. Coarsely chop the flesh.

In a blender or small food processor, combine the roasted pepper, sun-dried tomatoes, olive oil, salt, and dried red pepper and process with short bursts until almost smooth.

Transfer the purée to a crock or bowl and cover. *The purée can be prepared up to 3 days ahead and refrigerated; return it to room temperature before serving.*

For the chicken liver spread Warm the olive oil in a medium skillet over moderate heat. Add the onion and garlic and cook, stirring often, until tender and translucent, 3 to 4 minutes. Raise the heat slightly, add the chicken livers, and cook, tossing and stirring, until the livers are just cooked through but still slightly pink at the center and juicy, about 5 minutes. Cool to room temperature.

On a cutting board, with a long, sharp knife, chop the liver mixture almost to a purée. Transfer the livers and any juices remaining in the skillet to a bowl, stir in the capers and anchovy paste, and season with a pinch of salt and a generous grinding of black pepper. Cover and reserve at room temperature.

Serve both spreads, accompanied by the toasted slices of baguette.

●

roast pork loin with madeira mushroom gravy

serves 6

A boneless pork loin is attractive, tidy, and simple to carve. The creamy sauce, rich with Madeira, is delicious when made with white mushrooms but sublime if you spring for cremini, shiitake, or porcini.

1 boneless pork loin roast (about 3 pounds), rolled and tied
Salt
Freshly ground black pepper
1 cup medium-dry Madeira, such as Rainwater
3 tablespoons unsalted butter
¼ cup minced shallots
1 tablespoon minced fresh thyme, or 1 teaspoon dried thyme, crumbled
12 ounces fresh mushrooms, wiped clean, trimmed, and sliced thick (if using shiitakes, buy
    1 pound and discard the tough stems)
2 tablespoons unbleached all-purpose flour
1½ cups Chicken Stock (page 90) or canned broth
½ cup whipping cream

Position a rack in the middle of the oven and preheat the oven to 350° F.

Sprinkle the roast with ½ teaspoon salt and ¼ teaspoon pepper. Set the roast on a rack in a shallow, flameproof baking dish just large enough to accommodate it. Roast for 1 hour; pour off any fat.

Pour the Madeira over the roast and bake another 30 to 40 minutes, basting often, until an instant-reading thermometer inserted into the center of the roast registers 150°

to 160° F. Transfer the roast to a cutting board and tent with foil. Pour off and defat the juices; do not clean the roasting pan.

In the roasting pan over low heat, melt the butter. Add the shallots and thyme; cook, stirring and scraping browned bits from the bottom, for 5 minutes. Raise the heat to medium and stir in the mushrooms. Add ½ teaspoon salt and ¼ teaspoon pepper and cook, tossing and stirring, until the mushrooms render their juices, about 5 minutes.

Sprinkle the flour over the mushrooms and cook, stirring, for 3 minutes. Whisk in the reserved pan juices, the stock, and the cream and bring to a boil. Cook, stirring occasionally, for about 4 minutes, until the gravy has thickened. Remove from the heat and adjust the seasoning.

Carve the roast and serve, accompanied by the gravy.

●

patricia wells's provençal baked tomatoes

serves 6 to 8

Pat Wells has done what seemed impossible—an American, she writes about French restaurants for the French! At the same time, she has educated more Americans about contemporary French food than almost anyone. I find her recipe (from *Bistro Cooking*) for slowly baked, garlicky tomatoes is so easy, so good, and so appropriate in so many menus, it's become almost indispensable.

2 pounds firm, ripe tomatoes (see Note), halved and cored
¾ teaspoon salt
½ teaspoon freshly ground black pepper
8 garlic cloves, peeled and thinly sliced
¾ cup fresh homemade bread crumbs
½ cup minced wide-leaf parsley
3 tablespoons olive oil

Position a rack in the upper third of the oven and preheat the oven to 400° F.

Arrange the tomatoes cut side up in a shallow baking dish just large enough to hold them in a single layer. Season them with salt and pepper. In a small bowl combine the garlic, bread crumbs, and parsley. Sprinkle the mixture evenly over the tomatoes and drizzle with the olive oil. Bake, uncovered, until the tomatoes are soft and the crumbs are lightly browned, about 1 hour.

NOTE *Most of the year I find that Italian-style plum tomatoes are the most reliable for use in this dish, although during prime tomato season, medium-sized, sun-ripened garden tomatoes (of any color) make superior eating.*

●

mashed sweets

serves 6

Every bit as comforting as the other sort of mashed potato, these sweets are blessedly free of marshmallows, brown sugar, pineapple, etc. Pass additional sweet butter at the table if desired.

3½ pounds sweet potatoes, peeled and cut into 1-inch chunks
1 cup milk
½ stick (4 tablespoons) unsalted butter, softened
½ teaspoon salt
Freshly ground black pepper

In a large saucepan cover the potatoes with cold water. Bring to a boil over high heat, lower the heat slightly, and cook until the potatoes are very tender, about 25 minutes. Drain the potatoes and immediately force them through the medium blade of a food mill or mash them with a potato masher. Return the potatoes to the saucepan, set it over low heat, and cook, stirring, until the potatoes are steaming.

Meanwhile, in a small saucepan over medium heat bring the milk to a simmer. Beat the hot milk, the butter, the salt, and a generous grinding of pepper into the sweet potatoes. Adjust the seasoning and serve immediately.

●

pecan butter-rum tart

serves 6

Less goo, more nuts—those were my goals when I renovated the venerable pecan pie into this rather classy little tart. Like its inspiration, the dessert is rich as sin, a condition partially compensated for by the modest portions and somewhat alleviated by the garnish of unsweetened whipped cream. (One-quarter cup of the pecans can be replaced, if you wish, by an equal amount of semisweet chocolate chips.)

PECAN CRUST

½ cup (about 2 ounces) pecans
1¼ cups sifted unbleached all-purpose flour (measure by sifting it into dry-measure cups, then sweeping the tops level with a knife)
2 tablespoons granulated sugar
¼ teaspoon salt

¾ stick (6 tablespoons) unsalted butter, well chilled and cut into pieces
4 tablespoons whipping cream, chilled

FILLING

¼ cup packed dark brown sugar

1 egg

1 egg yolk

⅔ cup light corn syrup

⅓ cup whipping cream

3 tablespoons Vanilla Rum (page 66) or dark rum

3 tablespoons unsalted butter, melted

¼ teaspoon salt

1½ cups (about 6 ounces) pecans, coarsely chopped

Unsweetened whipped cream, for serving

For the pecan crust In a food processor, using short bursts of power, partially grind the pecans. Add the flour, sugar, and salt and pulse to blend. Add the butter and process until the mixture resembles coarse meal. With the machine running, add the cream through the feed tube 1 tablespoon at a time; do not let the dough form a ball. Scrape the dough onto a lightly floured work surface and divide it in half. Form each half into a flat disk, wrap the disks separately in plastic, and chill for at least 30 minutes.

Roll out 1 piece of the chilled dough between sheets of waxed paper into a 9-inch round. Pat the round into the bottom of a fluted 9-inch tart pan with a removable bottom. Cut the remaining dough in half. Shape each piece of dough on a floured surface into a ½-inch-thick rope. Fit the ropes around the edge of the tart pan and, using your fingers, seal them with the lower crust as you press them evenly up the sides of the pan. Refrigerate the pastry shell while preparing the filling.

For the filling In a bowl whisk together the brown sugar, egg, and yolk. Whisk in the corn syrup and then the cream, vanilla rum, butter, and salt.

Position a rack in the upper third of the oven and preheat the oven to 325° F.

Spread the pecans over the crust. Whisk the filling and pour it evenly over the pecans. Bake until the pecans turn a rich brown and the filling is set, about 40 minutes. Cool in the pan on a rack for 30 minutes. Remove the side of the pan and cool completely before cutting.

Serve, accompanied by unsweetened whipped cream.

leftovers

Any remaining red pepper spread can be used on sandwiches or as the basis for delicious deviled eggs (mash the hard-cooked yolks with the spread, and add a bit of mayonnaise if desired, and pipe into the whites). Although the chicken liver spread will not be as good the next day, it still can make an acceptable sandwich, either alone or along with leftover red pepper spread. Cold pork roast makes a delicious sandwich filling, or it can be mixed with leftover gravy and reheated to make a kind of comforting (if not particularly subtle) hash.

WINES FOR THE WEEKEND

What in the world are "weekend" wines? Since almost any type of meal, from informal to grand, featuring almost any ingredient, can be served up on a weekend in any season of the year, doesn't that mean almost any wine could be a weekend wine? And can't anything that is drunk on the weekend also be drunk during the week? Well, yes. So what *am* I talking about when I say weekend wines?

First, what I am *not* talking about is starting a wine cellar. If you have the patience, the space, and the cash, by all means begin one of these demanding investments in the future. You have my admiration, and I hope you'll invite me to dinner and pour me your best. And of course if you do collect fine wines, then analyzing them with equally serious friends is how you *should* spend your weekend.

But for me, and for many people, weekend wines are less single-minded than that, part of a larger picture of food, friends, and socializing. While that doesn't preclude quality, it does move wine back a step from the serious collector's intensely analytical approach. My weekend wines are affordable and food-compatible, are user-friendly rather than intimidating, include wines that are more suited to quaffing than comparing and contrasting, and are at their most useful when they work almost as well as apéritifs as they do on the table, letting me pour a single wine throughout the evening. Stock up, by all means, on the weekend wines suggested below, and refer to them as your "wine cellar" if you wish. But also open, enjoy, and share these friendly wines to the fullest with your weekend guests. Because of the vagaries of the market, these recommendations are general rather than specific and include no vintages. Use them to help you communicate with your neighborhood wine professional to select the best possible wines for your weekend menus.

Among the most food-compatible of white wines you will find some names that may be unfamiliar to you. Those who rank wine by taste rather than price tag will be pleasantly surprised—even impressed—by these "dark horse" white wines and how well they combine with and complement food.

Consider French Sancerre, for example. These crisp, herbal, even grassy wines, once little more than bistro plonk, have gone up somewhat in price but remain very drinkable, and are particularly good with simple fish and shellfish dishes and with goat cheeses. The California varietals (Sauvignon Blanc or Fumé Blanc) made from the same grape vary in quality but can be equally successful with similar foods.

French Muscadets are crisp and very dry, perfect for partnering clams, oysters, mussels, grilled fish, and seafood pastas. Two Italian whites—Pinot Grigio and Vernaccia—work well both as apéritifs and with grilled or baked chicken or fish, as well as with lighter pastas. Rieslings—from Germany, Alsace, or California—are made in a variety of styles, ranging from crisp and dry to lush and honeyed. The former are especially fine with lobster, and the latter can accompany modestly sweetened fruit or cheese desserts.

If you do choose to pour a more familiar Chardonnay, you now have a variety of styles from a number of countries to choose from. The hugely buttery, complex, and magnificent Chardonnays, aged in oak, that once characterized the California style have been joined by wines that are more elegant and restrained and at times even lively and very accessible. The venerable Chardonnay giants still give more pleasure in the mouth, dollar for dollar, than any wines I've ever tasted, but the elegant Chardonnays (superb with lobster, salmon, and halibut) and the lively ones (fine with chicken and pastas) make better matches with food and are more useful in weekend menu planning.

Among the red wines that are particularly suited to lazy-day meals and laid-back imbibing, several have proved their compatibility with many of the menus in this book. Among the best and most versatile are the Italian Dolcettos, Barberas, Barolos, Arneis, and Barbarescos. Together with lighter and livelier (as opposed to massively alcoholic and tannic) red Zinfandels from California, these wines combine fruit and acid, so they pair well with tart salads, perform perfectly with tomato sauces, and cut through the fat and smoke of grilled meats and even some seafoods. Chiantis from Tuscany will complement meals ranging from pristine grilled steaks to roast game to pepperoni pizza. Where the lighter, more elegant touch is needed, Pinot Noirs, never all that successful in California, have come into their own in the Pacific Northwest. Pinot Noirs are less complex (and less pricey) than the red Burgundies that are their French counterparts, and the best of them go well with hearty seafood, chicken, pork, beef, and cheese.

In addition to these multipurpose, food-friendly reds and whites, my weekend wines include a medium-priced French or California champagne (suitable as an apéritif or for any generally celebratory event) and a case each of a red and a white "premium" jug wine. Endowed with balance and good varietal flavor and free from the off flavors of cheaper bulk-produced wines, premium jug wines will cost between twelve and twenty dollars a magnum and are indispensable for casual meals where quantity is at least as important as quality. Two reliable labels are the Woodbridge Cabernet Sauvignon from Charles Mondavi and the Glen Ellen Proprietor's Reserve Chardonnay.

mixed seafood fry with green aioli

ginger-sesame rack of lamb

carrot and lentil gratin

patricia wells's provençal baked tomatoes (page 127)

cheese board (pages 150–51)

adrienne welch's chocolate-walnut fudge (page 136)

vintage port

This zesty, eclectic menu is a favorite of mine, and the one that invariably comes up, in some form or other, when food friends and I plan our personal "Last Suppers." It is vividly flavored with garlic, ginger, garlic, sesame, mustard, and *garlic*, and is perfectly suited for a lively celebration on a cold winter night.

The aioli, most of the gratin, and the dessert can be prepared a day ahead. The lamb roasts in about 30 minutes, making it just about the quickest-cooking piece of red meat on the market. The seafood, which does need to be deep-fried just before serving, takes only minutes, particularly if you set up two fryers. The lamb and vegetables can be individually plated or can be set on the table family-style, a particularly congenial way to enjoy this meal. Pour a crisp and lively Sauvignon Blanc with the seafood, offer your best Bordeaux or Cabernet Sauvignon with the lamb and the cheeses (see page 151 for advice on combining wine and cheese), and by all means experience the remarkable pairing of chocolate fudge and vintage port by way of conclusion.

mixed seafood fry with green aioli

serves 8

Though there is an inevitable last-minute scramble inherent in deep frying, this seafood appetizer, featuring a trio of lightly coated shellfish with a garlicky green dipping mayonnaise, is otherwise so easy and so satisfying to eat that the effort is worth the fuss. With two fryers, the whole process will take about 5 minutes.

Corn oil for deep frying
Green Aioli (page 77)
1 cup yellow cornmeal
1 cup unbleached all-purpose flour
¾ teaspoon salt
¾ teaspoon freshly ground black pepper
⅔ pound (4 or 5 small) squid, cleaned, bodies cut crosswise into ¼-inch rings
¾ pound medium shrimp, shelled and deveined
⅔ pound small sea scallops
Lemon wedges

In one or two deep fryers or wide, heavy pans fitted with deep-fry thermometers, heat 4 inches oil to between 360° and 375° F. Spoon about ⅓ cup green aioli into each of 8 ramekins.

In a wide, shallow plate (like a pie plate) stir together the cornmeal, flour, salt, and pepper. Coat half the squid with the cornmeal mixture. Transfer to a sieve and shake the seafood to remove any excess coating. Coat the remaining squid in the cornmeal mixture and shake off the excess. Lower half the squid into the hot oil in each fryer, stir, and then cook 1 minute, until crisp and golden. With a slotted spoon transfer the squid to paper towels to drain. Repeat with the remaining seafood.

Arrange the seafood on napkin-lined plates, set a ramekin of aioli on each plate, and garnish each plate with a wedge of lemon. Serve immediately.

•

ginger-sesame rack of lamb

serves 8

The lamb is subtly perfumed with the ginger, sesame, and orange of its marinade, resulting in a delicious but not at all "Oriental" flavor. The rack is tender and mild, roasts in a very short time, is easy to carve, and is automatically festive-looking on the plate—four qualities that more than justify the expense.

⅔ cup fresh orange juice, strained
1 long piece (2 inches) fresh ginger, peeled and chopped
4 medium garlic cloves, peeled and chopped
¼ cup soy sauce
2 tablespoons toasted sesame oil
1 tablespoon minced orange zest
4 racks of lamb, 8 ribs each, chine bones removed and ribs frenched
Freshly ground black pepper

In a food processor combine the orange juice, ginger, garlic, soy sauce, sesame oil, and orange zest; process until smooth. In a large, shallow bowl pour the marinade over the racks of lamb. Cover and refrigerate for 24 hours, turning the racks in the marinade once or twice.

Bring the lamb to room temperature before roasting. Position a rack in the upper third of the oven and preheat the oven to 450° F.

Wrap the frenched tops of the rib bones in foil. Lay the racks meaty side up and spaced well apart in a shallow roasting pan (such as a jelly-roll pan). Spread a third of the remaining marinade over the racks, season generously with pepper, and roast 10 minutes. Lower the oven temperature to 350° F. Spread half the remaining marinade over the lamb and roast 10 minutes. Spread the lamb with the remaining marinade and roast another 10 to 12 minutes, until a thermometer inserted into the thickest part of the meat registers 130° F.

Remove the racks from the oven, tent with foil, and let stand 5 minutes. With a sharp knife cut each rack in half between the fourth and fifth rib bones or cut each rack into separate chops. Transfer to plates or a platter and serve immediately.

carrot and lentil gratin

serves 8

This mustardy carrot and lentil casserole, with its crunchy topping of Parmesan and bread crumbs, is a good accompaniment to all sorts of plain roasted meats and poultry. You can customize the dish with your choice of mustard (tarragon to accompany chicken, green peppercorn with beef, honey if the main dish is pork).

5 tablespoons olive oil
1 cup finely chopped yellow onions
12 ounces (about 6 medium) carrots, peeled and sliced
1½ teaspoons dried thyme, crumbled
1 bay leaf
2 cups dried brown lentils, picked over and rinsed
3½ cups Chicken Stock (page 90) or canned broth
1½ teaspoons salt
½ cup Dijon-style mustard
½ teaspoon freshly ground black pepper
1 cup minced wide-leaf parsley
½ cup grated Parmesan cheese
3 tablespoons dried bread crumbs, preferably homemade

In a medium saucepan warm 3 tablespoons of the oil over moderate heat. Add the onion, carrots, thyme, and bay leaf; cook, covered, stirring once or twice, for 10 minutes.

Add the lentils, chicken stock, and salt and bring to a boil. Lower the heat, cover the pan, and cook, stirring once or twice, until the lentils are tender and have absorbed most of the stock, about 25 minutes.

Transfer the lentil mixture to a large bowl and cool to room temperature. Stir in the mustard, pepper, and parsley. *The dish can be prepared to this point 24 hours ahead. Refrigerate, covered, but bring it to room temperature before proceeding.*

Position a rack in the middle of the oven and preheat the oven to 400° F. Spoon the lentils into a shallow casserole of about 6-cup capacity. Smooth the top. Combine the Parmesan and crumbs. Sprinkle the mixture evenly over the lentils. Drizzle the crumbs with the remaining 2 tablespoons olive oil and bake the casserole until the top is crisp and brown and the lentils are sizzling, about 25 minutes. Serve immediately.

l e f t o v e r s

The seafood is not a successful leftover, but the aioli can be used to enliven sandwiches and salads for several days. The lamb chops make elegant eating, whether reheated or enjoyed cold atop a lusty green luncheon salad, or merely nibbled with a glass of red wine as an end-of-the-day treat. The lentils can be reheated, and any remaining tomatoes are delicious as the filling for an omelet. The fudge will keep up to a week in an airtight container.

adrienne welch's chocolate-walnut fudge

makes 16 pieces

There is no finer expression of chocolate than a square of perfect fudge. Such perfection does not come easily, however, and fudge making is fraught with complications. For those serious about their chocolate and their fudge, Adrienne Welch details the process in the recipe below, which first appeared in *Chocolatier* magazine. Her professional candymaker's approach is a bit daunting—mostly because of the precision of the directions—but actually less work than some so-called home versions, and the intense creamy fudge that it produces is worth the fuss. (If you ever believed the charming story that fudge was invented by coeds at Wellesley who used to cook it over light bulbs as an impromptu dormitory snack, working your way through Adrienne's formula will quickly disabuse you of that notion.) This recipe isn't for kids either (too much molten syrup and upper body strength required), but they will enjoy watching the process and eating the results.

You will need an accurate candymaking thermometer, a marble slab, an 8-inch-square flan form (see Cook's and Gardener's Sources), and the kind of stiff-bladed broad knife used for spreading spackling compound and found in hardware stores. Do not attempt to make fudge during humid weather.

3 cups sifted sugar
1¼ cups half-and-half
⅓ cup light corn syrup
Pinch of salt
7 ounces unsweetened chocolate, finely chopped
3 tablespoons unsalted butter, cut into ½-inch cubes
1½ teaspoons Vanilla Rum (page 66) or vanilla extract
2 cups walnut halves, coarsely broken

Lay a 10-inch square of heavy-duty aluminum foil on a baking sheet. Butter an 8-inch square in the center of the foil. Lightly butter the insides of an 8-inch-square flan form and set it on top of the buttered square on the foil. (Or line an 8-inch-square baking pan with foil so that the foil extends 2 inches beyond 2 opposite sides of the pan; lightly butter the bottom and sides of the foil-lined pan.)

Lightly butter the sides of a heavy, nonreactive 2-quart saucepan. Add the sugar, half-and-half, corn syrup, and salt. Set over medium-low heat and cook, stirring constantly, until the sugar crystals are completely dissolved. Do not let the mixture come to a boil. Remove the pan from the heat and, using a damp kitchen towel, wipe the sides of the pan above the liquid to remove any undissolved sugar crystals. Add the chocolate and stir until completely smooth.

Return the pan to the heat and attach a candy thermometer to the side of the pan so that it does not touch the bottom. (If using a thermometer that is mounted on a metal frame, do not worry about the base of the frame touching the bottom of the pan.) Bring the syrup to a gentle boil over medium-low heat. Cook the syrup without stirring for 1 hour to 1 hour 20 minutes, until the thermometer registers 234° F (soft-ball stage). If necessary, adjust the heat to low and use a Flame-Tamer; the surface of the syrup must boil evenly and gently to avoid scorching the fudge. Carefully take the pan off the heat and remove the candy thermometer. Immediately wash the thermometer in hot water.

Lightly sprinkle a marble slab with water and spread it with your hand so that there is a thin film covering the surface. Hold the saucepan of hot fudge close to the surface of the marble and slowly pour the fudge onto the marble. Do not scrape out the fudge that clings to the bottom and sides of the pan. Evenly distribute the butter cubes over the top of the hot fudge and let cool for 15 to 20 minutes, until the surface feels lukewarm (110° F).

Sprinkle the vanilla rum over the surface of the fudge. Using a 5- or 6-inch-wide flexible spackling knife, scrape and blend in the butter and vanilla by lifting and folding the fudge toward the center. When the butter and vanilla are completely incorporated, spread the fudge out into a 12- by 4-inch rectangle. Scrape the fudge back together and lift and fold the edges of the fudge back into the center. Continue working the fudge in this manner for 10 to 20 minutes, until the fudge thickens and starts to lose its shine. Blend in the walnuts. Quickly scrape the fudge into the prepared form or pan and spread it evenly with a small metal spatula. Set the fudge on a rack and let stand for 1 to 2 hours, until firm.

Take a warm sharp knife and run it around the edge of the fudge to loosen it from the sides of the form; remove the form. (If using the baking pan, lift the fudge out of the pan, using the two ends of aluminum foil as handles. Invert the fudge onto a small cutting board and carefully peel off the foil. Invert again onto a smooth cutting surface.) Using a large knife, score the fudge into 16 pieces. Cut the fudge, rinsing the knife with hot water and wiping it dry between each cut.

Let the finished fudge ripen for 1 to 2 days in an airtight container.

frisée and bacon salad with mustard-anchovy dressing

roasted chickens with basil-garlic sauce

carrot and potato gratin

mixed mushrooms with shallot persillade

crème café caramel

Noisy with rapid-fire tête-à-têtes and the clash of solid crockery, and hazy from the smoke of Gauloise cigarettes, the quintessential French bistro is a place of good will and hospitality. This menu is my attempt at recreating bistro grub (and the resulting good times) at home in the new American kitchen. Some details of authentic atmosphere will necessarily be missing (unless you speak French or smoke Gauloises), but the food can, for a few hours at least, transform your dining room into that of the best little bistro in Paris.

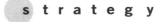 **s t r a t e g y**

There is no way to properly turn and baste the chickens without spending considerable time in the kitchen. I find that these days nearly everyone is willing to do *one* fairly sweaty culinary task as a favor to the host; so choose your company carefully and assign oven duty to the most pliable. Given the last-minute nature of both the salad and the mushroom side dish, volunteers for these jobs may also be necessary, and you may well end up with a dinner party that takes place almost entirely in the kitchen, a state of affairs that usually means the best of all possible times. Drink a Grand Cru Beaujolais such as one from Brouilly or Morgon.

frisée and bacon salad with mustard-anchovy dressing

serves 8

Bistro salads like this one are lusty things, generously portioned and vividly seasoned, designed to awaken the palate and prepare the appetite for the excellent meal to follow. If you can't locate the slightly bitter, slightly prickly green called frisée (French chicory), substitute a mixture of dandelion greens, arugula, and watercress.

12 ounces slab bacon, rind trimmed, cut into ½-inch dice
1 cup olive oil
2 garlic cloves, peeled and slightly crushed
4 cups bread cubes (¾ inch), about half a 14-inch loaf of Italian white bread
2 tablespoons Dijon-style mustard
2 tablespoons fresh lemon juice, strained
1 tablespoon anchovy paste
½ teaspoon freshly ground black pepper
2 large heads frisée (about 1 pound total), cored and torn into bite-sized pieces (about 16 cups)

In a large skillet set the bacon over medium heat. Cook, stirring occasionally, until crisp and brown, 10 to 12 minutes. With a slotted spoon transfer the bacon to paper towels to drain. Pour off all but 2 tablespoons of the bacon fat. Set the skillet over medium heat, add ⅓ cup of the olive oil and the garlic cloves, and cook, stirring, until the garlic is golden, about 5 minutes. Discard the garlic. Add the cubed bread to the skillet and stir well to coat the cubes. Cook, stirring occasionally, until the croutons are crisp and golden, 7 to 10 minutes.

Meanwhile, in a medium bowl whisk together the mustard, lemon juice, anchovy paste, and pepper. Gradually whisk in the remaining ⅔ cup olive oil; the dressing will thicken. Adjust the seasoning.

In a large bowl toss together the frisée, the browned bacon, and the dressing. Add the warm croutons and toss again. Divide the salad among plates, serve immediately, and pass a peppermill at the table.

roasted chickens with basil-garlic sauce

serves 8

A crisp and juicy chicken, presented in a fragrant, golden cloud of roasted garlic fumes, is found on many bistro menus. Repeated anointing with butter creates a crackly brown skin and frequent basting with pan juices produces moist, tender meat. Such necessary oven-hovering possibly might explain the rosy countenance of the typical bistro chef—or maybe it's just the Beaujolais. In any case, the sweaty effort is well worth it, as this basil-perfumed variation will prove.

2 chickens (about 3½ pounds each), at room temperature
Salt
Freshly ground black pepper
Stems from 1 large bunch basil
1 stick (4 ounces) unsalted butter, softened
40 large garlic cloves, unpeeled
½ cup dry white wine
1 cup tightly packed fresh basil leaves
1 cup Chicken Stock (page 90) or canned broth
1 tablespoon unbleached all-purpose flour

Position a rack in the middle of the oven and preheat the oven to 400° F.

Remove the fat from the chicken cavities. Pat the birds dry. Season the inside of each chicken with ¼ teaspoon salt and ⅛ teaspoon pepper. Tuck half the basil stems into each cavity and truss the chickens. Rub the chicken breasts and thighs with 2 tablespoons of the butter; season lightly with salt and pepper. Set the chickens breast side up in a shallow roasting pan.

Bake 15 minutes. Turn the chickens on their sides and brush with 1 tablespoon butter. Lower the oven temperature to 350° F and bake 15 minutes. Turn the chickens onto their other sides and brush with 1 tablespoon butter. Baste with any accumulated pan juices and bake 15 minutes.

Turn the chickens breast side up and brush with 1 tablespoon butter. Scatter the garlic cloves around chickens; baste the chickens with the wine. Brush the chickens with 2 tablespoons butter and roast 30 minutes longer, basting the chickens and the garlic every 10 minutes with the accumulated pan juices. The chickens, when pricked at the thickest part of the thigh, will yield clear yellow juices. Transfer the chickens to a cutting board and tent with foil.

Degrease the pan juices. Force the roasted garlic and pan juices through a sieve into a medium saucepan; discard the garlic skins. Cut the basil leaves into fine julienne. Add the chicken stock and basil to the saucepan and bring to a simmer over low heat.

Cook 1 minute; adjust the seasoning. Mash the remaining 1 tablespoon butter and the flour together in a small bowl. Whisk this paste into the sauce; simmer about 1 minute, until thickened.

Carve the chickens and serve, napped with sauce.

●

carrot and potato gratin

serves 8

This crusty, golden carrot-and-potato casserole is unique and delicious when made with the sweet and nutty French cheese Comté; if Comté is unavailable, use imported Gruyère.

2 pounds carrots, peeled and thinly sliced
Salt
2 pounds baking potatoes, peeled and thinly sliced
Freshly ground black pepper
6 ounces Comté (see Cook's and Gardener's Sources), grated
1 cup Chicken Stock (page 90) or canned broth
2 tablespoons unsalted butter

Position a rack in the upper third of the oven and preheat the oven to 375° F. Butter a 9- by 13- by 2-inch oval gratin dish.

Bring a large pan of water to a boil. Add the carrots and 1 tablespoon salt and cook 3 minutes; the carrots should remain slightly crunchy. Drain.

Arrange half the potatoes in the bottom of the prepared dish. Sprinkle with ¼ teaspoon salt and season to taste with pepper. Scatter one-quarter of the cheese over the potatoes. Arrange half the carrots over the cheese. Sprinkle with ¼ teaspoon salt and season to taste with pepper. Scatter another quarter of the cheese over the potatoes. Repeat layering with the remaining potatoes, carrots, and cheese, seasoning each vegetable layer with ¼ teaspoon salt and a grinding of pepper. Pour the stock over the vegetables and dot the top with the butter.

Bake for 70 minutes, until most of the stock has been absorbed, the potatoes are tender, and the top of the casserole is golden brown and crusty. Let stand 10 minutes before serving.

●

mixed mushrooms with shallot persillade

serves 6 to 8

Exotic mushrooms—some foraged from the wild, some cultivated—are now more widely available than ever before. Even Campbell's has entered the market, growing (along with uncounted tons of the white mushrooms used in their canned soups) shiitake, oyster, and cremini mushrooms, all of which turn up with reasonable regularity in the produce sections of supermarkets everywhere. (If you don't see them, ask the produce man. When he stocks up, honor your commitment by buying.) This dish is fairly plain, letting the mushrooms' deep, woodsy flavors shine through, with only a sprinkle of parsley and raw shallot added at the end for emphasis and color.

3 pounds assorted mushrooms, wiped clean and stems trimmed (discard the shiitake stems entirely)
¾ stick (6 tablespoons) unsalted butter
Salt
½ teaspoon freshly ground black pepper
⅓ cup finely minced shallots
⅓ cup minced wide-leaf parsley

Quarter the round mushrooms, such as the shiitake and cremini. Break the other mushrooms, such as the oysters, apart into separate caps.

In a large, deep skillet over medium heat, melt the butter. Add the mushrooms and stir to coat with butter. Cook, stirring once or twice, for 2 minutes. Add 1 teaspoon salt and continue to cook until the mushrooms begin to render their juices, about 1 minute. Raise the heat to medium-high and cook until the mushrooms are tender and the juices are reduced to a glaze that just coats them, about 3 minutes. Stir in the pepper and adjust the seasoning.

Stir in the shallots and parsley, transfer the mushrooms to a dish, and serve immediately.

crème café caramel

serves 8

Coffee adds a welcome edge of assertive flavor to the sweetly simple classic bistro dessert crème caramel. Use a full-flavored, regular-roasted coffee, such as mocha Java; dark-roasted beans will give the custard an unattractive oily appearance.

CARAMEL

1⅓ cups sugar
⅓ cup water

CUSTARD

2 cups whipping cream
1½ cups half-and-half
4 ounces whole coffee beans
3 eggs
5 egg yolks
2 teaspoons Vanilla Rum (page 66) or vanilla extract
¾ cup sugar
¼ teaspoon salt

For the caramel   In a heavy, medium saucepan stir together the sugar and water. Set over high heat and bring the mixture to a full boil. Cook without stirring until it turns a dark amber, 7 to 8 minutes. Immediately remove the pan from the heat and dip the bottom briefly into cold water to stop the cooking. Working quickly, spoon about 2 tablespoons of the caramel into a ¾-cup ramekin; tilt the ramekin to coat the bottom and sides with caramel. Repeat with the remaining caramel, coating a total of 8 ramekins and using all the caramel.

For the custard   In a medium saucepan combine the whipping cream and half-and-half. Set over medium heat and bring to a boil. Stir in the coffee beans, remove the pan from the heat, and let stand, covered, stirring once or twice, until cool. Strain and discard the coffee beans.

Position a rack in the middle of the oven and preheat the oven to 325° F.

In a mixing bowl whisk together the eggs, egg yolks, and vanilla rum. Whisk in ¾ cup sugar and the salt. In a saucepan over medium heat, bring the strained cream mixture just to a boil. Whisk the hot cream mixture into the eggs. Ladle the cream mixture into the ramekins, dividing it evenly and using it all.

Set the ramekins in a large baking dish and add enough hot water to the dish to come halfway up the sides of the ramekins. Set the baking dish in the oven and bake 50 minutes, until the custards are evenly, but not firmly, set. Remove the water bath from the oven; remove the ramekins from the water and let cool to room temperature. Cover and refrigerate at least 5 hours. *The desserts can be prepared up to 2 days ahead.*

To unmold, run a thin, sharp knife around the edge of each custard. Set a small dessert plate over a ramekin and invert the two together; the custard and the liquid caramel will drop onto the plate. Repeat with the remaining ramekins. Serve immediately, or return the custards, uncovered, to the refrigerator until serving time.

l e f t  v e r s

Chicken as moist and tender as that produced by the roasting method above makes a delicious leftover. Enjoy it in a sandwich with any unused Comté on crusty white bread with a generous schmear of Dijon mustard. The gratin can be reheated in a microwave oven or in a 325° F oven. Leftover mushrooms can be warmed and used as an omelet filling, along with any spare Comté. Any remaining crèmes caramel will keep up to 3 days in the refrigerator.

brine-cured breast of duck on a bed of

cabbage, apples, and leeks

mashed sweets (page 128)

mixed green salad with sherry dressing

cheese board (pages 150–51)

walnut whole-wheat bread

marmalade gingerbread

Here is another duck breast menu, but this one for winter is the antithesis of the summery one on page 86. In this meal the duck is cured in a spiced brine and served atop a sweet-and-sour sauté of cabbage, apples, and leeks. The remainder of the menu is equally rich, lavish, and altogether suitable to the season.

strategy

Although the brine-curing of the duck breasts is done well in advance, the final cooking of both the duck and the cabbage sauté are rather last-minute, hence the simplicity of the other accompaniments. Prepare 12 cups of Basic Mixed Green Salad (page 23), dressing it with sherry vinegar and a combination of walnut and sherry oils. I have not suggested an appetizer here, since there is a cheese board, but if you would like a nibble with drinks before heading to the table, consider Florence Fabricant's Crostini with Two Spreads on page 125. With this menu of subtle salty, sweet, and sour contrasts, drink a full-bodied, well-balanced Zinfandel or, more unexpectedly but perhaps more successfully, open a fairly dry (Halbtrocken) Riesling from West Germany.

brine-cured breast of duck on a bed of
cabbage, apples, and leeks

serves 6

The brine in which the boneless duck breasts (*magret*) cure for 48 hours is heavily spiced and salted, creating a flavor you may associate with corned beef, which is prepared similarly. The salt, which leaches out the duck breast's natural juices and allows the spices to penetrate, firms the meat, an effect that is partially offset by the sugar. After brining, the meat is soaked in plain water to remove some of its salt and then poached in wine, further desalting it. The result, napped with a slightly fruity sauce, is the same pleasant balance of salt and sweet enjoyed when eating a glazed ham.

BRINED DUCK BREASTS

6 cups water
1 cup coarse (kosher) salt
¾ cup packed light brown sugar
2 garlic cloves, peeled and slightly crushed
2 teaspoons white peppercorns
2 teaspoons yellow mustard seeds
2 teaspoons whole allspice
2 teaspoons juniper berries, lightly crushed
2 teaspoons dried thyme, crumbled
2 bay leaves
3 *magret,* about 2¼ pounds total (see Cook's and Gardener's Sources), skin removed
1 bottle (750 ml) hearty red wine, such as Merlot or Zinfandel

CABBAGE SAUTÉ

½ stick (4 tablespoons) unsalted butter
4 medium leeks (white part only), well cleaned and coarsely chopped (about 3 cups)
8 cups finely shredded red cabbage (about half a 2½-pound cabbage)
3 Golden Delicious apples, peeled, cored, and sliced ¼ inch thick
Salt
Freshly ground black pepper
⅓ cup balsamic vinegar

¾ stick (6 tablespoons) unsalted butter
2⅓ tablespoons balsamic vinegar
1 cup Chicken Stock (page 90) or canned broth

For the brined duck breasts   In a medium saucepan over moderate heat, combine the water, coarse salt, sugar, garlic, peppercorns, mustard seeds, allspice, juniper berries, thyme, and bay leaves. Bring to a boil, then lower the heat and simmer, partially covered, for 15 minutes. Cool to room temperature. Transfer the brine to a deep bowl. Add the *magret,* weighting them with a small plate heavy enough to keep them below the surface of the brine. Refrigerate 48 hours, turning the duck breasts in the brine once or twice.

Remove the *magret* to a large bowl and discard the brine. Cover the duck breasts with fresh, cold water and let stand at room temperature, stirring occasionally, for 2 hours. Drain.

In a large, deep skillet over medium heat, bring the red wine to a simmer. Add the duck breasts and cook gently, turning once or twice, for 10 minutes (the duck meat should be no more than medium rare at this point). Remove the *magret* from the wine, cool, and pat dry. Reserve ⅓ cup of the poaching wine. *The recipe can be prepared to this point 1 hour in advance.*

For the cabbage sauté   In a large, deep skillet over low heat, melt 4 tablespoons butter. Add the leeks and cook uncovered, stirring once or twice, for 5 minutes. Add the cabbage and apples, season with ¼ teaspoon each salt and pepper, and cook, stirring and tossing, until the cabbage is wilted and tender, about 10 minutes. Stir in ⅓ cup of the balsamic vinegar and cook another 2 minutes. Adjust the seasoning.

To finish   While the cabbage is cooking, in a large skillet heat 3 tablespoons of the butter over medium-high heat. When it foams, add the poached duck breasts and cook, turning once or twice, until lightly browned and heated through, 5 to 7 minutes. Transfer the duck breasts to a cutting board and tent with foil.

Pour off any fat in the skillet but do not clean it. Add 2⅓ tablespoons balsamic vinegar and the reserved poaching wine to the skillet and set over high heat. Bring to a boil, scraping to dissolve the browned bits in the skillet, and cook for 1 minute. Add the chicken stock and cook for another 3 to 4 minutes, until the sauce has reduced by about one-third. Turn the heat to low and whisk in the remaining 3 tablespoons butter, a small piece at a time, always adding another piece before the previous piece is completely absorbed; the sauce will thicken slightly. Adjust the seasoning.

Carve the *magret* across the grain and at a slight angle into thin slices. Divide the cabbage mixture among 6 plates. Top the cabbage mixture with slices of duck breast, overlapping them slightly. Spoon the sauce over the duck and the cabbage and serve immediately.

•

walnut whole-wheat bread

makes 2 oval loaves

This grainy, walnut-studded country loaf is the perfect bread to serve with a selection of ripe cheeses and a tart green salad. It can also be formed, if you wish, into three long baguette-type loaves.

2 cups lukewarm (105° to 115° F) water
1 package dry yeast
4 cups (about) unbleached all-purpose flour
1 tablespoon salt
2 cups whole-wheat flour
1 tablespoon walnut or olive oil
1½ cups (about 6 ounces) shelled walnuts
¼ cup yellow cornmeal
1 egg, well beaten

In a large bowl stir together the water and yeast; let stand 5 minutes. Whisk in 2 cups of the all-purpose flour to form a thin batter. Cover and refrigerate 12 hours.

Whisk the salt into the batter. Add the whole-wheat flour and an additional 1 to 1½ cups of the all-purpose flour and stir until a soft and sticky dough is formed. Generously flour the work surface, turn out the dough, and knead, incorporating additional flour as required, until the dough becomes firm and elastic, about 5 minutes. Coat a large bowl with the walnut oil. Form the dough into a ball, turn the ball of dough in the oil to coat it, and cover the bowl with a towel. Let stand at room temperature until the dough has doubled in bulk, about 2 hours.

Meanwhile, preheat the oven to 375° F.

Spread the walnuts in a single layer in a metal baking pan and toast them in the oven, stirring once or twice, until crisp, fragrant, and lightly browned, 7 to 10 minutes. Remove the walnuts from the pan, cool to room temperature, and coarsely chop.

Punch the dough down and turn it out onto a lightly floured surface. Flatten the dough into a large rectangle. Scatter the walnuts over the dough, then gather the dough into a ball, enclosing the walnuts, and knead briefly to distribute the walnuts through the dough. Form the dough into a ball, return it to the bowl, and cover with a towel. Let stand until almost doubled in bulk, about 1½ hours.

Sprinkle a baking sheet evenly with the cornmeal. Turn the dough out onto a lightly floured surface, divide it in half, and form each half into an oval loaf. Transfer the loaves to the prepared baking sheet and cover with a towel. Let stand 30 minutes, until slightly risen and puffy.

Position a rack in the middle of the oven and preheat the oven to 400° F.

With a serrated knife, cut 2 shallow parallel slashes in the top of each loaf. Brush the loaves generously with the beaten egg and bake 20 minutes. Remove the loaves from the baking sheet, brush off any clinging cornmeal, and bake them directly on the oven racks for another 5 to 7 minutes, until the crusts are crisp and brown and the loaves sound hollow when the bottoms are thumped. Cool completely on a rack before slicing.

●

marmalade gingerbread

serves 12

This moist, citrusy spice cake makes a fine dessert, but it can also be enjoyed sliced thin and spread with a bit of sweet butter at teatime. It's a good keeper, making it an ideal weekend snacking cake, and it's sweet enough that even kids enjoy it. The marmalade need not be the expensive, imported stuff—supermarket brands work fine.

1 cup orange marmalade
¾ cup unsulphured molasses
1¼ sticks (5 ounces) unsalted butter
3½ cups unbleached all-purpose flour
2 teaspoons baking powder
1¾ teaspoons ground ginger
1½ teaspoons ground cinnamon
1 teaspoon baking soda
½ teaspoon salt
¼ teaspoon ground cloves
⅔ cup sugar
3 eggs
Unsweetened whipped cream, for serving

In a small saucepan over low heat, melt together the marmalade, molasses, and butter. Let cool to room temperature.

Position a rack in the middle of the oven and preheat the oven to 350° F. Grease a 10-cup ring or bundt pan.

In a medium bowl sift together the flour, baking powder, ginger, cinnamon, baking soda, salt, and cloves. In a large bowl, whisk together the sugar and eggs. Stir in the marmalade mixture. Add the dry ingredients and stir until just combined; do not overmix. Pour the batter into the prepared pan and bake the cake about 40 minutes, until a tester inserted in the center comes out almost clean.

Cool the cake in the pan on a rack for 10 minutes. Turn the cake out of the pan onto the rack and cool completely before cutting. *The cake can be baked 2 days ahead. Wrap it well and store it at room temperature.* Slice the cake and serve it garnished with the whipped cream.

l e f t  e r s

If there is leftover duck breast, slice it and sandwich it with rye bread generously spread with mustard. Leftover walnut whole-wheat bread keeps for several days and can be toasted or cubed and sautéed to make fantastic croutons for a green salad.

W E E K E N D   K N O W – H O W

COMPOSING A CHEESE BOARD

Serving guests a selection of fine cheeses is, like preparing a green salad, a civilized touch that can make a good dining experience into a great one. In fact a salad course served after the entrée can segue nicely into the cheese service, continuing and enhancing the general conversation and good will, providing an opportunity for enjoying an extra glass or two of wine, and creating a pleasant interlude between the main course and dessert.

Although a cheese "board" can be as simple as a single cheese on a modest plate, a certain amount of skill at selecting and combining a variety of good cheeses, as well as a bit of effort applied to the presentation, will increase the eating pleasure considerably.

Ideally you should shop for cheese at a reliable specialty shop, one with a knowledgeable cheesemonger and a brisk turnover of product. Good cheese sometimes is also found precut in upscale supermarkets, but your chances of finding something really excellent there will be considerably reduced.

As when shopping for produce, it's better not to arrive with preconceived notions of what you want. Take the cheesemonger's advice on what's in peak condition and compose your array of cheeses on the spot. A quarter pound of cheese per person is usually sufficient, depending on the rest of your menu. You could choose to feature a single, terrific cheese; you might select a tasting of several examples of the same cheese from different makers or countries; or you can put together a variety of contrasting types of cheese, preferably not more than three or four. A reasonable list from which to choose might include a chèvre; a soft, rich triple crème, a Camembert, or a Brie; a blue cheese of some kind; and a harder cheese, such as Parmigiano Reggiano, a French Tomme, or an excellent domestic Cheddar.

Buy the cheeses as close to the day you will be serving them as possible. Good cheese stores wrap their wares in plain paper, or sometimes in plastic wrap that is pierced to allow the cheese to breathe. If you buy precut plastic-wrapped cheese, loosely rewrap it at home in waxed paper. Store the cheeses in the refrigerator unless otherwise instructed by the cheesemonger and serve them within a day or two at the most.

Let the cheeses come to room temperature—most will take about an hour, although soft ripened cheese may require longer; ask the cheesemonger. Arrange them on a cutting board or a marble slab, or just use a platter that is large enough to allow guests easy access. Cheese knives (one for each cheese, to avoid mixing) are a luxury, but plain table knives will do. Remove any labels from the wrappings or from the cheeses themselves and lay them next to their respective cheeses to allow guests easy identification.

Pass the board around the table often, letting guests sample at will. (Cheese board etiquette says a piece of cheese should always be cut so as to leave it in approximately the same shape it was when it reached you. In other words don't hack the tip off a wedge of Brie. The host can only instruct by example.) Accompany the board with good bread (the Walnut Whole-Wheat Bread on page 148 is delicious with cheese) or plain crackers and some softened unsalted butter—especially nice with the stronger blue cheeses.

Serving an additional bottle of wine with the cheese course is a fine idea, but care must be made to balance the wine with the cheeses chosen. The twin rules of thumb that older wines are served later in the meal and that white wines are served before reds would lead you to believe that a mature, elegant red wine would be ideal to accompany the cheese. In fact, aggressive cheeses, like Roquefort or Gorgonzola, even mild but rich cheeses like St. André or Explorateur, will devastate a fine old Burgundy or Bordeaux. Try such cheeses instead with a younger, fruitier red wine, like a Zinfandel; pair them with a crisp and well-balanced white, such as a Gewürztraminer; or enjoy a chilled (sweet) Sauternes or a young and vigorous vintage port instead—all are excellent alternative companions to a mixed selection of good cheeses.

sautéed softshell crabs with pecans

old bay slaw (page 69)

peppered curly fries with cajun catsup

raspberry—key lime squares (page 69)

When the spring softshell crab season begins in May (sometimes earlier), East Coast crab lovers (and others around the country with diligent fishmongers) can take advantage of this menu, which offers up the crunchy crustaceans with various hot and spicy Southern touches.

s t r a t e g y

The slaw, catsup, and dessert should be completed in advance, leaving the cook free for some real fancy last-minute footwork, sautéing the softshells and deep-frying the potatoes simultaneously. If this sounds too stressful, substitute a double portion of Tangy Mashed Potato Salad without the dill (page 54) for the fries, which will ease the pressure considerably. Serve a chilled Sauvignon Blanc or icy lager beer.

sautéed softshell crabs with pecans

serves 6

Softshell crabs are blue crabs harvested after they have shed their old shells and before they form their new shells. They are kept alive, but, unlike lobsters, they are stored on ice and dampened seaweed (if held in water they would regrow their shells) and thus are quite perishable. Fished primarily from Georgia up the coast to the Chesapeake Bay, softshells can be rushed by air freight almost anywhere (though at some expense), and I have seen lively specimens for sale in Indiana. They must be killed and cleaned before cooking, and there is a good reason for learning how: While live crabs can be kept at home, covered with damp towels and refrigerated on ice for 24 hours or so, dressed crabs (should you have the fishmonger do the job for you) quickly lose their sweet, fresh flavor and must be cooked within hours. Use a thick and flavorful hot sauce, such as Trappey's Red Devil in this recipe.

1 cup unbleached all-purpose flour
½ teaspoon salt
½ teaspoon freshly ground black pepper
12 medium-sized softshell crabs, dressed (see Note)
½ cup olive oil
1 stick (4 ounces) unsalted butter
1 cup (about 4 ounces) coarsely chopped pecans
2 tablespoons hot pepper sauce
½ cup minced wide-leaf parsley

In a shallow, wide dish (like a pie plate), stir together the flour, salt, and pepper. Coat the crabs with the seasoned flour, shaking off the excess.

In each of 2 very large skillets warm half the olive oil over medium-high heat. When the oil is hot, add the crabs (they may spatter) and cook, turning them once, until they are crisp, about 3 minutes per side. (The upper surfaces of the crabs will turn red.) With a spatula transfer the crabs to plates.

Wipe one of the skillets clean and set it over medium-high heat. Add the butter and when it has melted, add the pecans. Cook, stirring constantly, until the pecans are hot and fragrant, about 1 minute. Remove from the heat, stir in the hot pepper sauce and parsley, and spoon the sauce over the crabs. Serve immediately.

NOTE *Live softshell crabs should be vigorous and struggling visibly when picked up. To clean them, slip the blade of a knife under the apron—the flat flap on the underside—and pull it away. Cut away the horny beak and eyes. Under the soft upper flaps on both sides of each crab is a ridged, fan-shaped spongy mass (the "dead man's fingers"); with the blade of a knife scrape this away and discard. Pat the crabs dry. They are now ready to be cooked.*

•

peppered curly fries

serves 6

In my youth, my family ate often at an authentic drive-in (fake drive-ins having not yet been invented), complete with carhops, malted milks, and moistly greasy, deep-fried potatoes that somehow had been cut before cooking into dramatically long cork-screws. Packed into the back seat of the Chevy with two brothers, my chocolate malted, and a cardboard dish of those potatoes, I hardly bothered with my burger. Happily I've located a gizmo (see Cook's and Gardener's Sources) that is designed to produce those same long curls of potato. Similar to but even more Rube Goldberg-ish than the more familiar apple peeler-and-corer, it's a wonderful kitchen gadget for all potato lovers. (There's also an electric device on the market that does the same thing with more efficiency and less charm.) I've cut back a bit on the malteds, but thanks to my new potato cutter I make golden curly fries often. Now that I'm grown up, I like them under a veritable shower of fresh black pepper and—for extra fire—with a sweet-hot Cajun-style catsup.

3 pounds (about 6 medium) red-skinned potatoes
Corn oil, for deep frying
Coarse (kosher) salt
Freshly ground black pepper
Cajun Catsup (recipe follows), for serving

Scrub and dry the potatoes and cut away any sprouted eyes or blemishes.

Set up the potato-curl–cutting machine and cut the potatoes according to the manufacturer's instructions.

Meanwhile, in a deep-fat fryer or in a deep, heavy pan over medium heat, pour enough oil to come halfway up the sides of the fryer. Heat the oil to between 390° and 400° F. Fry the potatoes in batches, stirring them once or twice, until crisp and golden, 4 to 5 minutes. With a slotted spoon transfer the potatoes to paper towels to drain. Sprinkle them lightly with coarse salt and generously with fresh black pepper. Serve immediately, accompanied by Cajun Catsup if desired.

cajun catsup

makes about 3 cups

I spent considerable time trying to come up with a spicy, chunky catsup from scratch, but the results always lacked the shine, the thickness, and the improbable but essential neon color of the bottled product. Changing gears and using commercial catsup as a base for my Cajun flavors proved to be the solution, as outlined below. This catsup is not meant to be canned; store it in the refrigerator and use it up (on whatever you enjoy with catsup) within 2 weeks.

2 tablespoons olive oil
½ cup finely minced yellow onions
½ cup sliced green onions
½ cup finely minced sweet red pepper
3 pickled jalapeños, stemmed and minced
2 garlic cloves, peeled and minced
¼ teaspoon dried thyme, crumbled
1½ cups bottled tomato catsup
¾ cup canned crushed tomatoes in heavy purée

In a small heavy saucepan over low heat, warm the olive oil. Add the yellow and green onions, red pepper, jalapeños, garlic, and thyme; cook, covered, stirring once or twice, for 10 minutes. Stir in the catsup and crushed tomatoes and bring to a simmer. Partially cover (the mixture is thick and may spatter) and cook, stirring occasionally, for 5 minutes.

Transfer the catsup to a heatproof container, cool to room temperature, and refrigerate, covered.

 l e f t o v e r s

Cold sautéed softshells are about as successful as cold fried potatoes: Persevere while both are hot and freshly cooked.

oven-baked asparagus with green sauce

roast leg of lamb with caramelized shallots

sorrel and white bean purée

patricia wells's provençal baked tomatoes (page 127)

coeurs à la créme (page 78) with two sauces

A handsomely browned leg of lamb is the centerpiece of this grand springtime feast, one composed of seasonal specialties and worthy of your best linen, china, and crystal. Put the extra leaves in the dining room table, invite everyone you know, and celebrate the season in style.

s t r a t e g y

The asparagus is intended as a sit-down first course (proper respect for this harbinger of spring). The rest of the meal takes a certain amount of time at the stove, especially near the end, when the lamb sauce is made (enlist a volunteer to handle the carving chores). The purée only requires reheating. Make a double portion of the Coeurs à la Créme. Prepare a double portion of Mango Sauce (page 79) and a single portion of Raspberry Sauce (page 34). Serve each heart-shaped custard framed with a bit of both sauces, and garnish each portion with a perfect strawberry. Although asparagus is supposed to be difficult to match with wine, the sauce provides a flavor bridge and you can feel free to pour a light and uncomplicated California Chardonnay. Either a Bordeaux or a Cabernet Sauvignon, both reds traditional with lamb, are appropriate with this grand feast. Pour the finest you can afford.

oven-baked asparagus with green sauce

serves 8

This dry-heat method of cooking asparagus concentrates and sweetens the vegetable's subtle flavor, while the robust salsa verde adds a pungent accent.

2 pounds medium asparagus, trimmed and peeled (page 74)
2 tablespoons olive oil
Salt
Green Sauce (recipe follows)

Position a rack in the upper third of the oven and preheat the oven to 450° F.

On a jelly-roll pan toss the asparagus with the olive oil. Set on the rack and bake, stirring once or twice, until the asparagus is just tender and lightly browned, 12 to 15 minutes.

Arrange the asparagus, hot or warm, on individual serving plates. Drizzle generously with green sauce and serve immediately.

green sauce

makes about 1¾ cups

2 cups loosely packed wide-leaf parsley leaves
2 cups loosely packed fresh basil leaves
3 tablespoons fresh lemon juice, strained
1 egg, at room temperature
5 oil-packed anchovy fillets
2 tablespoons small (nonpareil) capers, drained
1 garlic clove, peeled
1 teaspoon Dijon-style mustard
½ teaspoon salt
½ teaspoon freshly ground black pepper
¾ cup olive oil

In a food processor combine all ingredients except the olive oil; process until smooth. With the machine running, slowly add the oil through the feed tube; the sauce will thicken. Adjust the seasoning. *The sauce can be prepared up to 3 days ahead. Cover and refrigerate, but return to room temperature before use.*

roast leg of lamb with caramelized shallots

serves 8 to 10

Excellent American lamb is available now year round, although in spring it seems particularly tender and delicious. This handsome, crusty, bone-in roast is a rarity and particularly welcome in these days of processed chicken nuggets and other insipid fare. Half the sweetly caramelized shallots are puréed, providing the basis for the sauce, while the rest are served whole as a savory garnish. The "fell" is a tough, strong-flavored, parchmentlike membrane that covers the outside of the roast; it should be removed by the butcher along with the aitch bone, to facilitate carving.

1 leg of lamb (7 to 8 pounds), fell and aitch bone removed
2 garlic cloves, peeled and cut into slivers
½ teaspoon dried thyme, crumbled
2 tablespoons olive oil
Salt
Freshly ground black pepper
2 pounds large shallots, peeled
2 cups Chicken Stock (page 90) or canned broth
3 tablespoons sherry vinegar
½ cup dry red wine
2 tablespoons unsalted butter, cut into 4 pieces

With the tip of a small knife cut shallow, evenly spaced incisions on both sides of the leg. In a small bowl toss together the garlic slivers and thyme. Slip a sliver of thyme-coated garlic into each incision. Set the leg meaty side up in a shallow flameproof baking dish; cover and let stand at room temperature for 1 hour.

Position a rack in the lower third of the oven and preheat the oven to 450° F.

Rub the lamb with the olive oil and season with ½ teaspoon each salt and pepper. Set the lamb in the oven and bake for 15 minutes. Lower the oven temperature to 350° F, scatter the shallots in the roasting pan around the lamb, and return it to the oven. Bake another 50 to 60 minutes, stirring the shallots occasionally, until the internal temperature of the lamb at its thickest registers 130° F (medium-rare).

Transfer the lamb to a cutting board and tent with foil. With a slotted spoon remove the shallots from the pan. Cover half of them and keep warm. In a saucepan over high heat, combine the remaining shallots with the chicken stock and vinegar and bring to a boil. Lower the heat slightly and cook, stirring and mashing the shallots occasionally, for 15 minutes. Meanwhile, pour the grease out of the roasting pan and set it over medium heat. Add the wine and bring it to a boil, stirring and scraping the browned deposits on the bottom. Cook for 2 minutes, until the wine is reduced by half.

Force the stock-and-shallot mixture through the medium blade of a food mill. Return the mixture to the saucepan and stir in the red wine reduction. Bring to a simmer over low heat; adjust the seasoning. Whisk in the butter 1 piece at a time, adding the next piece before the first piece is completely absorbed. Keep the sauce warm.

Carve the lamb and arrange the meat on a platter. Scatter the whole shallots over the lamb and serve immediately, accompanied by the sauce.

●

sorrel and white bean purée

serves 8

Sorrel (or sourgrass) melts when heated into a tart, green puddle, which is used to color and flavor the puréed white beans. The entire dish can be prepared one day ahead and reheated just before serving.

1 pound dried white beans, such as Great Northern, picked over and soaked for 24 hours in
        cold water to cover
2 teaspoons salt
½ stick (4 tablespoons) unsalted butter
2 medium leeks (white part only), well cleaned and coarsely chopped
1 pound sorrel, rinsed, tough stems removed, and leaves chopped
1 cup Chicken Stock (page 90) or canned broth
1 teaspoon freshly ground black pepper

Drain the beans and pour them into a large pan. Add fresh cold water to cover by at least 3 inches. Set over medium heat and bring to a boil. Lower the heat and simmer, partially covered, for 20 minutes. Stir in the salt and cook another 15 to 20 minutes, until very tender. Drain and cool.

In a large, deep skillet over low heat, melt the butter. Add the leeks and cook, covered, stirring once or twice, for 10 minutes. Add the beans and stir to coat with butter. Stir in the sorrel and chicken stock; cook, covered, stirring once or twice, until the sorrel is completely soft and tender, about 5 minutes.

In a food processor, working in batches if necessary, purée the bean-and-sorrel mixture until very smooth. Transfer to a bowl, stir in the pepper, and adjust the seasoning. *The purée can be prepared 1 day ahead. Cool completely, cover, and refrigerate.*

Just before serving, in a medium saucepan over low heat, warm the purée, covered, just until it is heated through and steaming.

leftovers

Green sauce will keep for several days and can be served with hot or cool shrimp, chicken, or vegetables such as broccoli. Cold roast lamb is a great treasure, and depending on the amount, leftovers can be turned into anything from a single sandwich to lamb hash. If there is leftover purée, rewarm it gently and enjoy it with a dollop of butter.

SPRING

creamed fiddlehead ferns and mushrooms on toast

clay-baker tarragon chicken with potatoes and carrots

mesclun salad

strawberry-lemon tart

These days spring is necessarily a state of mind, since so much formerly seasonal produce is now readily available year round. When you're of a mind to celebrate spring (hopefully when spring is actually in the air and not merely being imported from south of the equator) and want to experience some of its clear, simple flavors and delicate colors, consider this meal.

strategy

The clay baker (brand name Römertopf) required here is commonly sold in housewares stores or by mail (see Cook's and Gardener's Sources). It's a great, lazy-day way to roast a chicken, since the bird and its garnish of vegetables bake almost unattended, leaving the cook free to prepare and serve the luscious (rather last-minute) hot appetizer. Prepare 12 cups of the Basic Mixed Green Salad, using a light French olive or walnut oil, red wine vinegar, and—ideally—the mixture of baby lettuces, herbs, and edible flowers known as mesclun, although more readily available salad greens can be substituted. The tart can be completed several hours in advance of serving. Drink a light and herbal California Chardonnay.

●

creamed fiddlehead ferns and mushrooms

on toast

serves 6

Fiddleheads are the infant stages of several types of wild ferns. Skilled foragers know the best varieties to pick, but the rest of us should be content to purchase from knowledgeable greengrocers (or by mail; see Cook's and Gardener's Sources). The season for fiddleheads is short, moving from south to north as spring warms the land, and lasts only about two weeks in a given area. Prices for such a rare and hand-harvested commodity are steep, but the eating experience, especially when celebrated in this simple but elegant recipe, is worth the cost.

1 pound fiddlehead ferns, cleaned and trimmed (see Note)
Salt
3 egg yolks
1 cup whipping cream
2½ tablespoons fresh lemon juice, strained
¼ teaspoon freshly ground black pepper
5 tablespoons unsalted butter
12 ounces cultivated white or brown (cremini) mushrooms, wiped clean, trimmed, and sliced
6 thick (1 inch) slices country-style bread

Bring a large pot of water to a boil. Stir in the fiddleheads and 1 tablespoon salt; cook, stirring once or twice, until just tender, 4 to 6 minutes. Drain immediately and transfer to a large bowl of ice water. Cool completely and drain well. *The fiddleheads can be prepared to this point several hours ahead. Wrap well and store at room temperature.*

In a medium bowl whisk the egg yolks. Whisk in the cream, lemon juice, ½ teaspoon salt, and the pepper.

In a large skillet over medium heat, melt 3 tablespoons of the butter. Add the mushrooms and cook, tossing and stirring constantly, for 2 minutes. Stir in ¼ teaspoon salt and cook another 2 minutes. Add the fiddleheads and cook, stirring often, until just heated through, 2 to 3 minutes. Stir in the cream mixture, lower the heat, and cook, stirring often, until the sauce thickens, 2 to 3 minutes. Do not boil. Adjust the seasoning.

Meanwhile, in a toaster or under a preheated broiler, toast the bread. Butter the toast on one side with the remaining 2 tablespoons butter. Set a slice of toast on each of 6 plates. Spoon the fiddlehead mixture over and around the toast and serve immediately.

NOTE *Purchase fiddleheads that are firm and tightly curled with stems that are not brown. Cut away the dried tip of each stem and soak the ferns in several changes of cold water, rubbing gently to remove any clinging brown fluff.*

clay-baker tarragon chicken with potatoes

and carrots

serves 6

Baked in the covered clay roasting vessel known as a Römertopf (see Cook's and Gardener's Sources), this chicken requires no basting (merely a little rubbing with butter near the end, which produces a crisp skin) and becomes deliciously infused with the flavor of tarragon, which is stuffed under the skin.

1 roasting chicken (about 6 pounds), at room temperature
1 bunch (about 4 good-sized sprigs) fresh tarragon
Salt
Freshly ground black pepper
1 pound medium carrots, peeled and cut into 1½-inch chunks
1½ pounds (about 12) new red-skinned potatoes, well scrubbed
2 tablespoons unsalted butter, softened
⅓ cup minced wide-leaf parsley

Immerse the top and bottom of a 4-quart clay baker in cold water for 15 minutes. Pat the chicken dry and remove all visible fat. Loosen the skin over the breast meat by sliding your hand between the skin and the meat. Slip the sprigs of tarragon under the skin on both sides of the chicken's breastbone. Season the cavity with ¼ teaspoon each salt and pepper. Rub ¼ teaspoon each salt and pepper into the skin of the breast. Set the chicken, breast side up, in the bottom of the baker. Scatter the chunks of carrot over the chicken. With a swivel-bladed vegetable peeler or a small paring knife, remove a ¼-inch-wide band of peel from around the middle of each potato. Scatter the potatoes over the chicken and sprinkle with ¼ teaspoon each salt and pepper.

Cover the baker and set it in a cold oven. Turn the oven to 450° F and bake, without uncovering, for 60 minutes. Remove the lid. Rub the chicken breast with 1 tablespoon butter and bake, uncovered, for 10 minutes. Remove any vegetables that are tender and keep warm. Rub the chicken breast with the remaining 1 tablespoon butter and bake another 10 to 15 minutes, removing the remaining vegetables as they become tender. The chicken breast should be juicy and just cooked through, while the legs and thighs will be very tender and may fall off the bone.

Transfer the chicken to a cutting board and tent with foil. Degrease the juices from the baker. Carve the chicken, discarding the softened tarragon from under the skin, and arrange the meat and the vegetables on a platter. Drizzle the pan juices over the chicken and vegetables, sprinkle with parsley, and serve immediately.

strawberry-lemon tart

serves 6

Good strawberries come from California, but better ones will be grown closer to home, coming from farmer's markets or supermarkets that advertise local produce. Such berries will be smaller but fresher and more intensely flavorful than the over-irrigated imports, and they will make this a dessert that tastes as good as it looks.

TART SHELL

1½ cups unbleached all-purpose flour

2 tablespoons sugar

Pinch of salt

5 tablespoons unsalted butter, well chilled and cut into small pieces

¼ cup solid vegetable shortening, well chilled and cut into small pieces

3 to 4 tablespoons ice water

FILLING

3 large eggs

3 large egg yolks

¾ cup plus 1 tablespoon sugar

⅔ cup fresh lemon juice, strained

2 tablespoons *fraise eau-de-vie* (clear strawberry brandy) or other clear berry-flavored brandy

1½ tablespoons finely minced lemon zest

TOPPING

⅓ cup strawberry jelly

2 teaspoons sugar

4 cups strawberries, hulled, rinsed only if necessary

For the tart shell In a bowl or food processor combine the flour, sugar, and salt. Cut in the chilled butter and shortening until the mixture resembles coarse meal. Blend in the water, 1 tablespoon at a time, until a soft dough forms. Turn the dough out onto a lightly floured surface, flatten it into a disk, and wrap tightly in plastic. Refrigerate at least 45 minutes. *The dough can be prepared up to 1 day ahead.*

On a lightly floured surface roll out the dough into a ⅛-inch-thick round. Fit it into a 9-inch fluted tart pan with a removable bottom and trim the edges. Refrigerate at least 30 minutes. *The unbaked tart shell can be wrapped and kept refrigerated up to 1 day.*

Position a rack in the middle of the oven and preheat the oven to 400° F. Line the tart shell with parchment paper, fill it with dried beans or pie weights, and bake until the pastry is set, about 10 minutes. Remove the beans and parchment and bake until the shell is golden, about 10 minutes more. With the back of a fork, gently flatten any steam pockets in the crust. (Do not prick with the fork.) Cool the tart shell on a rack.

Position a rack in the middle of the oven and preheat the oven to 350° F.

For the filling In a medium bowl whisk the eggs and egg yolks. Whisk in the sugar, lemon juice, *eau-de-vie*, and lemon zest. Transfer the filling to a container with a pouring lip.

Set the tart shell on the rack in the oven. Pour the filling carefully into the shell and bake until firm, 20 to 25 minutes. Cool on a rack to room temperature.

For the topping In a small, heavy saucepan over medium heat, melt the jelly and sugar together. Bring to a simmer and cook 3 minutes, stirring. Remove from the heat and cool to room temperature.

Cut the strawberries into thin slices. Brush the top of the tart with some of the glaze. Arrange the strawberry slices in overlapping concentric circles atop the tart, beginning with the outside edge of the tart and covering it completely. Brush the strawberries with the remaining glaze. Let stand at least 30 minutes but no longer than 2 hours. Cut into wedges and serve.

 l e f t o v e r s

The moist, tarragon-scented chicken, mixed with a little mayonnaise, diced celery, and some chopped walnuts, makes a fine chicken salad. Slice or dice any leftover roasted vegetables, dress with a mustardy vinaigrette, and serve them along with the chicken salad.

W E E K E N D   K N O W – H O W

HANDLING A COUNTRY HAM

Dorothy Parker, it is said, once defined Eternity as "two people and a ham," thereby sealing her reputation as a witty cynic but doing irreparable harm to her status as an eater. Those of us less scornful, and hungrier, will recognize a truth known by much of mankind since the pig was first domesticated: Hams—the cured and preserved hind legs of pigs—make delicious eating, no matter how long it takes us to finish the last morsel. With a house full of guests, or merely a heavy schedule of company on the way, sooner or later the weekend cook will succumb to the convenient (crowd-feeding) lure of the country ham.

Acquiring such a ham can be something of a mixed blessing. On the one hand, you have before you a prime example of an eminently edible product of the American ham-making art. On the other hand, once that attractive cloth bag is slipped off the ham, you are faced with a fairly unlovely piece of goods—a dense, salty, smoky hunk of pork, mahogany brown and heavily spangled with pepper and mold. To the modern government-regulated sensibility, which expects food products—and especially meat products—to be sanitized and rather predictable, a genuine country ham can be a strange and confusing thing.

By "country" ham let me say I mean dry-cured or Smithfield-type ham (not all of them produced in or around Smithfield County, Virginia; see Cook's and Gardener's Sources). These hams are arrived at by a unique three-step process. Following an application (or several applications) of a dry rub consisting of salt, possibly sugar, and other spices (especially pepper), plus nitrates and nitrites, the hams are slow-smoked over fragrant hardwoods and then hung or aged, sometimes for a year or longer. This process transforms the ham into something deeply flavorful, firmly textured, and as complex as great cheese or fine wine. There is also a loss of water inherent in the process, which concentrates the flavor and results in a considerable increase in price per pound. (There are also high-quality, brine-cured, heavily smoked country hams that, while not produced by the Smithfield method, are similarly firm, smoky, and salty.)

On the other hand, "city" hams, as they are sometimes called, are wet-cured and have been injected with a salt-water solution and then lightly smoked, returning, through dehydration during the smoking process, to something like their original weight. "Water-added" hams have also been injected and smoked but retain a larger proportion of the injected solution. Some city hams can be delicious (look for the Esskay label, among others), but water-added hams, in addition to being a poor value (who wants to pay five dollars a pound for salt water?), lack genuine ham character and taste like nothing more than luncheon meat.

Hams that are fully cooked (and most are these days) have been heated during smoking to an internal temperature of at least 137° F and are considered ready to eat. In actual practice city hams are more tender and flavorful if they are baked, not only heating them through (if they are to be served hot) but also allowing the cook to coat them with an attractive glaze as well. And, although there are those who enjoy country hams "as is"—sliced paper thin and tasting like a distant smoky cousin of the more familiar prosciutto—I recommend the process outlined below, whereby the ham is soaked, removing some of the salt, and then simmered, removing more of the salt and making the ham more tender. Non–Smithfield-type brine-cured country hams sometimes need a soaking, but usually not a simmering—follow the packer's directions.

Certainly this is more work than opening a can (and recognizing this, most smoke-houses also offer precooked hams), but it's an interesting process and probably one every curious cook should try at least once. The feasting and nibbling that follow are what weekend eating is all about.

TO PREPARE A DRY-CURED COUNTRY HAM

Remove the ham from its cloth bag (or poke). Under cold running water scrub the ham with a stiff brush to remove as much of the mold (it's harmless) and pepper coating as possible. In a very large stockpot or in a deep sink, cover the ham with cold water and soak it, changing the water every 6 hours, for 48 hours. After soaking, again scrub the ham with the brush to remove the last of the mold and spice coating.

In a 16- to 20-quart stockpot cover the ham with cold water. Set it over medium heat and bring the water slowly to a simmer. Simmer the ham gently for 4 hours. Remove the stockpot from the heat and cool the ham to room temperature in the simmering liquid. Drain and pat dry.

The ham now can be sliced and served, or used as an ingredient in the several recipes in this book that call for country ham, or it can be glazed and baked (page 297) for a handsome presentation. Leftover ham can be refrigerated up to five days or frozen up to one month. Remember to save the bone for making soup.

sunday breakfasts and brunches

cappuccino coolers

honey-oat waffles with raspberries and ricotta

mail-order smokehouse bacon

This breakfast menu, intended for one of the first hot weekends of the summer, is light but satisfying. Before the kitchen gets too steamy, turn out these crisp high-fiber waffles and get your Sunday off to a great start.

s t r a t e g y

Brew the double-strength coffee the night before, then whip up the coolers in the blender in seconds the next morning. The bacon needn't necessarily come by mail, but because eating it is a rare treat these days, don't waste the calories and cholesterol on the insipid mass-produced stuff. Try a nearby smokehouse, look for a premium brand of bacon in the supermarket, or see Cook's and Gardener's Sources.

●

cappuccino coolers

serves 4

The espresso base can be brewed in an ordinary automatic drip coffee maker. The recipe makes enough for four but doubles easily should you want seconds.

3 cups double-strength coffee, brewed from ground espresso and chilled until very cold
¾ cup chilled milk
¼ cup chilled whipping cream
¼ teaspoon cinnamon
1 tablespoon unsweetened cocoa powder

In a blender combine the coffee, milk, whipping cream, and cinnamon. Add 6 large ice cubes and blend on high speed until foamy and very cold.

Spoon the foam into 4 stemmed glasses, dividing it evenly. Pour the liquid portion of the cooler over the foam. Transfer the cocoa to a small sieve and sift it onto the tops of the coolers. Serve immediately.

●

honey-oat waffles with raspberries and ricotta

serves 4

Use coarse Irish or steel-cut oats, available in gourmet shops and health food stores.

3 baskets (6 ounces each) fresh raspberries, picked over, rinsed only if necessary
½ cup orange, raspberry, or wildflower honey
2 tablespoons fresh lemon juice, strained
1 cup water
¼ cup Irish or steel-cut oats (see Cook's and Gardener's Sources)
Pinch of salt
½ cup buttermilk
2 eggs, well beaten
1 cup unbleached all-purpose flour
1 teaspoon baking powder
½ teaspoon baking soda
¾ stick (6 tablespoons) unsalted butter, melted, plus additional softened butter for the waffle iron
8 ounces ricotta cheese, at room temperature, whisked until light and fluffy

In a small bowl crush the raspberries coarsely with a fork. Stir in ¼ cup of the honey and the lemon juice and let stand while preparing the batter.

In a small, heavy saucepan bring 1 cup water to a boil. Stir in the oatmeal and salt, turn the heat to very low, and cook, stirring often, until very thick, about 15 minutes. (The oats will remain slightly al dente.) Scrape the oats into a medium bowl. Whisk in the buttermilk, the remaining ¼ cup honey, and the eggs.

Sift together the flour, baking powder, and soda. Stir the dry ingredients into the oat mixture until partially combined. Add the melted butter and stir until just combined.

Heat a waffle iron and butter it according to the manufacturer's directions. Spoon ½ cup batter onto the prepared iron and cook until the waffle is crisp and golden, about 5 minutes. Repeat with the remaining batter.

Set the waffles on plates. Spoon the raspberry mixture over the waffles, dividing it evenly. Top each waffle with a generous dollop of ricotta and serve immediately.

l e f t o v e r s

Cook extra bacon; it reheats quickly in a microwave oven, perfect for a spontaneous BLT sandwich.

W E E K E N D   K N O W – H O W

SUNDAY
BREAKFASTS
AND
BRUNCHES

•

173

A GREAT CUP OF COFFEE

What is your totem for the weekend, the visual symbol, the sign or the logo that sums up everything a weekend should be? A calendar composed only of two-day weeks? A kite floating against a deep blue sky? An open door? A stack of Sunday morning papers? A stack of Sunday morning flapjacks? For me it is steaming coffee, perfectly brewed, piping hot, served up in an oversized blue cup that I have used and treasured for years. Even in the midst of a houseful of raucous weekend company, this cup and the coffee it holds are my quiet, personal island of calm. Such a cup (to quote a man who was actually talking about soup) "breathes reassurance."

Like many who treasure a truly fine cup of coffee, I'm mystified (sometimes appalled) by what gets served under that name. America apparently gets most of its work done under the influence of hot java, and yet so much of it is so bad. The rank brew from the office coffee maker or a cardboard cup of dishwater from a fast-food chain may be necessary for getting through the week, but come the weekend, if the coffee isn't good it might as well be Monday and here we go again. Like many great things, brewing good coffee is rather simple, the result of following a few clear rules. Do that and fine coffee is yours.

To begin, the better the bean the better the cup. All beans are not created equal, despite what you may be hearing on television commercials. The best coffee comes from freshly roasted, estate-grown beans of the type known as *arabica*, ideally purchased from a company that roasts its own or from a specialty retailer with a high turnover. (Most supermarket coffees are made from inferior *robusta* beans.) Once roasted, coffee beans quickly begin to go stale. Once ground, coffee goes stale even faster. Buy only whole beans and store those not to be used up within a week in the freezer in an airtight container.

Coffee should be ground just before it is brewed. If this seems too challenging while in a morning fog, purchase an automatic grinder/coffee maker combination that will let you set the time and will then do all the work.

Use cold, fresh water. Hot tap water is flat, lacking oxygen and producing coffee without snap. I filter my coffee water through a simple charcoal filter that sits on the top of a pitcher and use it immediately. (Apparently such filters don't do much to remove lead and other impurities in the water but do well against off odors and flavors like those of chlorine.)

Of the mainstream coffee-brewing methods, experts recommend drip (automatic or otherwise) and French press (the plunger-style Melior system). The coffee maker's carafe should be absolutely clean, free from any residual coffee oils (which quickly turn rancid) and of course from the smell or taste of dishwashing soap.

Grind the coffee beans to the fineness recommended by the manufacturer of the coffee-making system you are using. Measure the coffee accurately—the industry standard is two tablespoons (one coffee-measuring spoonful) to each six ounces of water. If you are using the proper grind, this will produce a full-strength cup of coffee, neither too weak nor too strong. Try these proportions once, then adjust for your personal taste.

For best brewing the water should be heated to 195° F—just slightly below the boil. With an automatic coffee maker, you will have to trust the manufacturer.

If you have brewed more than one cup, store the remainder in a thermos. Sitting on a hot plate will quickly ruin the wonderful coffee that you have spent so much time achieving.

Beyond this straightforward method, which is designed to combine the right amount of the best and freshest coffee, with the purest water, at the correct temperature, everything else is fine tuning. You may enjoy flavored coffees, for example (though many in the coffee industry campaign actively against them), or you may prefer decaffeinated coffee (again, many experts just don't find decaf drinkable). Many people who take their coffee seriously drink only dark roast, believing, somehow, that this is what the connoisseur should do. Drink what you like, of course, but experts wish more coffee drinkers would experiment with medium or even light roasts, feeling that there is a whole world of nuance to coffee that is missing from dark roasts.

Beyond the morning cup, there is room in the weekend for coffee in many forms. If you enjoy making espresso or cappuccino, or like to savor a big cup of *café au lait*, or require a tall iced coffee as a summertime cooler, follow the advice above regarding beans, grinds, and water and you'll always produce a cup worthy of the weekend.

tomato and farmstead goat-cheese omelets

tiny green beans with dill vinaigrette

double-corn muffins with sour cream and chives

melon and blueberries with wildflower honey

The farmer's market is not only an essential resource for the weekend cook, it's an opulent celebration of the season's abundance. Here is a height-of-summer breakfast or brunch from the farmer's market or the roadside stand (or your own approximation thereof), celebrating straight-from-the-garden produce, herbs, and fruits, plus new-laid eggs and fresh, mild goat's-milk (or sheep's-milk) cheese.

s t r a t e g y

Omelet making is a weekend skill worth acquiring and one that, while not difficult, is showy and appealing, as this menu will prove. All it takes is an egg chef willing to dedicate part of his day off to standing at the stove. Happily the rewards are great, and an omelet expert will never lack an appreciative audience. Enlist the kids (or other volunteers) to stir up the muffins. For the simple fruit dessert, select several kinds of ripe, juicy melon, slice them thin, and fan the slices on plates. Drizzle each with honey (wildflower honey if you can), spritz with fresh lime juice, and scatter a handful of fresh blueberries over all. A sprig of fresh mint will add a cool, green note.

●

tomato and farmstead goat-cheese omelets

serves 6

As with the rest of the menu, the ingredients for these omelets need not actually come from the farmer's market as long as they're the best, ripest, and freshest you can locate. Making six omelets may sound like sweaty, short-order work, but it gets easier with practice and will earn you no end of kitchen kudos. Two omelet pans (nonstick professional pans are recommended; see Cook's and Gardener's Sources) make the work at least twice as fast—and twice as much fun.

18 fresh large eggs
Salt
Freshly ground black pepper
¾ stick (6 tablespoons) unsalted butter, plus additional softened butter (optional)
1 pound fresh goat's-milk or sheep's-milk cheese, cut into ½-inch chunks, at room
    temperature
1 pound (about 4 medium) ripe red plum tomatoes, trimmed and cut into chunks, at room
    temperature
Fresh herb sprigs, for garnish

In a small bowl, with a fork, briefly whisk 3 eggs together with a generous pinch each of salt and pepper. In a 6-inch nonstick omelet pan heat 1 tablespoon of the butter over medium-high heat. When it foams, add the eggs and with a rubber scraper stir once or twice. As the eggs begin to set on the bottom, stir one-sixth of the cheese into the eggs. As the omelet approaches doneness (2 to 3 minutes' total cooking time for a soft French-style omelet; 3 to 4 minutes for a firmer American-style omelet), sprinkle one-sixth of the tomatoes over the surface. With the scraper release the omelet from the sides of the pan; tilt the pan and roll the omelet onto a waiting plate. Tuck the omelet into a tidy oval shape and spread an additional pat of softened butter over the omelet (optional, but nice). Garnish with a fresh herb sprig and serve immediately.

Repeat with the remaining ingredients.

NOTE *If you have 6 small bowls, the 6 sets of eggs can be beaten ahead of time; the truly organized may also want to portion out the cheese and tomatoes, to keep fumbling to a minimum once the eggs hit hot butter. Silicon scrapers, recently available (see Cook's and Gardener's Sources), don't melt and thus are perfect for omelet making. My general observation is that people are so flattered you bothered to make omelets, they really don't care if the finished product isn't a food stylist's perfect vision. And you* will *get better with practice.*

tiny green beans with dill vinaigrette

serves 6

Some accommodating farmers (or gardeners) willingly commit vegetable infanticide to pick green beans at their skinniest, while others come from the redwood school, believing bigger is better. Differences of opinion make the world go round, but for this salad, at least, the produce of the former makes for better, more tender eating, and you are encouraged to seek them out.

Salt
1¼ pounds small, tender green beans, tipped and tailed
3 tablespoons red wine vinegar
1 tablespoon Dijon-style mustard
¾ teaspoon sugar
½ teaspoon freshly ground black pepper
5 tablespoons vegetable oil
¼ cup finely diced red onions
1 tablespoon finely minced fresh dill

Bring a medium saucepan of water to a boil. Stir in 1 tablespoon salt and the green beans and cook until just crisp-tender, about 4 minutes. Drain and immediately transfer to a bowl of ice water. Cool completely, then drain thoroughly. *The beans can be cooked 1 day ahead. Wrap well and refrigerate.*

In a medium bowl whisk together the vinegar, mustard, sugar, and ½ teaspoon each salt and pepper. Gradually whisk in the vegetable oil; the dressing will thicken.

Just before serving, toss the beans, onions, and dill with the vinaigrette. Adjust the seasoning and serve immediately.

double-corn muffins with sour cream and chives

makes 9 large muffins

Even though it's corn season, for muffins like these, frozen corn actually yields better and more visible results. Save the sweet, tender, and juicy ears you'll surely find at your farmer's market and boil or grill them to enjoy with butter, salt, and pepper at another summertime meal.

1 cup unbleached all-purpose flour
1 cup yellow cornmeal, preferably stone-ground
¼ cup sugar
2½ teaspoons baking powder
¼ teaspoon baking soda
½ teaspoon salt
1 cup sour cream, at room temperature
1 cup well-drained canned or thawed frozen corn kernels
¾ stick (6 tablespoons) unsalted butter, melted and cooled to room temperature
¼ cup minced fresh chives (about 1 large bunch)

Preheat the oven to 400° F. Grease 9 cups of a muffin tin.

In a large bowl stir together the flour, cornmeal, sugar, baking powder, soda, and salt. In a medium bowl whisk together the sour cream, corn, butter, and chives. Stir the sour cream mixture into the cornmeal mixture until just combined; do not overmix.

Spoon the batter into the prepared muffin cups, dividing it evenly. Bake about 25 minutes, until the muffins are puffed, golden, and crunchy. Cool in the pan on a rack for 5 minutes. Serve warm.

l e f t  v e r s

There are endless uses for leftover goat cheese and tomatoes (in a sandwich on a crusty baguette, for example), but if there is a quantity (or you've doubled your shopping list to provide extras), toss the crumbled cheese with chunked tomatoes, red wine vinegar, olive oil, minced fresh basil, and salt and pepper to taste for a rustic salad. Once dressed, the green bean salad will quickly lose its color, but the flavor will remain. The muffins will reheat nicely in the microwave oven. Purée leftover melon, thin the purée with sparkling sweet wine, and garnish with leftover blueberries. Serve as a chilled dessert soup.

chilled fresh orange juice

herbed turkey sausage cakes

three-b flapjacks

Blueberries, buttermilk, and buckwheat are the three Bs that make up this breakfast's light and tender flapjacks. Pancakes from scratch are a treat any time of the year but are particularly welcome in summer, when they are least expected and when blueberries are at their best.

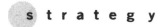

strategy

The sausage cakes, mixed up from fresh herbs and purchased ground turkey meat, are seasoned, formed into patties, and chilled overnight. Pancake making is an intensive but otherwise easy enough operation, and if there are kids present they can help. (This menu multiplies beautifully and, if you're blessed, as some of my friends are, with a commercial range equipped with a griddle, don't hesitate to feed these pancakes to a crowd.) If you would like to make this a full-scale diner breakfast, add fried or scrambled eggs. Squeeze fresh juice for this quick menu's final, special touch, and since flapjacks always seem to go with coffee—brew up a big pot.

●

herbed turkey sausage cakes

serves 4

To turn lower-fat, lower-cholesterol, sensible ground turkey into sausages remotely resembling those made from unsensible (but delicious) ground pork, add a measure of minced onion that has been sautéed in olive oil for moisture, use bread crumbs for tenderness, and cook the sausage cakes at a lower temperature for a longer time.

5 tablespoons olive oil
⅓ cup finely diced yellow onions
1½ pounds ground turkey, including some dark meat
2 tablespoons fine dry bread crumbs
3 tablespoons minced wide-leaf parsley
1 tablespoon minced fresh thyme
½ teaspoon salt
¾ teaspoon freshly ground black pepper

In a small skillet over low heat, warm 2 tablespoons of the olive oil. Add the onion and cook, covered, stirring once or twice, until the onion is tender, about 7 minutes. Cool to room temperature.

In a medium bowl lightly mix together the sautéed onion with its oil, the turkey, bread crumbs, parsley, thyme, salt, and pepper. Divide the turkey mixture into eighths and shape each portion into a cake about ½ inch thick and about 3 inches in diameter. Arrange the cakes on a plate, wrap them tightly, and refrigerate for 12 hours.

Warm the remaining 3 tablespoons oil in a large skillet over medium heat. Add the sausage cakes and cook, turning them once or twice, until they are lightly browned and cooked through but still juicy, about 8 minutes per side. Drain the cakes briefly on paper towels before serving.

●

three-b flapjacks

makes about ten 5-inch pancakes, serving 4

Although maple syrup is deliciously traditional, try the flapjacks with a dollop of Concord grape jelly (preferably homemade, page 182). The pairing of purple grapes with purple berries is wonderful. Later in the year, when fresh blueberries are not available, substitute frozen (do not thaw them) or skip the berries and enjoy the flapjacks plain.

¾ cup unbleached all-purpose flour
¾ cup buckwheat flour
2 tablespoons sugar
1½ teaspoons baking powder
1 teaspoon salt
¾ stick (6 tablespoons) unsalted butter
2 eggs, separated
1½ cups buttermilk, at room temperature
2½ cups blueberries, picked over, rinsed, and drained
Maple syrup and unsalted butter, for serving

In a medium bowl sift together the all-purpose flour, buckwheat flour, sugar, baking powder, and salt.

Melt 3 tablespoons of the butter and cool to room temperature. In a large bowl whisk the egg yolks. Whisk in the buttermilk and the melted butter.

In a medium bowl whisk the egg whites until soft peaks form. Stir the dry ingredients into the buttermilk mixture until just combined. Fold in the egg whites; do not overmix.

Warm a griddle over medium heat. Lightly grease it with some of the remaining 3 tablespoons butter. Working in batches and greasing the griddle with additional butter when necessary, drop the batter onto the griddle by ⅓ cupfuls. Onto each flapjack scatter about ¼ cup blueberries and cook about 4 minutes, until bubbles begin to appear on the pancakes' upper surfaces. Turn and cook about 1 minute more, until the flapjacks are just cooked through and the blueberries are beginning to sizzle.

Serve immediately, accompanied by maple syrup and additional butter.

aunt adrienne's concord grape jelly

makes about 14 pints

When the frost is on the pumpkin, it's Concord grape season in Massachusetts, and my friend Lisa Ekus is once again on the phone to her Aunt Adrienne Dahncke in Illinois, requesting once again the recipe she makes every year but never writes down. Adrienne's patience is exceeded only by her skill in jelly making: The recipe is a wonder. How is it possible that so few ingredients can combine to make a jelly so aromatically flavorful, so intensely colored, so tender, so purple-*tasting?* Although I have standardized the formula for the purposes of this book, you can make the jelly with any amount of grapes. Measure the juice after straining and add 1½ cups sugar per cup of juice. The jelly requires no added pectin, by the way, and in fact the flavor and texture are better without it.

10 pounds (about 6 quarts) Concord grapes
1 cup water
12 cups (about) sugar

Rinse the grapes well under cold running water. Remove and discard the stems.

In a large, deep nonreactive pan over medium heat, combine the grapes and the water. Cover and bring to a boil. Lower the heat, partially cover, and simmer, stirring once or twice, for 15 minutes. Remove from the heat and cool slightly.

Transfer the mixture to a jelly bag or a colander lined with a triple thickness of cheesecloth set over a large bowl. Let the mixture drain, gently stirring it but not forcing the mixture through the cloth, for 30 minutes. Gently press the bag to extract a little additional juice but stop immediately when the juice mixture shows any sign of turning cloudy. Discard the pulp in the jelly bag (see Note).

Measure the juice. For each 1 cup juice measure out 1½ cups sugar and in a deep nonreactive saucepan combine the juice and sugar. Set over medium heat and bring to a boil, stirring often and thoroughly to dissolve the sugar. When the jelly reaches a boil that cannot be stirred down, adjust the heat to prevent the pan from boiling over and cook, stirring occasionally, for exactly 5 minutes.

Remove the jelly from the heat and pack it into hot sterilized jars. Seal the jars according to the manufacturer's directions. Let stand 1 week before using.

NOTE   *Lisa's husband Lou is working on a sorbet recipe that will take advantage of all the juice and flavor left in the grape pulp. Stay tuned.*

rum-spiced cider

apple scrapple with maple syrup

eggs scrambled with toast

Keep it simple but make sure it's hearty, delicious, and interesting—these are good rules for designing a weekend breakfast menu. Serve this one when the first snap and crackle of autumn frost are in the air—and when apples are at their finest.

s t r a t e g y

The centerpiece of this menu, the scrapple, can be cooked and chilled in its loaf pan several days in advance, requiring only slicing and browning at the last minute. In a second skillet scramble the eggs, timing both to be ready and piping hot at the same time.

●

rum-spiced cider

serves 8

Begin your brunch with this hot cider drink (omit the rum if you wish), and if you have an electric juicer, you may substitute fresh pear juice for some or all of the apple cider. A pat of butter melting on top of the hot cider is a voluptuous—but optional—touch.

2 quarts apple cider, preferably fresh and unfiltered
⅓ cup packed light brown sugar
2 pieces (2 inches each) cinnamon stick
12 whole cloves
12 allspice berries
2 cups dark rum
½ stick (4 tablespoons) unsalted butter, sliced into 8 pats (optional)
8 long cinnamon sticks, for garnish

In a nonreactive pan combine the cider, brown sugar, short cinnamon sticks, cloves, and allspice. Set over medium-low heat, partially cover, and slowly bring just to a boil, stirring occasionally and skimming any scum that forms on the surface.

Meanwhile, divide the rum among 8 large mugs. Drop a pat of butter and a long cinnamon stick into each mug if desired. Strain the cider into the mugs and serve immediately.

●

apple scrapple

serves 8

Even those who adore scrapple—a frugal, hard-times combination of cornmeal and less-than-prime pig parts—admit it is an acquired taste. I acquired it years ago and now when I'm in scrapple country (Pennsylvania in particular) I always enjoy a breakfast plateful of the genuine article, accompanied by scrambled eggs and napped with maple syrup.

When company comes calling, though, I abandon authenticity and turn instead to this apple-studded variation. A hybrid of cornmeal mush, Italian polenta, and the scrapple of my dreams, it's too sophisticated to do more than remind me of the real thing, with which it nevertheless shares a hearty, stick-to-the-ribs quality.

1½ pounds mildly seasoned bulk sausage meat, preferably coarsely ground

1 stick (4 ounces) unsalted butter

1 cup finely diced yellow onions

1 large red apple (such as Red Delicious), cored and cut into ¼-inch dice

1½ tablespoons finely minced fresh thyme, or 1 teaspoon dried thyme, crumbled

1½ tablespoons finely minced fresh sage or 1 teaspoon ground dried sage

1 teaspoon freshly ground black pepper

6 cups water

1½ cups yellow cornmeal, preferably stone-ground

2 teaspoons salt

1 cup unbleached all-purpose flour

Maple syrup, for serving

Crumble the sausage into a large skillet and set over medium heat. Cook, stirring and breaking up any large lumps, until the meat is cooked through and lightly browned, 15 to 20 minutes. With a slotted spoon, transfer the sausage to paper towels to drain. Discard the fat but do not clean the skillet.

Set the skillet over low heat. Add 2 tablespoons of the butter and when it foams, stir in the onions. Cover and cook, stirring once or twice and scraping the pan, for 5 minutes. Stir in the apple, thyme, and sage; cook, uncovered, stirring once or twice, for 5 minutes. The apple should retain its shape and most of its texture. Return the sausage to the skillet, stir in the pepper, and mix thoroughly. Set aside.

Lightly oil a 9- by 5- by 3-inch loaf pan. In a heavy 4½- to 5-quart pot, gradually whisk the water into the cornmeal. Whisk in the salt. Set the pot over medium heat and bring to a boil, stirring once or twice. Lower the heat, partially cover, and simmer, stirring often, until the cornmeal is very thick, about 40 minutes.

Stir the sausage mixture into the hot cornmeal, combining well. Transfer the mixture while still hot to the loaf pan and smooth the top. Cool to room temperature, wrap well, and refrigerate until firm. *The scrapple can be prepared up to 3 days ahead.*

Run a sharp knife between the scrapple and the sides of the loaf pan. Invert the pan onto a cutting board; the scrapple will drop out. Cut the scrapple into 8 thick slices. In a large skillet heat the remaining 6 tablespoons butter over medium heat. On a plate dredge the scrapple slices with the flour, tapping off the excess. Fry the scrapple, turning it once, until well browned and crisp, about 4 minutes per side. Serve immediately, passing maple syrup at the table.

eggs scrambled with toast

serves 8

When good-quality (flavorful, firm!) bread is scrambled along with eggs, it becomes partly crunchy, partly custardy, utterly delectable. Use either white or whole-wheat bread and preferably day-old rather than fresh.

4 thick (½ inch) slices good-quality sandwich bread
16 eggs
1 teaspoon salt
½ teaspoon freshly ground black pepper
¾ stick (6 tablespoons) unsalted butter
½ cup minced wide-leaf parsley

Preheat the oven to 450° F.

With a serrated knife cut the bread slices into ½-inch cubes; there should be about 4½ cups. Lay the bread cubes in a pan large enough to hold them in a single layer and bake, stirring once or twice, until the bread is crisp and lightly colored, about 15 minutes.

In a large bowl beat the eggs. Whisk in the salt and pepper. In a large skillet over medium heat, melt the butter. Add the bread cubes and toss to coat them lightly with melted butter. Add the eggs and cook, stirring often, for about 7 minutes, until they are done to your liking. Stir in the parsley and serve immediately.

l e f t o v e r s

Scrapple that has not been fried can be refrigerated and sautéed at another meal.

assorted fresh juices

five-grain porridge with apple butter, brown sugar, and yogurt

sprouted wheat berry and walnut bread

herbal tea

The aim of this breakfast is health, but when there are grains on the menu, satisfaction and good eating are the primary effects, the healthful benefits secondary.

s t r a t e g y

The sprouts for the bread should be started at least three days in advance, although the porridge, of course, should be hot, thick, and freshly made. Spoon the porridge into bowls and let guests add dollops of unsweetened apple butter, plain low-fat yogurt, and brown sugar to taste. Toast the bread or serve it as is, passing honey or preserves on the side. There are a number of good electric juicers now available for the home market. Offer guests a choice of apple, citrus, tomato, or vegetable juices (or stick to simple fresh OJ). Herb tea completes the healthful picture, but don't be surprised by requests for coffee as well.

●

five-grain porridge

These five grains were chosen for the greatest possible contrast of flavor, texture, and color. If you use one of the increasingly available gourmet brown rice blends, you'll end up with more than five grains in your porridge. Flaxseed, steel-cut oats, and millet can be located at health food stores and, increasingly, in some supermarkets.

6½ cups water
⅓ cup brown rice, rinsed
⅓ cup millet, rinsed
⅓ cup barley, rinsed
⅓ cup wild rice, rinsed
2 tablespoons flaxseed
½ teaspoon salt
½ cup dark or golden raisins
⅓ cup Irish or steel-cut oats

In a medium, heavy pot over high heat, bring the water to a boil. Stir in the brown rice, millet, barley, wild rice, flaxseed, and salt; return to a boil. Lower the heat, partially cover, and simmer for 15 minutes. Stir in the raisins and the Irish oats; simmer, partially covered, stirring often, until the porridge is very thick and the grains are tender, about 30 minutes. Serve immediately.

sprouted wheat berry and walnut bread

makes 2 loaves

Seeds and grains contain powerful concentrations of nutrients, food intended for the growing plant. Sprouting the grains helps release those nutrients and make them more readily available to us. It's also a fascinating kitchen project, and the added texture makes the bread simply delicious. Don't limit this loaf to health-conscious breakfasts—it's also good with soups or on a cheese board.

Be sure your wheat berries are organic or at least untreated. The best source is a health food store. The bread takes time but not technique, and it freezes well, so that you can enjoy the fruits of your labors over more than one weekend.

¼ cup organic wheat berries

1 tablespoon molasses

2 cups lukewarm (105° to 115° F) water

1 package dry yeast

2 cups unbleached all-purpose flour

1 tablespoon salt

4 cups (about) whole-wheat flour, preferably stone-ground

1 tablespoon walnut or olive oil

1 cup (about 4 ounces) walnuts, coarsely chopped

¼ cup yellow cornmeal

Three to four days before making the bread, in a small bowl combine the wheat berries with enough cold water to cover them by 2 inches. Let stand at room temperature for 24 hours.

Drain the wheat berries and transfer them to a pint jar. Cover the jar with a piece of cheesecloth and fasten it in place with string. Set the jar in a dark place. Wet the wheat berries by filling the jar with water and draining it through the cheesecloth 3 or 4 times a day, returning the jar to a dark place each time. Repeat the process until the berries have sprouted and the sprouts are about ½ inch long. It will take 2 to 3 days. Remove the sprouts from the jar, wrap them in dry paper towels, put the towels loosely in a plastic bag, and refrigerate. *The sprouts can be prepared up to 1 week ahead.*

In a mixing bowl combine the molasses and the warm water. Stir in the yeast and let stand 5 minutes. Stir in the all-purpose flour and salt. Add whole-wheat flour, 1 cup at a time, until a sticky but manageable dough is formed.

Turn the dough out onto a work surface heavily dusted with some of the remaining whole-wheat flour. Dust the dough with more whole-wheat flour and knead, adding additional flour in small amounts when the dough becomes sticky, until the dough is relatively smooth and elastic, about 7 minutes. Coat a large bowl with the walnut oil. Gather the dough into a ball, turn the ball in the bowl to coat it with oil, and cover with a towel. Let the dough rise until doubled in bulk, 1½ to 2 hours.

Punch down the dough and turn it out onto a lightly floured work surface. Knead 3 to 4 minutes, dusting lightly with whole-wheat flour if necessary. Form the dough into a ball and return it to the bowl. Cover with a towel and let rise until doubled in bulk, 1½ to 2 hours.

Preheat the oven to 375° F.

Spread the walnuts in a shallow metal baking pan and toast, stirring them once or twice, until they are crisp, brown, and fragrant, 7 to 10 minutes. Remove from the pan and cool.

Sprinkle a large, heavy baking sheet with the cornmeal. Punch down the dough and divide it in half. Pat one piece out about ½ inch thick. Sprinkle half the walnuts over the dough. Untangle the sprouts and sprinkle half of them over the walnuts. Fold up the dough to enclose the walnuts and sprouts and knead briefly to distribute them throughout the dough. Form the dough into a round or oval loaf and transfer it to the prepared baking sheet. Repeat with the remaining dough, sprouts, and walnuts. Cover the loaves with a towel and let rise until almost doubled in bulk, about 1 hour.

Position a rack in the middle of the oven and preheat the oven to 400° F.

Lightly slash the tops of each loaf once or twice with a sharp knife and bake for 25 minutes. Remove the loaves from the baking sheet, brush off any clinging cornmeal, and return the loaves to the oven, setting them directly on the oven rack. Bake another 10 to 12 minutes, until the crusts are crisp and brown and the loaves sound hollow when the bottoms are thumped. Cool the loaves completely on a rack before cutting.

l e f t o v e r s

The porridge reheats well in a microwave oven and during hot weather can even be enjoyed cold. The bread keeps well, tightly wrapped or frozen. It makes delicious toast (I like it as the basis for a tuna salad sandwich).

cider doughnuts with maple-cream icing

makes about 12 doughnuts and 12 holes

I can buy good cider year round, but I only feel like making these snacks when there's a nip of fall in the air. Like sticky buns, they don't really fit into a meal plan, so just fry up a batch and enjoy them whenever your sweet tooth acts up. (Don't forget to brew a pot of java.) If there are kids in the house and colored sprinkles in the cupboard, the former should be encouraged to apply the latter to the just-glazed tops of the doughnuts and holes before the icing sets. Since leftover doughnuts are not very successful, this recipe makes a fairly small batch; enjoy them while they're warm and fresh.

MAPLE-CREAM ICING

¼ cup genuine maple syrup (see Cook's and Gardener's Sources)
¼ cup whipping cream
1 tablespoon unsalted butter
1 teaspoon Vanilla Rum (page 66) or vanilla extract
2 cups confectioners' sugar

DOUGHNUTS

Corn oil for deep frying
5 cups (about) bleached all-purpose flour
1½ teaspoons baking powder
1 teaspoon baking soda
½ teaspoon ground cinnamon
½ teaspoon salt
2 eggs
1 egg yolk
1 tablespoon unsalted butter, melted
1 cup sugar
¾ cup fresh, unfiltered apple cider

For the icing In the top of a double boiler over simmering water, heat the maple syrup, cream, butter, and vanilla rum until the butter is melted. Whisking constantly, sift in the confectioners' sugar. Remove the double boiler from the heat, cover, and set aside over the hot water.

For the doughnuts In a deep fryer or in a wide, heavy pan fitted with a deep-fry thermometer, heat 4 inches corn oil to between 350° and 375° F.

On a piece of waxed paper sift together 4¼ cups of the flour, the baking powder, soda, cinnamon, and salt.

In a large bowl whisk together the eggs and egg yolk. Whisk in the butter and sugar and then the cider. Add the dry ingredients and stir until a soft dough forms. Turn it out onto a surface heavily sprinkled with the remaining flour and knead about 20 seconds. The dough should remain somewhat soft and sticky. Pat the dough out about ½ inch thick. Using a 3-inch and a 1½-inch round cutter, each dipped before each use in flour, cut out 10 to 12 doughnuts and 10 to 12 holes. Let the dough rest 5 minutes.

Working in batches, fry the doughnuts and the holes in the hot oil, turning them once, for about 3 minutes total, until they are lightly browned and cooked through. Gather the dough scraps together, pat out ½ inch thick, cut out additional doughnuts and holes, and fry them. Drain on paper towels.

Stir the icing. Dip the doughnuts and the holes, one at a time, into the icing, letting the excess drip back into the double boiler. Set the doughnuts and holes on a rack and let stand until the icing is set, about 10 minutes.

sherried chicken hash

mixed mushrooms with shallot persillade (page 142)

tomato, sugar snap pea, and watercress salad

lemon-glazed bourbon black-walnut cake

Chicken hash is the solidly comforting main course for this brunch menu, a favorite in my house. In days when leftover roast chicken and gravy was common, hash was just a frugal way to stretch one meal into two. Nowadays it's made on purpose, using tender, juicy poached chicken white meat, rich velouté sauce, leeks, red peppers, and dry sherry—a treatment that turns frugal hash into a sublime dish for company.

s t r a t e g y

The hash can be completed, except for the final baking, the day before, leaving the cook plenty of time for the last-minute accompaniments—the mushrooms and the salad are not suitable dishes for preparing in advance. If you're serving the black-walnut cake, know that it keeps well for a day or two, although it may not last that long if discovered by hungry weekend nibblers.

●

sherried chicken hash

This creamy chicken hash would also make a fine lunch or supper dish.

3 pounds boneless, skinless chicken breasts
Salt
2 bay leaves
1¼ pounds (about 4 medium) red-skinned potatoes, peeled and cut into ½-inch dice
5 tablespoons unsalted butter
1 large, meaty sweet red pepper, preferably Dutch, trimmed and cut into ¼-inch dice
2 medium leeks (white part only), well cleaned and coarsely chopped (about 1¼ cups)
¼ cup Amontillado sherry
2 tablespoons minced fresh thyme
Velouté Sauce (recipe follows)
½ cup fresh homemade bread crumbs

Arrange the chicken breasts in a single layer in a large skillet and cover with cold water. Stir in 2 teaspoons salt, add the bay leaves, and set over medium heat. Bring slowly to a simmer, turning the chicken breasts once. Simmer until just cooked through, about 5 minutes. Check the chicken for doneness. Remove the skillet from the heat and cool the chicken to room temperature in the poaching liquid. Drain and pat dry. Trim any fat or cartilage and cut the chicken into ½-inch cubes.

In a saucepan cover the potatoes with cold water. Stir in 2 teaspoons salt, set over medium heat, and bring to a boil. Lower the heat slightly and cook, stirring once or twice, until the potatoes are barely tender, about 5 minutes. Drain immediately.

In a medium skillet over moderate heat, melt 2 tablespoons of the butter. Add the sweet pepper and leeks; cook, covered, stirring once or twice, for 10 minutes. Uncover, add the sherry, and raise the heat. Cook, stirring often, until the sherry is reduced to a glaze that just coats the vegetables, 2 to 3 minutes. Remove from the heat and stir in the thyme.

In a large bowl combine the cooked chicken, potatoes, glazed vegetable mixture, and velouté sauce. *The recipe can be prepared to this point 1 day ahead. Cool completely, cover, and refrigerate. Return to room temperature before proceeding.*

Position a rack in the upper third of the oven and preheat the oven to 400° F.

Spoon the hash mixture evenly into a shallow baking dish, such as a 9- by 13-inch oval gratin. Sprinkle the top evenly with the bread crumbs. Melt the remaining 3 tablespoons butter and drizzle it evenly over the bread crumbs. Bake for about 40 minutes, until the top is lightly browned and the hash is bubbling.

velouté sauce

makes about 3 ½ cups

¾ stick (6 tablespoons) unsalted butter
½ cup unbleached all-purpose flour
3 cups Chicken Stock (page 90) or canned broth
¾ teaspoon salt
½ teaspoon freshly ground black pepper
Pinch of freshly grated nutmeg

In a medium, heavy saucepan over low heat, melt the butter. Whisk in the flour and cook, stirring occasionally, for 5 minutes. Do not allow the flour to brown.

Off the heat, whisk in the stock. Return the pan to low heat, whisk in the salt, pepper, and nutmeg, and cook, stirring often, until the sauce is thick and glossy, about 20 minutes. Remove from the heat and cool to room temperature. *The recipe can be prepared up to 3 days in advance. Refrigerate, covered.*

tomato, sugar snap pea, and
watercress salad

serves 8

This colorful, crunchy salad is also good alongside plain roasted chicken, grilled fish, or broiled steak.

1 pound sugar snap peas
Salt
1½ tablespoons Dijon-style mustard
2 tablespoons sherry vinegar
½ teaspoon freshly ground black pepper
½ cup olive oil
2 pounds (about 10) ripe plum tomatoes, seeded, juiced, and diced (about 3 cups)
2 large bunches watercress, trimmed, rinsed and spun dry

Trim the sugar snap peas and string them if necessary. Bring a large pot of water to a boil. Stir in 1 tablespoon salt, add the peas, and cook until just tender, about 4 minutes.

Drain immediately and transfer to a large bowl of ice water. Cool completely and drain thoroughly.

In a medium bowl whisk together the mustard, the vinegar, ½ teaspoon salt, and the pepper. Gradually whisk in the oil; the dressing will thicken.

In a large bowl combine the peas, tomatoes, watercress, and dressing and toss to mix. Adjust the seasoning, toss again, and serve immediately.

•

lemon-glazed bourbon black-walnut cake

makes one 10-inch cake

This lemon-glazed, abundantly walnut-filled cake is adapted from a recipe in Susan Herrmann Loomis's *Farm House Cookbook* (Workman). It is moist and firm—a good keeper—and thus an ideal weekend sweet. Sliced thin, the cake is great for snacking on or for enjoying at teatime, while in more generous slices, it concludes a brunch or supper in a very satisfying fashion. The original recipe calls for coffee in the cake; I've substituted good bourbon and also added a jot of the same to the glittering glaze. The cake is delicious either way.

CAKE

2¼ cups sifted unbleached all-purpose flour

¼ teaspoon plus 1 pinch salt

1 teaspoon baking powder

2 sticks (8 ounces) unsalted butter, softened

¾ cup granulated sugar

¾ cup packed light brown sugar

6 eggs, at room temperature, separated

¼ cup milk

2 tablespoons bourbon

½ teaspoon Vanilla Rum (page 66) or vanilla extract

2½ cups (about 9½ ounces) black walnuts or regular walnuts, coarsely chopped

GLAZE

½ cup extra-fine sugar

Finely julienned zest of 2 large lemons

3 tablespoons fresh lemon juice, strained

3 tablespoons bourbon

Preheat the oven to 350° F. Butter a 10-inch tube or bundt pan.

For the cake Sift together the flour, ¼ teaspoon salt, and the baking powder.

In a large bowl cream the butter. Reserving 1 tablespoon of the granulated sugar, add the remaining granulated sugar and the brown sugar and mix until the mixture is light and fluffy. Add the egg yolks one at a time, beating well after each addition.

In a small bowl stir together the milk, bourbon, and vanilla rum. Add this to the butter mixture alternately with the dry ingredients, beginning and ending with the dry ingredients. Fold in the walnuts; do not overmix. The batter will be thick.

Beat the egg whites with a pinch of salt until they are foamy and begin to thicken. Add the reserved 1 tablespoon granulated sugar and continue beating until the whites are glossy and hold stiff peaks. Mix one-quarter of the egg whites into the batter to lighten it. Fold in the remaining egg whites, until just incorporated; do not overmix.

Pour the batter into the prepared pan and smooth the top. Bake until the cake is golden and puffed and springs back when lightly touched, about 55 minutes. Cool in the pan on a rack for 10 minutes.

For the glaze Meanwhile, in a small nonreactive saucepan over medium heat, combine the sugar, lemon zest and juice, and the bourbon. Cook, stirring, until the glaze just comes to a boil.

Unmold the warm cake onto a wire rack set over waxed paper to catch the drips. With a metal skewer poke several holes in the top of the cake. Slowly spoon the warm glaze over the cake, using it all. Cool completely before serving.

l e f t  v e r s

Any remaining sautéed mushrooms can be used as an omelet filling or mixed with a bit of whipping cream to make a rich pasta sauce for one or two. Leftover chicken hash can be rewarmed for a comforting midweek supper. Toast thin slices of cake for breakfast, teatime, or midday snack.

baja breezes or

fresh limeade plus! (page 64)

breakfast burritos with avocado and tomato

pinto bean fritters with

goat-cheese cream and salsa

santa fe bran muffins with honey butter

Lovers of spicy Southwestern food are never happier than when they can enjoy that fiery fare at the first meal of the day. Here's a warming winter menu, based on a New Mexican specialty—the burrito *desayuno*, or breakfast burrito.

 s t r a t e g y

The scrambled eggs and the deep-fried pinto bean fritters make this a breakfast/ brunch of the slightly clattery, last-minute kind. Snag a volunteer or two to help with the assembling, plating, and serving. Such an adrenaline-drenched session of kitchen brouhaha isn't out of place with the zesty food (if you want peace and quiet, eat cornflakes), and there's just no better way to get the day started. If you would like a dessert, serve a selection of chilled fruit. Drink Fresh Limeade Plus! (page 64) or Baja Breezes (recipe follows); or even simpler, pour cold Mexican beer, with or without a squeeze of fresh lime.

●

baja breezes

makes 1 cocktail

This fiery beer and fruit juice combination was inspired by the Mexican cocktail called *sangrita*. Make it with a mellow amber brew such as Dos Equis.

¼ cup fresh orange juice, strained
¼ cup tomato juice
Dash of hot pepper sauce
½ cup (about) beer
1 fresh lime wedge

In a tall glass stir together the orange juice, tomato juice, and hot pepper sauce. Fill the glass with ice. Slowly pour in the beer until the glass is full. Squeeze the wedge of lime into the cocktail and serve immediately.

●

breakfast burritos with avocado and tomato

serves 8

In Santa Fe and other Southwestern parts, the breakfast burrito can hold any number of savory ingredients (chorizo, cheese, chiles) and can sometimes jump right off the Richter scale heatwise. My version is somewhat tamer, although the pinto bean fritter recipe below includes enough extra salsa for any hotheads in the crowd.

16 eggs
2 teaspoons salt
1 teaspoon freshly ground black pepper
½ stick (4 tablespoons) unsalted butter
2 cups diced red onions
1 pound (about 5) Italian plum tomatoes, trimmed and cut into 1-inch chunks
2 buttery-ripe black-skinned avocados, pitted and cut into 1-inch chunks
8 flour tortillas (10-inch), warmed slightly

In a large bowl whisk together the eggs, salt, and pepper.

Melt the butter in a large skillet, preferably nonstick, over low heat. Add the onions and cook, stirring once or twice, until translucent but still slightly crunchy, about 5 minutes. Stir in the eggs and cook, stirring often, until softly set, about 7 minutes. Gently fold in the tomatoes and avocados and remove the eggs from the heat.

Spoon one-eighth of the egg mixture onto a warmed tortilla. Fold the 2 sides of the tortilla partially over the egg mixture, then roll up the tortilla, enclosing the filling. Transfer to a plate; repeat with the remaining eggs and tortillas. Serve immediately.

•

pinto bean fritters with goat-cheese cream and salsa

serves 8

These fritters were inspired by the chickpea-based Middle Eastern dish falafel and make similarly addictive eating. Please note that the beans first must soak for 48 hours.

2 cups (about 12 ounces) dried pinto beans, picked over and soaked in water to cover for 48 hours
2 medium garlic cloves, peeled and minced
2 teaspoons salt
2 teaspoons freshly ground black pepper
6 green onions, trimmed and thinly sliced
8 ounces fresh mild goat cheese, such as Montrachet, at room temperature
1 cup sour cream
Corn oil for deep frying
2 cups prepared hot red salsa
2 cups prepared hot green salsa
4 cups finely shredded romaine lettuce (optional)

Drain the beans. In a food processor combine the beans, garlic, salt, and pepper and process until almost smooth. Transfer the mixture to a bowl and stir in the green onions.

In a small bowl whisk together the goat cheese and sour cream until smooth and shiny.

In a deep fryer or in a deep, heavy pot fitted with a deep-fry thermometer, heat about 4 inches corn oil to 375° F. The fryer or pot should be no more than half full. Form the bean fritters by scooping up a heaping tablespoon of the bean mixture and firmly squeezing it into a ball. Lower the fritters carefully into the hot fat, working in batches to avoid crowding the fryer, and cook, turning once, about 2 minutes, until crisp and golden. Drain on paper towels.

Spoon a dollop of goat-cheese cream onto each plate (right beside the breakfast burritos, if you are preparing the complete menu). Set the hot fritters on the goat-cheese cream. Spoon red and green salsa onto the fritters and the goat-cheese cream, garnish with a mound of shredded lettuce if desired, and serve immediately. Pass any remaining salsa at the table.

●

santa fe bran muffins with honey butter

makes 10 large muffins

These rugged, oversized muffins are studded with toasted pine nuts and dried apricots—both grown in New Mexico, hence the title of the recipe.

⅓ cup pine nuts
2 cups unprocessed bran
1½ cups whole-wheat flour
1¼ teaspoons salt
1 teaspoon baking powder
½ cup packed light brown sugar
½ cup corn oil
2 eggs
1½ cups buttermilk, at room temperature
¾ cup diced dried apricots
Honey Butter (recipe follows), at room temperature

Preheat the oven to 375° F.

In a metal baking pan, toast the pine nuts, stirring them once or twice, until crisp, fragrant, and lightly colored, about 8 minutes. Transfer to a bowl and cool.

Raise the oven temperature to 400° F. Generously butter 10 cups of a muffin tin.

In a medium bowl stir together the bran, whole-wheat flour, salt, and baking powder. In a large bowl whisk together the brown sugar and corn oil. One at a time, whisk in the eggs. Stir in the buttermilk, apricots, and toasted pine nuts. Add the dry ingredients and stir until just combined; do not overmix. Divide the batter among the prepared muffin cups.

Bake 20 to 25 minutes, until the muffins are puffed and browned and a tester inserted into the center of a muffin comes out clean. Cool the muffins in the tin for 5 minutes. Remove carefully and serve hot or warm, accompanied by honey butter.

●

honey butter

makes about ⅔ cup

1 stick (4 ounces) unsalted butter, softened
¼ cup honey, preferably citrus honey

In a small bowl cream together the butter and honey. Transfer to a crock, cover, and refrigerate. *The butter can be prepared several days in advance.*

l e f t  v e r s

Any remaining goat-cheese cream is unexpectedly delicious on a hot baked potato or atop a bowl of chili. The cream also can be enjoyed spread on crackers or on slices of baguette, topped with sun-dried tomatoes or tapenade. Leftover muffins can be reheated in a microwave oven or split and toasted. The honey butter also will keep for a number of days and is good on pancakes, waffles, and toast.

spiced cranberry jam

makes 5 pints

Here is an easy but delicious preserve, perfect for enjoying on biscuits at a holiday brunch or breakfast, and also nice to have on hand for tucking into gift baskets for a final, seasonal fillip.

8 cups sugar
5 cups water
4 bags (12 ounces each) cranberries, rinsed and picked over
2 teaspoons ground cinnamon
2 teaspoons freshly grated nutmeg
1 teaspoon ground cloves

In a 6- to 7-quart nonreactive, heavy-bottomed pan combine the sugar and water. Set over medium heat and bring the mixture to a boil, stirring constantly to be certain the sugar is dissolved.

Stir in the cranberries, cinnamon, nutmeg, and cloves and bring to a boil. Lower the heat and simmer, uncovered, stirring often and thoroughly, for 1 hour, until the jam has begun to darken and is thick and shiny.

Spoon the hot jam into hot sterilized jars and seal according to the manufacturer's directions for jams. Process for 15 minutes in a hot water bath, again following the manufacturer's directions.

NOTE The jam can also be cooled and then refrigerated in a clean, tightly covered container without processing. It will keep several months.

grits, country ham, and sweet pepper cakes

with poached eggs

patricia wells's provençal baked tomatoes (page 132)

apple, orange, and cranberry compote

chewy granola thins (page 286)

The central players in this winter brunch—grits and eggs and ham—are country hearty, although I've rearranged the combinations slightly for a fresh approach.

s t r a t e g y

This is a relatively low-pressure brunch to turn out, since so much is completed in advance. Only the frying of the grits cakes and the poaching of the eggs require last-minute fussing, and like most egg cookery, poaching is merely a matter of practice. Serve the eggs in small bowls (like restaurant "monkey" dishes) set on larger plates with the grits cakes next to the baked tomatoes; diners can then combine the three elements as they wish. Though—or perhaps because—the menu has a down-home touch, I like to serve champagne with it.

grits, country ham, and sweet pepper

cakes with poached eggs

serves 6

This recipe is adapted from one I served when I was a partner in the Manhattan Chili Company, and that recipe was in turn adapted from one I enjoyed at Commander's Palace, in New Orleans, when Emeril Lagasse was chef there. For those of you who think of grits as something irredeemably soft and bland, these cakes will be a crisp and savory revelation.

GRITS CAKES

3 tablespoons unsalted butter

½ cup finely diced yellow onions

8 ounces ham, preferably ready-to-eat country ham (pages 165–66), trimmed and finely diced

1 large, meaty sweet red pepper, preferably Dutch, trimmed and finely diced

4 cups canned chicken broth

1 cup regular cooking (not instant) white hominy grits

¾ teaspoon freshly ground black pepper

2 eggs, well beaten

TO ASSEMBLE

3 eggs, well beaten

2 cups yellow cornmeal

3 tablespoons unsalted butter

3 tablespoons corn oil

Poached Eggs (recipe follows)

For the grits cakes Lightly grease a 9- by 13-inch baking dish. In a medium saucepan over low heat, melt the butter. Add the onion, ham, and sweet pepper; cook, stirring once or twice, until the pepper is tender, about 10 minutes. Add the broth and bring to a boil. Stir in the grits and pepper and bring to a boil. Lower the heat and cook, uncovered, stirring often, until the grits mixture is very thick, about 15 minutes.

Remove from the heat and immediately whisk in the beaten eggs. Pour the grits mixture into the prepared dish and smooth the top with the back of a spoon. Cool to room temperature, cover, and refrigerate until firm, about 5 hours. *The grits mixture can be prepared up to 3 days ahead.*

To assemble With a 2-inch round cookie cutter, cut out 12 grits cakes. One at a time, dip each cake into the beaten eggs and then into the cornmeal, turning to coat thoroughly. Let the cakes stand on a rack at room temperature for 1 hour to firm the coating.

In a large skillet heat 2 tablespoons each butter and corn oil over medium heat. Working in batches if necessary and adding additional butter and oil if the skillet becomes dry, fry the grits cakes, turning once or twice, until they are crisp and brown, about 4 minutes per side. Drain the grits cakes on paper towels and keep them warm in a 250° F oven until all the cakes are fried. Serve the grits cakes with the poached eggs.

•

poached eggs

makes 12 eggs, serving 6

For the best results, the eggs should be as fresh as possible. Be certain the skillet is impeccably clean in order not to discolor the eggs. Once you are experienced in egg poaching, you can cook the eggs in two skillets at the same time, which will speed the process considerably.

1 tablespoon red wine vinegar
2 teaspoons salt
12 extra-large eggs

Fill a clean large skillet with water. Set it over medium heat and stir in the vinegar and salt. When the water boils, lower the heat slightly to a moderate simmer. Working in 2 or 3 batches, crack the eggs and slip them into the simmering water. Regulate the heat so that the water neither boils (which will break up the eggs) nor becomes too cool (which will prevent the eggs from holding together in neat ovals). With a slotted spoon gently move the eggs around in the water until they are done to your liking. Using the slotted spoon, drain the eggs well and transfer them to the bowls or plates on which they will be served; keep warm. Repeat with the remaining eggs.

apple, orange, and cranberry compote

serves 6 to 8

This compote is undercooked slightly, so that the apples and cranberries retain a chunky texture. For a completely different approach (wonderful beside a Thanksgiving turkey), cook the compote another 5 minutes and then force the fruit through a food mill or purée in a food processor.

4 firm tart apples (such as Granny Smith), peeled, cored, and cut into 1-inch chunks
2 cups fresh orange juice, strained
1⅓ cups sugar
1 piece (2 inches) cinnamon stick
1 bag (12 ounces) cranberries, picked over and rinsed
Sour cream or crème fraîche, homemade (page 217) or purchased (optional)

In a medium nonreactive saucepan combine the apples, orange juice, sugar, and cinnamon stick. Set over medium heat and bring to a simmer, stirring to dissolve the sugar.

Stir in the cranberries and bring to a boil. Lower the heat, partially cover, and cook, stirring once or twice, just until the cranberries have burst, about 10 minutes.

Remove from the heat, transfer to a bowl, and cool to room temperature. Cover and refrigerate. *The compote can be prepared up to 3 days ahead.*

Spoon into bowls and top with sour cream or crème fraîche if desired.

leftovers

The unused portion of the firm grits mixture can be refrigerated, to be dipped in egg and cornmeal and sautéed for another meal. It's also good served like polenta, topped with tomato sauce and some melted mozzarella. Leftover compote can be served at another breakfast (dolloped onto hot oatmeal, for example) or enjoyed on ice cream as a fruit topping.

maple-walnut sticky buns

---

m a k e s   1 2

The scent of home-baked sticky buns, wafting into weekend bedrooms, will have hungry lazybones up in short order. Too huge and rich to follow most meals and too like dessert to be called breakfast, these sticky buns fall somewhere in between and exist for their own sweet sake—the ultimate weekend nibble. Not that they need either, need but these are delicious spread with unsweetened apple butter or drizzled with Maple Cream Icing (page 191).

DOUGH

2 cups milk

1 stick (4 ounces) unsalted butter

3 tablespoons granulated sugar

1 tablespoon salt

1 package dry yeast

3 eggs, at room temperature, well beaten

7 cups (about) unbleached all-purpose flour

TOPPING AND FILLING

1¾ sticks (7 ounces) unsalted butter, softened

1 tablespoon granulated sugar

1 teaspoon ground cinnamon

1½ cups coarsely chopped walnuts

1¼ cups raisins (see Note)

½ cup packed light brown sugar

½ cup genuine maple syrup (see Cook's and Gardener's Sources)

For the dough   In a saucepan over medium heat, combine the milk, butter, sugar, and salt. Heat, stirring once or twice, until the milk is hot and the butter is melted. Remove from the heat and pour into a large mixing bowl.

Cool the milk to lukewarm (105° to 115° F). Add the yeast, stir to dissolve, and let stand 5 minutes. Stir in the beaten eggs and then the flour, 1 cup at a time, until a soft dough forms. Turn out onto a floured surface and knead, adding flour as necessary, until the dough is smooth and elastic, 5 to 7 minutes. Butter a large bowl. Put the dough in the bowl and turn it to coat with butter. Cover with a clean towel and let rise at room temperature until doubled in bulk, about 2 hours. Punch down the dough, knead it briefly, and return it to the bowl. Cover with plastic wrap and refrigerate for 24 hours.

For the topping and filling Turn the chilled dough out onto a lightly floured work surface and pat and roll it out into a 12- by 17-inch rectangle about ⅓ inch thick. With a pizza wheel or a long sharp knife, trim the edges of the rectangle straight. Evenly spread 6 tablespoons of the softened butter over the dough. In a small bowl combine the granulated sugar and cinnamon and sprinkle it evenly over the buttered surface of the dough. Evenly sprinkle ½ cup each walnuts and raisins over the buttered dough. Starting with one long side, roll the dough into a long cylinder. Cut the cylinder crosswise into 12 equal slices.

In a small saucepan melt the remaining butter. With a pastry brush, brush the sides of a 9- by 13-inch baking pan with some of the melted butter. Combine the remaining melted butter, brown sugar, maple syrup, and remaining walnuts and raisins in the baking pan and mix thoroughly. Arrange the 12 slices of dough, cut side down, in the maple mixture. Cover with a towel and let rise at room temperature for 2 hours.

Preheat the oven to 350° F.

Bake the buns until puffed and golden brown, about 30 minutes. Cool in the pan on a rack for 5 minutes, then turn out onto a platter or baking sheet. Spoon any syrup remaining in the baking dish over the sticky buns and serve them hot, warm, or cool.

NOTE *Dried cherries can be substituted for the raisins; you may use a mixture of dark and golden raisins.*

lemon bloody marys

eggs and eggs in crisp potato skins

watercress salad with champagne vinaigrette

buttered toast

maple-walnut sticky buns (page 208)

cognac-and-wine-poached dried fruit compote (page 43)

This is a sybarite's brunch, perfect for New Year's Day or for any other morning after, when you and your guests require a little tenderness and cosseting. It could also be scaled down to feed two, as a romantic Valentine's celebration.

strategy

Although they're a little more work, this menu is also nice with poached eggs (page 206). (Set a poached egg into each potato skin, top the eggs with the caviar, and omit the crème fraîche or sour cream and the chives.) Prepare the salad following the directions for Basic Mixed Green Salad on page 23, using 16 cups watercress, and dressing it with champagne vinegar and a delicate olive oil. Serve the stuffed potato skins and the salad on the same plate, and pass the toast (firm white sandwich bread, crusts trimmed, would be ideal) in a napkin-lined basket. Set the sticky buns and fruit compote out on the sideboard and let guests help themselves when they're ready for something sweet. Although the Bloody Marys, made with your own homemade or purchased lemon vodka, are delicious, you could offer champagne instead.

lemon bloody marys

makes 8 cocktails

These tart, almost elegant Bloody Marys are in strong contrast to the chewy, horse-radish-laden cocktails that are all too prevalent today. Try these and get a whole new perspective on a classic libation. To best appreciate the flavor, serve the Bloody Marys well chilled but without additional ice.

4 cups tomato juice
1⅓ cups lemon vodka, homemade (page 213) or purchased
½ cup fresh lemon juice, strained
3 tablespoons hot pepper sauce
3 tablespoons Worcestershire sauce

In a pitcher stir together the tomato juice, vodka, lemon juice, hot pepper sauce, and Worcestershire sauce. Refrigerate at least 5 hours, until well chilled. Serve straight up or over ice.

eggs and eggs in crisp potato skins

serves 8

Don't let caviar scare you off. It's expensive, sure, but it doesn't take a lot to make a big effect, and if you buy from a reputable dealer (see Cook's and Gardener's Sources), your money will be well spent. Topped with a modest amount of nutty, complex-flavored osetra caviar, plus a few grains of salmon roe for bright color, these potato skins stuffed with both chicken and fish eggs are a luxurious treat.

8 russet baking potatoes (about 6 ounces each), well scrubbed
½ stick (4 tablespoons) unsalted butter, melted
Rich Scrambled Eggs (recipe follows)
6 ounces crème fraîche, homemade (page 217) or purchased, or sour cream, well chilled
1 ounce black caviar, such as osetra
½ ounce salmon roe caviar
2 tablespoons minced fresh chives

Position a rack in the middle of the oven and preheat the oven to 400° F.

Pierce each potato several times with a fork. Place the potatoes directly on the oven rack and bake until tender, about 50 minutes. Let stand until cool enough to handle, about 20 minutes.

Halve the potatoes lengthwise and scoop out the insides of the potatoes, leaving a shell about ¼ inch thick. *The potato shells can be prepared up to 1 day ahead. Wrap well and refrigerate.*

Position a rack in the upper third of the oven and preheat the oven to 425° F.

Lightly brush the potato shells inside and out with melted butter. Arrange them, cut side down, on a baking sheet and bake 12 minutes. Turn the shells upright and bake until the edges are crisp and golden brown, about 12 minutes more.

Arrange 2 potato shells on each of 8 plates. Fill one of the shells on each plate with scrambled eggs. Spoon a generous dollop of crème fraîche into the remaining potato shells. Divide the black and salmon caviars atop the crème fraîche. Sprinkle the chives over the scrambled eggs and serve immediately, accompanied by the watercress salad.

●

rich scrambled eggs.

serves 8

16 eggs
½ cup whipping cream
1 teaspoon salt
1 teaspoon freshly ground black pepper
½ stick (4 tablespoons) unsalted butter

In a large bowl whisk together the eggs, cream, salt, and pepper.

Melt the butter in a large skillet, preferably nonstick, over low heat. Stir in the eggs and cook, stirring often, until softly set, about 7 minutes.

 leftovers

The Bloody Mary mixture will keep in the refrigerator for several days. Unused potato skins can be crisped for use on another day. Leftover caviar is an oxymoron: Not only is it expensive, it's perishable. Eat up.

lemon vodka

---

makes 1 bottle (7 5 0 m l)

There's plenty of lemon vodka for sale at any decent liquor store, but when I mix up my own from this simple recipe, it always tastes fresher and more lemony. Start with a good-quality vodka and don't let the lemon peel macerate for more than 24 hours or the taste will be too strong. I store the bottle in the freezer—there's something particularly refreshing about syrupy-thick, icy-cold, lemon-flavored vodka that will take the steam out of the hottest day of the year. The vodka is perfectly delicious with caviar (actually better than champagne), and needless to say, it makes a terrific Bloody Mary.

1 bottle (750 ml) best-quality imported vodka
Zest (colored peel) of 1 large lemon, removed in large strips with a vegetable peeler

In a jar or other container with a lid, combine the vodka and lemon zest. Cover and let stand at room temperature, stirring once or twice, for 24 hours. Remove and discard the lemon zest. Return the vodka to its bottle and store it in the freezer.

campfire trout with hazelnut sauce

carrot and potato pancakes

buttermilk biscuits (page 297)

strawberries and cream

orange-cornmeal butter cookies
(page 97)

The best thing about a weekend spent camping out is the food, hence this trail-inspired spring brunch, for which you needn't tramp any farther than the back yard.

strategy

Except for the cookies, this is last-minute food, but everything goes quickly. Because the menu is divided between indoor and outdoor cooking, it's a good place to ask for a volunteer or two. I keep a big old cast-iron skillet dedicated exclusively to cooking on the grill, because I cook that way a lot, but if you only do so occasionally, the smoke will scrub off whatever utensil you choose rather easily. Look for intensely flavored local strawberries, slice a big bowl of them, add a bit of sugar to taste, and then just set the bowl out on the table, along with a pitcher of cream and additional sugar, to let guests help themselves.

campfire trout with hazelnut sauce

serves 4

Your back-yard grill provides all the necessary heat and smoke, and the nearest fishmonger will supply the requisite rainbows, brookies, or browns, making this outdoor fish fry about as effortless as it's possible to get. The seductively creamy hazelnut sauce may not be in the Boy Scout manual, but the results are still worthy of a merit badge.

3 cups aromatic wood smoking chips, preferably hickory or apple (see Cook's and Gardener's Sources)
½ cup unbleached all-purpose flour
Salt
Freshly ground black pepper
4 medium trout (about 3 pounds total), cleaned and scaled
7 tablespoons unsalted butter
½ cup coarsely chopped hazelnuts
3 green onions, trimmed and sliced
¾ cup crème fraîche, homemade (page 217) or purchased
2 tablespoons fresh lemon juice, strained

Soak the wood chips in water for 30 minutes. Light a charcoal fire and let it burn until the coals are evenly white or preheat a gas grill (high heat).

In a wide, deep plate (like a pie plate) stir together the flour, ¾ teaspoon salt, and ½ teaspoon pepper. Dredge the trout in the flour; shake off the excess.

Drain the wood chips and scatter them around the edges of the coals or grill stones. Position a rack about 6 inches from the heat source. Set a very large, heavy skillet on the grill rack. Melt 4 tablespoons of the butter in the skillet. When it foams, add the trout. Cover the grill and cook 4 minutes. Carefully turn the trout (use a long spatula), cover the grill, and cook until done but still moist, another 3 to 4 minutes. Transfer the trout to plates and keep warm.

Wipe the skillet. Add the remaining 3 tablespoons butter and set the skillet on the grill. Add the hazelnuts and cook, stirring, until golden brown, about 2 minutes. Stir in the green onions and cook 30 seconds. Remove the skillet from the heat and whisk in the crème fraîche, lemon juice, ½ teaspoon salt, and ¼ teaspoon pepper. Spoon the sauce over the trout, dividing it evenly, and serve immediately.

•

carrot and potato pancakes

serves   4

Use two skillets to speed things along or keep half the pancakes warm in a 325° F oven while you fry the rest. The strands of carrot and potato should be long and coarse to give the pancakes a crisp, lacy texture. Use the grating blade of a food processor. The potato should be grated and added to the carrot mixture just before you begin frying the pancakes.

1 small yellow onion (about 3 ounces), peeled and finely grated
2 eggs
2 tablespoons unbleached all-purpose flour
½ teaspoon salt
¼ teaspoon freshly ground black pepper
3 medium carrots (about 10 ounces), peeled and coarsely grated
1 large russet baking potato (about 12 ounces), peeled and coarsely grated
5 tablespoons unsalted butter

In a large bowl whisk together the onion, eggs, flour, salt, and pepper. Stir in the carrots and potato.

In each of two large skillets over medium heat, melt half the butter. Divide the carrot mixture into 8 equal portions (each about ½ cup). Transfer to the hot skillets and flatten each portion with a spatula into a 3-inch cake. Fry the pancakes, turning them once, until crisp and golden brown, about 5 minutes per side.

H A P P Y   H A N D S   R E C I P E

crème fraîche
---
m a k e s   2   c u p s

Crème fraîche—cultured heavy cream—is regularly found for sale these days in gourmet shops or cheese stores. Imported or domestic, it is expensive, but it is also tart, thick, and luscious. Spoon it over fresh berries or poached fruit, use it as the basis for a rich sauce (unlike sour cream, it won't curdle when boiled), spread it on a hot biscuit along with a dollop of strawberry jam, and so on. Making your own crème fraîche is an interesting and easy process, one of the puttering tasks that can fill a pleasant weekend in the kitchen. This works more reliably and tastes better if you can locate cream that has not been ultra-pasteurized.

2 cups whipping, or heavy, cream, preferably not ultra-pasteurized
2 tablespoons cultured buttermilk

In a container whisk the cream and buttermilk together. Cover with a clean kitchen towel and let stand at room temperature for 24 hours. The mixture will thicken slightly. Cover the container and refrigerate the crème fraîche; it will thicken further as it chills. *The crème fraîche will keep, refrigerated, for up to 10 days.*

asparagus, bacon, and ricotta tart

watercress salad with champagne vinaigrette

toasted english muffins

strawberry, pineapple, and mango compote

orange-cornmeal butter cookies (page 97)

Light, elegant, and fresh—three words that sum up spring can also be applied to this brunch menu.

strategy

The tart shell can be partially baked the day before, but it should be filled and the tart finished shortly before serving—the tart is best hot or slightly warm. Prepare the salad with 12 cups watercress and dress it with Champagne vinegar and olive oil, following the directions for Basic Mixed Green Salad on page 23. Make the mango sauce ahead but combine it with the strawberries less than an hour before serving. Drink a chilled Riesling or Sauvignon Blanc.

asparagus, bacon, and ricotta tart

s e r v e s   6

Since quiche, in some trendy circles at least, has been deemed "out," I've called this a tart, but the name change will fool few. Studded with nubbins of asparagus and smoky bacon, the creamy ricotta-based you-know-what is delicious for lunch or supper, and, cut into smaller wedges, it's also good with a preprandial glass of cool white wine.

8 ounces sliced bacon
1 pound medium asparagus, trimmed and peeled (page 74)
Salt
4 large eggs
15 ounces ricotta cheese
¾ teaspoon freshly ground black pepper
Pinch of freshly grated nutmeg
3 green onions, trimmed and sliced
1 partially baked Deep Tart Crust (page 152)

Spread the bacon in a cold skillet and set it over medium heat. Cook, turning once or twice, until the bacon is crisp, about 10 minutes. Drain on paper towels and finely chop.

Cut the asparagus into ½-inch pieces. Bring a pot of water to a boil. Stir in 1 tablespoon salt and the asparagus and cook, stirring once or twice, until very tender, 6 to 7 minutes. Drain and transfer immediately to a bowl of ice water. Cool completely, drain, and pat dry.

Position a rack in the middle of the oven and set a baking sheet on the rack. Preheat the oven to 375° F.

In a medium bowl whisk together the eggs, the ricotta, 1 teaspoon salt, the pepper, and the nutmeg. Fold in the bacon, asparagus, and green onions. Pour the filling into the prepared tart shell and spread it evenly.

Set the tart on the preheated baking sheet and bake about 35 minutes, until puffed, golden, and firm. Cool on a rack 5 minutes. Remove the side of the tart pan. Cut the tart into wedges and serve hot or warm.

•

strawberry, pineapple, and mango compote

serves 6

One cup of Raspberry Sauce (page 341) or Blackberry Sauce (page 96) can be substituted for the Mango Sauce. Spoon the compote into tall, elegant goblets and top it with sour cream, crème fraîche, or plain yogurt.

1½ pints fresh strawberries, hulled and quartered
¾ medium pineapple, trimmed and cut into ½-inch chunks (about 3 cups)
Mango Sauce (page 79)
3 tablespoons dark rum
1 cup sour cream; crème fraîche, homemade (page 217) or purchased; or plain yogurt.
Fresh mint sprigs, for garnish

In a bowl toss together the strawberries, pineapple, mango sauce, and rum and let the fruit mixture stand at room temperature at least 30 minutes or up to 1 hour.

Divide the fruit among stemmed goblets. Whisk the sour cream, crème fraîche, or yogurt until smooth. Garnish each serving with a generous dollop, and a sprig of mint if desired. Serve immediately, accompanied by Orange-Cornmeal Butter Cookies.

l e f to v e r s

Although the tart isn't at its best cold, it still makes a tasty nibble. Try it for lunch with a green salad or tuck it into some lucky someone's brown bag. The fruit in the compote will soften, but the mixture will still be delicious spooned over plain yogurt or vanilla ice cream.

kir royale

sautéed salmon with asparagus, new potatoes, and

minted hollandaise sauce

raspberry brown-rice pudding

Salmon is a favorite fish of mine and, thanks to aquaculture, there is more of it around these days. Experts argue the relative merits of wild versus cultivated fish, as well as Atlantic versus Pacific denizens, but no one disputes that salmon makes great eating. Here is a brunch that might also serve as a light supper or lunch, featuring an elegant plateful of salmon and other spring bounty, napped with an herbal green hollandaise.

strategy

The dessert can be baked a day in advance, the asparagus and potatoes can be precooked a few hours ahead, and even the hollandaise can be held for an hour or so in a warmed thermos. Sautéing the salmon and reheating the vegetables are both necessarily last-minute tasks, albeit quick ones. Offer hot and flaky Buttermilk Biscuits (page 297) if you wish, or just slice a crisp baguette. Begin with the classic champagne-and-cassis apéritif known as kir royale; drink an acidic, low-alcohol white wine, such as Sancerre or Sauvignon Blanc, with the salmon.

●

kir royale

<u>makes 4 apéritifs</u>

Buy decent (though not great) champagne. Even though it's embellished with a dollop of cassis (black currant liqueur), the wine's inherent quality will remain apparent.

1 bottle chilled champagne
1½ tablespoons (about) crème de cassis

Divide the champagne among 4 glasses, preferably champagne flutes. Pour about 1 teaspoon crème de cassis into each glass and serve immediately.

●

sautéed salmon with asparagus, new
potatoes, and minted hollandaise sauce

<u>serves 4</u>

In order to keep the cooking times for all four pieces of salmon the same, ask the fishmonger to cut them from the gill or head end of four separate salmon fillets and to be certain they are of the same thickness. If the idea appeals to you, add a poached egg to each plate along with the salmon, asparagus, and potatoes.

8 new red-skinned potatoes (about 1 pound), scrubbed
Salt
12 ounces medium asparagus, trimmed and peeled (page 74)
4 equal pieces salmon fillet (about 1⅓ pounds total)
½ stick (4 tablespoons) unsalted butter
Freshly ground black pepper
Minted Hollandaise Sauce (recipe follows)
Fresh mint sprigs, for garnish

With a swivel-bladed vegetable peeler or a small paring knife, remove a ¼-inch-wide band of peel from around the middle of each potato. In a medium pan cover the potatoes with cold water. Stir in 1 tablespoon salt, set over medium heat, and bring to a boil. Lower the heat slightly and cook until just tender, about 12 minutes. With a slotted spoon remove the potatoes from the water and drain.

Return the water to a boil, add the asparagus, and cook until crisp-tender, 3 to 4 minutes. Drain and transfer immediately to a bowl of ice water. Cool completely and drain well. *The recipe can be prepared to this point several hours in advance. Cover or wrap the potatoes and asparagus and store at room temperature.*

Lightly score the skin side of each piece of salmon. In each of 2 large skillets set over medium heat, melt half the butter. To one skillet add the salmon, skin side up, and cook 3 minutes.

Meanwhile, to the second skillet add the potatoes, cover, and cook, shaking the skillet and rolling them in the butter, for 3 minutes. Turn the salmon, season with salt and pepper to taste, and cook another 2 to 3 minutes, until barely cooked through. Meanwhile, add the asparagus to the skillet with the potatoes and cook, covered, stirring once or twice, until the salmon is done and the vegetables are heated through, 2 to 3 minutes. Remove from the heat.

Arrange the salmon fillets on each of 4 plates. Arrange the potatoes and asparagus around the salmon, dividing both evenly. Spoon the hollandaise over the salmon and asparagus, dividing it evenly and using it all. Garnish each serving with a sprig of mint and serve immediately.

●

minted hollandaise sauce

makes about ⅔ cup

2 large egg yolks
2 teaspoons fresh lemon juice, strained
¼ teaspoon salt
Freshly ground black pepper

1 tablespoon unsalted butter, well chilled
1 stick (4 ounces) unsalted butter, melted
2 tablespoons finely minced fresh mint

In a small, heavy, nonreactive saucepan whisk together the egg yolks, lemon juice, and salt and a generous grinding of pepper.

Set the pan over very low heat and cook, whisking constantly, until the yolks begin to thicken, about 1½ minutes.

Immediately remove the pan from the heat and add the tablespoon of chilled butter. Whisk until the butter is incorporated. Begin to whisk the melted butter, a few drops at a time, into the egg mixture. As the hollandaise thickens, you can begin to add the butter in a slow stream, whisking constantly. Whisk in all the clear melted butter, leaving behind the white residue of milk solids.

Whisk the mint into the hollandaise, taste, and correct the seasoning. Cover and keep warm (but not hot) until serving time.

NOTE *To hold the hollandaise longer than 15 minutes or so, rinse a small thermos with very hot tap water. Dry it well, spoon in the hollandaise, and cover.*

raspberry brown-rice pudding

Brown rice adds crunch and fiber to this simple, old-fashioned dessert. The recipe makes more than you will need for the brunch.

⅓ cup brown rice, rinsed
Pinch of salt
5 egg yolks
½ cup sugar
2¾ cups whipping cream
2 teaspoons Vanilla Rum (page 66) or vanilla extract
1 basket (6 ounces) fresh raspberries, picked over, rinsed only if necessary

Bring a medium saucepan of water to a boil. Stir in the brown rice and salt, lower the heat slightly, and simmer briskly for about 40 minutes, until the rice is just tender. Drain well.

Position a rack in the middle of the oven and preheat the oven to 350° F.

In a mixing bowl whisk the egg yolks. Whisk in the sugar, and then the whipping cream and vanilla rum. Divide the raspberries among eight ½-cup ramekins or custard cups. Divide the rice among the custard cups. Evenly pour the cream mixture over the rice and berries; with a chopstick or a paring knife, gently stir the berries and rice through the cream mixture.

Transfer the ramekins to a baking pan. Add hot tap water to the baking pan to come halfway up the sides of the ramekins. Set the pan in the oven and bake about 50 minutes, until the tops of the puddings are golden brown and the custard, although not firm, is evenly textured from the edges to the center.

Remove the baking pan from the oven and let it stand on a rack until the water is room temperature. Remove the puddings from the water bath, cover, and refrigerate at least 5 hours, until cold and firm.

l e f t  o v e r s

Any remaining rice puddings will keep up to 3 days and make a particularly cool and seductive midnight snack.

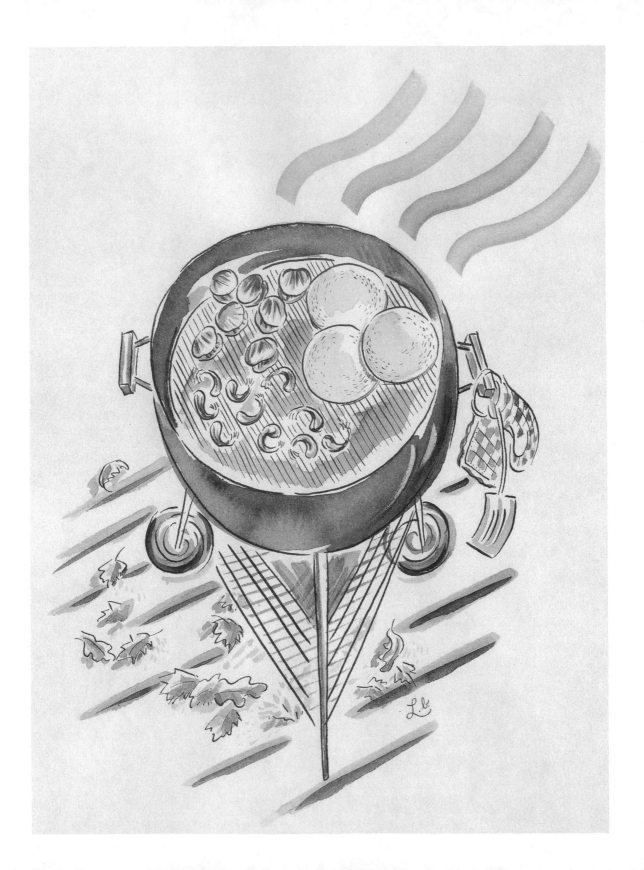

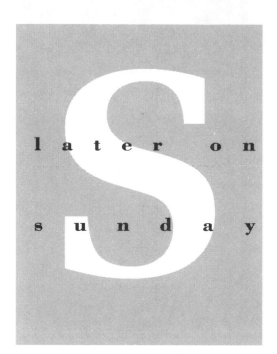

later on

sunday

warm barbecued chicken salad

tarragon mustard slaw (page 55)

succotash in basil vinaigrette

toasted focaccia (page 34)

red, white, and blueberries

orange-cornmeal butter cookies (page 97)

A salad of crisp, warm chicken morsels and greens, napped with a barbecue-sauce–spiked dressing, is the unusual main course in this summery all-salad Sunday supper. Although the menu has more than a few culinary twists, the results have a familiar, old-fashioned Fourth-of-July quality.

s t r a t e g y

Take advantage of the do-ahead steps in the side salads, but please sauté the chicken shortly before serving. This menu will look its best if it is served already plated. To prevent the several dressings from turning the plates swampy, I spoon the succotash into cups formed of radicchio leaves and serve the slaw in cups of Boston lettuce leaves. Use purchased focaccia or any other crusty bread instead of homemade if you wish. Split the focaccia horizontally, brush it with Savory Oil (page 232) or plain olive oil, and run it under the broiler for a few seconds until crisp. I serve the dessert in footed glass ice-cream-sundae dishes, ordered years ago (but still occasionally available) from Williams-Sonoma (see Cook's and Gardener's Sources).

•

warm barbecued chicken salad

serves 6

Use a good, thick barbecue sauce with a touch of molasses, heat, and smoke for the most genuine barbecue flavor.

½ cup unbleached all-purpose flour
1¼ teaspoons salt
¾ teaspoon dried thyme, crumbled
¾ teaspoon dried mustard
¾ teaspoon sweet paprika
¾ teaspoon freshly ground black pepper
2 pounds boneless chicken (light and/or dark meat), cut into 1-inch squares
¾ cup corn oil
8 cups torn mixed salad greens, such as romaine, watercress, and arugula, rinsed and spun dry
Barbecue Vinaigrette (recipe follows)

In a wide, deep plate (like a pie plate) mix together the flour, salt, thyme, mustard, paprika, and pepper. Coat the chicken with the flour and shake off the excess.

In a large skillet warm the corn oil over medium-high heat. Add the chicken and cook 5 minutes. Turn and cook 3 minutes (for light meat) to 5 minutes, until done. Drain on paper towels.

Divide the greens among 6 plates. Top the greens with hot or warm chicken. Drizzle the chicken and greens generously with the vinaigrette and serve immediately.

•

barbecue vinaigrette

makes about 1¼ cups

¼ cup tomato-based barbecue sauce
2 egg yolks, at room temperature
1 tablespoon red wine vinegar
2 teaspoons Dijon-style mustard

½ teaspoon salt
½ teaspoon freshly ground black pepper
¾ cup olive oil

In a medium bowl whisk together the barbecue sauce, egg yolks, vinegar, mustard, salt, and pepper. Gradually whisk in the oil; the dressing will thicken. Adjust the seasoning.

•

succotash in basil vinaigrette

serves 6

The useful idea of seasoning succotash with basil comes from John Thorne's book *Simple Cooking* and is attributed by him to Molly Finn. While Thorne's is a hot side dish, the match-up is equally successful in this cool salad variation.

2 cups frozen baby lima beans, thawed
Salt
2 cups well-drained canned or thawed frozen corn kernels
½ cup finely diced red onion
⅓ cup oil
2½ teaspoons red wine vinegar
¾ teaspoon freshly ground black pepper
3 medium plum tomatoes, seeded and diced
½ cup minced fresh basil
6 cup-shaped radicchio leaves

Bring a saucepan of water to a simmer. Stir in the lima beans and 2 teaspoons salt; simmer until the beans are just tender, about 5 minutes. Drain and cool.

In a large bowl combine the beans, corn, onion, oil, vinegar, 1 teaspoon salt, and the pepper. Cover and refrigerate. *The salad can be prepared up to 4 hours ahead; refrigerate, covered. Return the salad to room temperature before proceeding.*

Stir in the tomatoes and basil and adjust the seasoning. Divide the succotash and dressing among the radicchio cups just before serving.

•

red, white, and blueberries

serves 6

Unsweetened whipped cream or crème fraîche (page 217) can be used in place of the ice cream. Store-bought Scottish shortbreads will go nicely; the Orange-Cornmeal Butter Cookies (page 97) will go even better.

3 baskets (6 ounces each) fresh raspberries, picked over, rinsed only if necessary
½ cup sugar
1½ tablespoons fresh lemon juice, strained
2½ pints (5 cups) fresh blueberries, picked over, rinsed, and drained
Premium vanilla ice cream, softened slightly

In a medium bowl crush the raspberries. Stir in the sugar and lemon juice, cover, and refrigerate at least 1 hour. *The raspberry sauce can be prepared up to 3 days ahead.*

Divide the blueberries among bowls or stemmed goblets. Spoon the raspberry purée over the blueberries, using it all. Top each portion with a small scoop of ice cream and serve immediately.

l e f t o v e r s

Any remaining chicken nuggets can be nibbled on any time. Leftover coleslaw or succotash also will taste fine the next day. Unused raspberry purée is delicious over breakfast yogurt or a midnight bowl of ice cream.

savory oil

makes about 2 cups

This garlicky, herbal, slightly *picante* oil is patterned on one I receive each Christmas from Park Kerr, coproprietor with mom Norma, of the El Paso Chile Company. It's delicious in a salad dressing or as a dip for good bread (like Focaccia on page 32), and it can even be used for making popcorn (sorry, Park, but true). It's a flexible formula: The actual amounts of ingredients, as well as the combination of herbs, are up to you.

2 sprigs fresh rosemary
3 sprigs fresh oregano
3 sprigs fresh marjoram
3 sprigs fresh thyme
2 medium garlic cloves, peeled
2 small dried red chiles, such as *chiles de arbol* or *japones*
1 tablespoon whole white or black peppercorns
2 bay leaves
2 cups (about) extra-virgin olive oil, preferably Tuscan

In a 3-cup jar or bottle with a tight-fitting lid, arrange the rosemary, oregano, marjoram, thyme, garlic cloves, chiles, peppercorns, and bay leaves. Add enough olive oil to completely cover all the ingredients. Cap the jar and let the oil stand, refrigerated, at least 2 weeks before use. As you use the seasoned oil, add additional olive oil to keep the herbs covered or they will eventually mold.

pamela morgan's grill-smoked chicken

corn, barley, and bacon casserole

rainbow tomato salad with caesar dressing

orange-glazed raspberry loaf cake

Developed by Manhattan caterer Pamela Morgan, this menu's method of briefly smoking the almost fully oven-cooked chicken over wood flavoring chips gives the chef maximum control of both roasting and smoking times. The rest of the side dishes are a veritable flavor and color riot of prime summer produce.

strategy

Since the grill is only used for a few minutes, those with gas grills, which heat up quickly, have the advantage over those who use slower-to-get-started charcoal. With either method, the result is moist and flavorful chicken every time. The casserole is assembled a day ahead and will bake while you are smoking and carving the chicken. Since this chicken is particularly delicious cooled just to room temperature, you could do it an hour or so ahead, simplifying preparation even further. The salad dressing can be completed well in advance and the tomatoes take only rinsing and slicing. Because it is so moist, the loaf cake could be prepared a day ahead and stored, well wrapped (be careful of the glaze), at room temperature.

●

pamela morgan's grill-smoked chicken

Pamela says the general method outlined below for a whole bird (stuffed under the skin with garlic, herbs, and goat cheese, baked almost through in the oven, and then smoked briefly over wood chips) is equally successful with butterflied fryers, game hens, or chicken quarters. *Herbes de Provence* is a distinctive dried herb seasoning mixture that typically features fennel seeds, marjoram, thyme, and lavender.

7 large garlic cloves, unpeeled
3 tablespoons olive oil
⅔ cup (about 6 ounces) soft fresh goat cheese, at room temperature
½ cup minced wide-leaf parsley
1 shallot, minced
2 teaspoons minced fresh rosemary
2 teaspoons minced fresh thyme
1 teaspoon *herbes de Provence* (see Cook's and Gardener's Sources), crumbled
Salt
Freshly ground black pepper
1 roasting chicken (about 6 pounds)
1 cup Chicken Stock (page 90) or canned broth
½ cup dry white wine
2 cups aromatic wood smoking chips, preferably hickory (see Cook's and Gardener's Sources)
Fresh rosemary, thyme, or basil sprigs, for garnish

Preheat the oven to 400° F.

In a small ovenproof dish combine 3 garlic cloves and the olive oil. Bake, basting the cloves with the oil, for 15 to 20 minutes, until the garlic is tender and lightly browned. Cool slightly, reserving the oil.

Squeeze the baked garlic from the peels into a small bowl and mash it thoroughly. Stir in the goat cheese, reserved oil, parsley, shallot, 1½ teaspoons each rosemary and thyme, and ½ teaspoon each *herbes de Provence*, salt, and pepper.

Pat the chicken dry. Remove all visible fat from the chicken. Season the cavity lightly with salt and pepper. Loosen the skin over the breast meat, thighs, and as far down the legs as possible by sliding your hand between the skin and the meat. Stuff the cheese mixture under the skin of the breasts, thighs, and legs, using it all. Rub the remaining ½ teaspoon each rosemary, thyme, and *herbes de Provence*, plus a pinch of salt and a grind of pepper, into the skin of the chicken. Set it on a rack in a shallow baking dish just large enough to hold it; add the 4 remaining garlic cloves, the stock, and the wine to the pan.

Roast the chicken for 20 minutes, then begin basting every 10 minutes, until the chicken has baked for a total of 1 hour. The chicken will not quite be fully cooked but will finish cooking as it smokes on the grill.

Meanwhile, soak the hickory chips in water for 30 minutes. Preheat a gas grill (medium-high heat) or light a charcoal fire and let it burn down until the coals are evenly white. Drain the wood chips, scatter them over the grill stones or charcoal, and cover the grill until it is smoking.

Immediately transfer the hot chicken from the roaster to a shallow disposable foil pan just large enough to hold it. Reserve the juices in the baking dish. Set the foil pan on the grill, cover the grill, and smoke the chicken for 10 to 15 minutes, until the skin is browned and smoky and the thigh, when pricked at its thickest point, yields clear yellow juices. Remove from the grill and let stand for at least 30 minutes.

Degrease the pan juices. Force the garlic through a sieve into the pan juices, discarding the peels; adjust the seasoning. Carve the chicken, garnish with fresh herb sprigs if desired, and serve warm or cool, accompanied by the pan juices.

●

corn, barley, and bacon casserole

serves 6

This rich and hearty casserole is Pamela's recommended accompaniment to the handsomely smoked bird.

1 cup barley, rinsed well
Salt
8 ounces smoked slab bacon, trimmed and cut into ¼-inch dice
2 large, meaty sweet red peppers, preferably Dutch, trimmed and cut into ¼-inch dice
1 small fresh jalapeño, stemmed and minced
1 teaspoon dried thyme, crumbled
1 cup Chicken Stock (page 90) or canned broth
1 cup whipping cream
3 cups well-drained canned or thawed frozen corn kernels
4 green onions, trimmed and sliced

Bring a medium saucepan of water to a boil. Add the barley and 1 teaspoon salt, lower the heat slightly, and simmer briskly until the barley is just tender, about 25 minutes. Drain.

In a large skillet set the bacon over medium heat. Cook, stirring occasionally, until the bacon is lightly browned, about 10 minutes. Pour off all but 2 tablespoons of the bacon fat. Stir in the sweet peppers, jalapeño, and thyme; cook, covered, stirring once or twice, until the vegetables are slightly wilted, about 5 minutes. Add the stock and cream, raise the heat, and bring to a boil. Cook, stirring and scraping the bottom of the skillet, for 1 minute. Remove from the heat and cool to room temperature.

In a 10-cup casserole about 4 inches deep, stir together the barley, corn, cream mixture, and green onions and ¾ teaspoon salt. *The casserole can be prepared to this point 1 day ahead. Cool completely, cover, and refrigerate. Return to room temperature before proceeding.*

Preheat the oven to 350° F.

Cover the casserole tightly with foil and bake 15 minutes. Uncover and bake another 25 minutes, until hot, bubbling, and lightly browned.

●

rainbow tomato salad with caesar dressing

serves 6

Mix and match all the tomato shapes and colors your garden or market offers for the most vividly beautiful salad. Serve it on a big, cool pottery platter.

About 3 pounds assorted ripe and colorful garden tomatoes, such as beefsteak, yellow plum,
    sweet green, and red cherry
1¼ cups Caesar Dressing (page 49)
Freshly ground black pepper
Fresh basil sprigs, for garnish

Rinse and trim the tomatoes. Slice the larger tomatoes; cut the small tomatoes in half; leave any tiny tomatoes whole.

Arrange the sliced tomatoes on a large platter; scatter the halved and whole smaller tomatoes over them. Drizzle with some of the dressing, season with fresh black pepper, and garnish with basil sprigs. Serve immediately, passing the remaining dressing at the table.

l e f t  v e r s

Pam says the chicken is "divine" the next day and suggests combining it with a green salad with a red wine vinaigrette for a tasty lunch. Leftover barley casserole can be reheated and enjoyed with some leftover chicken. Because it's moist, the loaf cake keeps well and, if it survives that long, makes a delicious breakfast nibble.

●

orange-glazed raspberry loaf cake

makes one 9- by 5-inch cake

This moist, tangy, berry-studded cake is perfect for eating out of hand (for those impatient to get back to serious recreation), but it's pretty enough to serve on plates, accompanied by a little whipped cream or sherbet and a few perfect berries. The cake is also good made with blueberries.

CAKE

2½ cups bleached all-purpose flour
2 teaspoons baking powder
½ teaspoon salt
¾ stick (6 tablespoons) unsalted butter, softened
1 cup sugar
2 eggs, beaten
1 tablespoon grated orange zest
1 cup buttermilk
1½ cups fresh raspberries, picked over, rinsed only if necessary

GLAZE

⅓ cup sugar
2 tablespoons fresh orange juice, strained
1 tablespoon grated orange zest

For the cake Position a rack in the middle of the oven and preheat the oven to 325° F. Butter a 9- by 5- by 3-inch metal loaf pan. Line the bottom of the pan with waxed paper and butter the waxed paper.

In a small bowl thoroughly mix the flour, baking powder, and salt. In a large bowl cream the butter and sugar until light and fluffy. Whisk in the eggs and orange zest. By halves, alternately add the flour mixture and the buttermilk to the creamed mixture. Gently fold in the berries. Pour the batter into the prepared pan. Bake about 1 hour, until a tester inserted in the center of the cake comes out clean. Cool the cake in the pan on a rack for 15 minutes.

Preheat the broiler.

For the glaze In a small bowl whisk together the sugar, orange juice, and orange zest.

Remove the cake from the pan, peel off the waxed paper, and set the cake upright on a boilerproof baking pan. Slowly spoon the glaze over the loaf, allowing the cake to absorb as much of the glaze as possible. Set the cake under the broiler and broil until the glaze is bubbly and lightly colored, 3 to 4 minutes. Remove from the oven and cool completely on a rack before cutting.

blackberry-basil vinegar

makes about 1 quart

When basil and blackberries are at their most abundant and affordable, put up several bottles of this beautiful and delicious vinegar. It can be used to dress green salads or blanched vegetables, to glaze beets or carrots, to marinate chicken before broiling or grilling, or as the acid in a delicious pink mayonnaise.

4 cups white wine vinegar, preferably imported champagne vinegar (see Cook's and Gardener's Sources)
¼ cup sugar
1 cup fresh blackberries, plus additional berries for garnish, picked over, rinsed only if necessary
6 sprigs fresh basil, plus 2 sprigs for garnish

In a nonreactive saucepan over medium heat, combine the vinegar and sugar and bring just to a boil, stirring to dissolve the sugar.

In a 5-cup lidded bottle or jar (a decorative one if you wish), arrange the berries and basil sprigs. Pour the hot vinegar into the jar, cool to room temperature, and cover. Let stand 2 weeks before using.

If desired for a more attractive presentation, strain the vinegar, discarding the softened berries and basil and replacing them with fresh berries and basil. For long-term storage, keep the vinegar in a cool, dark place. Use it up within 1 year.

a mixed grill of shellfish:

clams with cilantro vinaigrette,

lobsters with lime mayonnaise, and

shrimp in honey-orange adobo

black bean, corn, tomato, and poblano chile salad

grill-warmed tortillas with garlic butter

red fruit sorbet

mexican chocolate shortbreads

A grand grill of assorted shellfish is automatically festive, inspiring the same good-natured seafood gluttony as a clambake on the beach, but without the discomfort of sand in your shorts. For extra excitement this menu includes a touch of the Southwest, adding the fire of chiles to the smoky heat of the grill.

s t r a t e g y

Serve the clams first, as an appetizer, shells set in a platter of salt to maintain them upright and hold the cilantro vinaigrette or (for traditionalists) a squirt of lemon juice. Employ an assistant to ferry the platters of lobsters and shrimp from grill to table as they become ready. Finally, over the dying coals, heat (and slightly scorch) a generous stack of soft flour tortillas—delicious when slathered with garlic butter, perfect for eating as is, or for enfolding shrimp, chunks of lobster, and dollops of lime mayonnaise—splendid impromptu tacos. And please remember that when seafood is grilled, it tastes as good warm as it does hot—so relax and enjoy the heat, the smoke, and the inevitable huzzahs.

•

a mixed grill of shellfish

s e r v e s   8

The hot, delicately flavored smoke of mesquite wood is ideal for opening clams, for giving an edge of sharp flavor to sweet lobster meat, and for adding a crisp crust to succulent chile-marinated shrimp.

24 large shrimp (about 1½ pounds), shelled and deveined

Honey-Orange Adobo (recipe follows)

3 cups aromatic wood smoking chips, preferably mesquite (see Cook's and Gardener's Sources)

1 pound (about) coarse (kosher) salt

24 large hard-shell clams, well scrubbed

Cilantro Vinaigrette (recipe follows)

3 lemons, quartered

4 lobsters (about 2 pounds each), split (see Note)

Lemony Mayonnaise (page 292), prepared with lime juice and zest instead of lemon juice and zest

In a medium nonreactive bowl combine the shrimp and adobo and marinate at room temperature, covered, stirring once or twice, for 2 hours. Soak the wood chips in water for 30 minutes.

Prepare a charcoal fire and allow it to burn until the coals are evenly white, or preheat a gas grill (medium-high). Pour the coarse salt in an even layer about 1 inch deep on 1 or 2 large platters. Drain the chips and scatter one-third of them over the coals or grill stones. When the chips are smoking, position a rack about 6 inches above the heat. Lay the clams directly on the grill, cover, and cook, turning the clams once or twice, until they open, 4 to 9 minutes. (The opening time of the clams in any particular batch varies widely; be patient.) With tongs, transfer the clams as they open to the platter with the salt, pressing the bottom shells lightly into the salt so that the clams are level. Spoon a dollop of cilantro vinaigrette into some clams, while leaving others unsauced. Serve immediately, accompanied by lemon wedges and the peppermill.

Scatter half the remaining wood chips over the coals or grill stones. Lay the lobsters, cut side up, on the grill. Cover and cook 7 minutes. Turn the lobsters, cover, and cook another 5 to 7 minutes, until just done. Transfer to a large platter; serve hot, warm, or cool, accompanied by lime mayonnaise.

Divide the shrimp among 8 short metal skewers. Scatter the remaining wood chips over the coals or grill stones. Lay the skewers on the grill, cover, and cook the shrimp

3 minutes. Turn and cook another 2 to 3 minutes, until just done. Serve the shrimp on the skewers, giving one to each diner.

NOTE *Just before grilling, kill the lobsters by inserting the point of a long knife into the top of the lobster where the head and body shell meet. Turn them over and, using the knife, split the lobsters lengthwise. Discard the sac from the head. With the heavy butt of the knife blade, crack the claws.*

●

honey-orange adobo

makes enough for 24 large shrimp

⅓ cup mild powdered chiles (see Cook's and Gardener's Sources)
¼ cup fresh orange juice, strained
2 tablespoons olive oil
2 garlic cloves, peeled and crushed through a garlic press
1 tablespoon finely minced orange zest
1 tablespoon fresh lime juice, strained
2 teaspoons ground cumin, preferably from toasted seeds (page 63)
1½ teaspoons honey
1½ teaspoons tomato paste
1 teaspoon dried oregano, crumbled
¾ teaspoon salt

In a small bowl stir together all the ingredients. *The adobo can be prepared 24 hours before use. Refrigerate, covered.*

NOTE *The adobo can also be used to season 3 pounds of spareribs. Slash the meat to the bone in a crosshatch pattern, rub the adobo into the ribs, and marinate in the refrigerator for 24 hours. Bake in a shallow baking dish in a 350° F oven until tender, about 1¼ hours, covering the ribs loosely with foil during the last half hour of baking.*

●

cilantro vinaigrette

1 tablespoon fresh lemon juice, strained
1 tablespoon red wine vinegar
1 tablespoon Dijon-style mustard
¼ teaspoon salt
½ teaspoon freshly ground black pepper
¼ cup corn oil
½ cup olive oil
⅓ cup finely minced cilantro

In a medium bowl whisk together the lemon juice, vinegar, mustard, salt, and pepper. Gradually whisk in the corn and olive oils. The vinaigrette will thicken. *The vinaigrette can be prepared 1 hour ahead.* Just before serving, rewhisk if necessary and stir in the cilantro.

●

black bean, corn, tomato, and poblano chile salad

If poblano chiles are unavailable, substitute red or green bell peppers. If you like cilantro as much as I do, you'll recognize this salad as the perfect vehicle for the pungent herb. Add lots, to taste.

1½ cups dried black beans, picked over and soaked in water to cover for 24 hours
Salt
4 poblano chiles (see Cook's and Gardener's Sources)
¼ cup sherry vinegar
1 tablespoon Dijon-style mustard
2 teaspoons ground cumin, from toasted seeds (page 63)
1½ teaspoons freshly ground black pepper
½ cup olive oil
2 cups well-drained canned or thawed frozen corn kernels
5 ripe red plum tomatoes, trimmed and cut into chunks
4 green onions, trimmed and sliced
2 buttery-ripe black-skinned avocados, pitted, unpeeled, and cut into thin wedges, for garnish

Drain the beans and transfer them to a large saucepan. Cover with fresh cold water, set over medium heat, and bring to a boil, skimming any scum that forms on the surface. Lower the heat and simmer, uncovered, for 30 minutes. Stir in 2 teaspoons salt and continue to cook until the beans are just tender, another 30 to 45 minutes; drain.

Meanwhile, over the open flame of a gas burner or under a preheated broiler, roast the chiles, turning them as needed, until the skins are lightly charred. Transfer the chiles to a paper bag or a plate covered with a large bowl and let stand until cool. Rub away the charred skins, then stem, core, and seed the chiles. Cut the flesh into ¾-inch squares.

In a small bowl whisk together the vinegar, mustard, cumin, and black pepper and 2 teaspoons salt. Gradually whisk in the oil; the dressing will thicken.

In a large bowl combine the beans, chiles, and corn. Pour the dressing over the salad and toss well. *The salad can be prepared to this point 1 day ahead. Cover and refrigerate. Allow the salad to return to room temperature before proceeding.*

Add the tomatoes and green onions to the salad and toss well. Adjust the seasoning. Serve at room temperature, garnished with slices of avocado if you wish.

●

grill-warmed tortillas with garlic butter

serves 8

Oddly enough, this simple garlic butter will have people asking for the "recipe." Make plenty—my tasters loved it slathered onto warmed tortillas rolled around the grilled shrimp and/or chunks of lobster pulled from the shell.

GARLIC BUTTER
2 sticks (8 ounces) unsalted butter, softened
2 garlic cloves, peeled
Pinch of salt
Freshly ground black pepper
18 large flour tortillas, at room temperature

For the garlic butter Cream the butter in a bowl. Remove any green shoots from the garlic and crush it through a garlic press into the butter. Add the salt and a generous grind of pepper and mix well. *The butter can be prepared ahead and refrigerated up to 1 day or frozen, well wrapped, up to 3 months. Let warm to room temperature before using.*

In batches, heat the tortillas on the grill, turning them once, until they are soft, puffed, and slightly charred, 2 to 3 minutes. Transfer to a napkin-lined basket and serve immediately, accompanied by the garlic butter.

●

red fruit sorbet

Icy cold and ruby red, this mixed fruit sorbet is a delicious relief after the zestily seasoned seafood. For this rustic outdoor menu, I leave the raspberry seeds in, but you may force the puréed berries through a strainer before cooking if you wish.

2 baskets (6 ounces each) fresh raspberries, picked over, rinsed only if necessary
1½ pounds red plums, such as Santa Rosa, pitted and cut into 1-inch chunks
12 ounces sweet black cherries, such as Bing, stemmed and pitted
1¼ cups sugar
¼ cup crème de cassis (black currant liqueur)
3 tablespoons fresh lemon juice, strained

In a food processor purée the raspberries. In a heavy, nonreactive saucepan over low heat, combine the puréed berries, plums, cherries, sugar, crème de cassis, and lemon juice. Bring slowly to a simmer, stirring carefully to dissolve all the sugar. Partially cover the pan and cook, stirring once or twice, for 30 minutes, until the plums and cherries are very tender.

Cool the mixture slightly, then force it through the medium blade of a food mill. Cover and refrigerate until very cold, at least 5 hours but preferably overnight.

Transfer the fruit mixture to the canister of an ice cream maker and churn according to the manufacturer's instructions. Cover and store in the freezer, softening the sorbet in the refrigerator if necessary before serving. *The sorbet can be prepared up to 2 days ahead.*

●

mexican chocolate shortbreads

makes about 24 cookies

Touches of cinnamon and black pepper add subtle spice to these crisp chocolate cookies.

2 cups unbleached all-purpose flour
⅔ cup lightly packed unsweetened cocoa powder
½ teaspoon cinnamon
½ teaspoon finely ground fresh black pepper
½ teaspoon salt
2 sticks (8 ounces) unsalted butter, softened
½ cup plus 2 tablespoons sugar, plus additional for coating the cookies
2 teaspoons Vanilla Rum (page 66) or vanilla extract

Sift the flour, cocoa, cinnamon, pepper, and salt together twice onto a piece of waxed paper. In a medium bowl cream together the butter and sugar until light and fluffy. Mix in the vanilla rum, then stir in the flour mixture. Stir and knead the dough (it will be dry and crumbly at first) until it is moist, dark, and supple. Between 2 sheets of waxed paper, roll the dough ¼ inch thick as evenly as possible. Chill for 30 minutes.

Position a rack in the middle of the oven and preheat the oven to 275° F. Lightly butter 2 baking sheets.

Cut out the cookies with a 2-inch round cutter. Pierce each cookie twice with the tines of a fork. Spread the coating sugar on a plate. Lightly press the top of each cookie in the sugar, so that the sugar clings to the dough. Arrange the cookies, sugar side up, on the prepared sheets, spacing them well apart.

Bake the cookies 40 to 45 minutes, until crisp and firm, exchanging the position of the sheets on the racks from top to bottom and from front to back at the halfway point. Cool the cookies on the sheets on a rack for 5 minutes. Transfer to paper towels and cool completely. Store the cookies in an airtight container at room temperature. *The cookies can be baked up to 1 week ahead.*

leftovers

Any remaining grilled shellfish can be refrigerated and served the next day. Combine it with mixed greens and a simple vinaigrette to make a grilled seafood salad. Leftover lime mayonnaise is delicious in tuna or chicken salad or on a sandwich. Any leftover garlic butter can be spread generously onto sliced baguettes or split focaccia and run under the broiler for a minute or two for a delicious garlic bread. The sorbet will be good for up to 3 days in the freezer; the cookies keep well, stored airtight and at room temperature.

end-of-summer chutney

When canning season is in full bloom and cases of Ball jars show up at your hardware store, it's difficult not to succumb to the lure of "putting by" some of the summer's abundant harvest. In the preserve category, chutneys are among the easier projects to undertake, and this one among the tastier. When prime tomatoes and abundant red or purple plums (but not the so-called prune plums) are at their affordable best, dedicate part of one weekend to simmering up this ruby condiment. While eight jars hardly constitute a pantry, you'll feel justifiably proud when you line them up on a counter or shelf. Let the chutney mature for 1 month, then serve it with ham, smoked turkey, grilled sausages, or roast pork or beef. Or spoon it over a mound of *fromage blanc* (page 80) or a block of cream cheese and spread it on crisp crackers.

Salt
6 pounds ripe tomatoes
5 cups cider vinegar
4 cups (about) sugar
6 pounds slightly underripe late-summer red or purple plums, such as Casselman, Rosa, and/or Angeleno, pitted and cut into eighths
3 pounds yellow onions, peeled and coarsely chopped
4 ounces (about 1 cup) yellow mustard seeds
4 ounces (about ½ cup) finely chopped crystallized ginger (see Cook's and Gardener's Sources)
2 cups golden raisins

Bring a large pot of water to a simmer. Stir in 1 tablespoon salt. Working in batches, add the tomatoes and turn them in the simmering water for 1 minute. With a slotted spoon, transfer the tomatoes to a large bowl of cold water. When they are cool, peel the tomatoes and halve them. Squeeze out and discard the seeds and liquid; coarsely chop the tomato flesh.

In a 9-quart, nonreactive, heavy-bottomed pot, combine the vinegar and 3 cups of the sugar. Over medium heat bring the mixture slowly to a boil, stirring constantly to be certain the sugar is dissolved.

Add the tomatoes, plums, onions, and mustard seeds; return to a boil, stirring often. Lower the heat, skim any scum that forms, and simmer, uncovered, for 1 hour. Stir often and thoroughly.

Add the ginger and raisins and simmer, stirring often, until the chutney begins to darken and is thick and shiny, about 45 minutes. Taste and add more sugar, if necessary, stirring thoroughly to be certain it is dissolved.

Pack the hot chutney into hot sterilized pint jars and seal according to the manufacturer's instructions for processing chutneys. Process 15 minutes in a hot water bath, again following the manufacturer's instructions. Allow the chutney to mellow 1 month before using.

NOTE *The chutney can also be cooled and then refrigerated in a clean, tightly covered container without processing. It will keep several months.*

crab-and-prosciutto-stuffed mushrooms

veal shanks braised in red wine

with garlic and orange

polenta with the last of the basil

mixed green salad

peach and blush tomato tart

Veal shanks, or *osso buco*, are tough cuts of working muscle that take a long, slow time to simmer into succulent tenderness, a process that illustrates the best of weekend cooking. As the nights grow cooler, the oven's warmth is welcome, and the rich meat, tender and falling off the bone, is the right food to eat at the time.

s t r a t e g y

This meal is a well-balanced mix of dishes that are done in advance, that cook virtually unattended, and that take a bit of last-minute fussing. It's a kitchen ballet all right, but with the varying tempos the cook is never under pressure. Prepare the fruit tart several hours before serving, let the veal shanks stew away in the oven, and concentrate your kitchen pyrotechnics on the quick-cooking crab-stuffed mushroom appetizer. Prepare 8 cups of Basic Mixed Green Salad (page 23), using red wine vinegar and olive oil for the vinaigrette. A cool, uncomplicated Italian white wine, like a Soave, will complement the mushrooms; with the rich veal serve a rich, oaky Chardonnay, one fairly low in alcohol but with a touch of fruit (especially citrus) and herb.

crab-and-prosciutto-stuffed mushrooms

serves 4

If you can locate brown, also called cremini, mushrooms, the earthier, sturdier cousins of the common cultivated white mushroom, this dish will be the better for it. Either way, it's a light but savory opener for the braised-veal main course.

16 large perfect mushrooms, preferably cremini
5 tablespoons olive oil
2 medium garlic cloves, peeled and minced
½ cup dry white wine
2 ounces sliced prosciutto, minced
1 tablespoon fresh thyme, minced
8 ounces fresh lump crabmeat, picked over
Freshly ground black pepper
⅓ cup coarse homemade bread crumbs (see Note)
Fresh lemon wedges, for serving

Wipe the mushrooms with a damp paper towel and trim the ends of the stems. Remove the stems and carve out the resulting cavities if they seem small. Mince the stems. In a small skillet warm 2 tablespoons of the olive oil over medium heat. Add the minced mushroom stems and the garlic; cook, stirring once or twice, for 5 minutes. Add the white wine, raise the heat, and bring to a boil. Cook, stirring once or twice, until the wine has almost evaporated, about 4 minutes. Remove the skillet from the heat, stir in the prosciutto and thyme, and cool to room temperature.

Position a rack in the upper third of the oven and preheat the oven to 450° F. In a medium bowl stir together the crabmeat and the prosciutto mixture. Season generously with fresh black pepper and stir again.

Drizzle 2 tablespoons of the remaining olive oil over the bottom of a shallow baking dish, such as a 9- by 13-inch oval gratin. Stuff the mushrooms with the crabmeat mixture, mounding it and using it all. Set the mushrooms in the baking dish and sprinkle with the bread crumbs. Drizzle the tops of the mushrooms with the remaining 1 tablespoon oil. Set the dish in the oven and bake the mushrooms about 10 minutes, until the tops are browned and the juices in the pan are sizzling.

Let the mushrooms stand in the pan on a rack for 5 minutes before transferring to small plates. Spoon any juices in the pan over the mushrooms, garnish each serving with a lemon wedge, and serve immediately.

NOTE   *To make bread crumbs, leave good-quality white bread unwrapped at room temperature for 24 hours. Trim, cutting away any dry, hard crusts. Cut the bread into 1-inch squares. In a food processor grind the bread to coarse or fine crumbs, as desired. Store, airtight, in the freezer and measure out crumbs as needed.*

●

veal shanks braised in red wine with
garlic and orange

serves 4

Forty cloves is just the right amount of garlic when cooked, as they are here, to a sweet, mellow richness.

2 cups unbleached all-purpose flour
Salt
Freshly ground black pepper
4 large, meaty center-cut sections of veal shank (about 4 pounds total)
¼ cup olive oil
2 cups finely chopped yellow onions
3 leeks (white part only), well cleaned and chopped
1 cup finely chopped carrots
Stems from 1 small bunch wide-leaf parsley
1 teaspoon dried thyme, crumbled
1 teaspoon dried oregano, crumbled
1 bay leaf
2 cups Chicken Stock (page 90) or canned broth
1 cup dry red wine
40 large garlic cloves, peeled
⅓ cup finely minced wide-leaf parsley
¼ cup finely minced fresh orange zest (from 2 large oranges)
½ stick (4 tablespoons) unsalted butter, cut into pieces

In a wide dish (like a pie plate) combine the flour, 1 teaspoon salt, and ½ teaspoon pepper. Pat the veal dry. Coat the shanks with the flour and shake off the excess.

In a 4½- to 5-quart, heavy, nonreactive pot warm the oil over high heat. Working in batches, cook the veal shanks, turning them often, until well browned on all sides, about 15 minutes. Set aside. Do not clean the pan.

Set the pan over medium heat and stir in the onions, leeks, carrots, parsley stems, thyme, oregano, and bay leaf. Cover and cook, stirring occasionally, until tender, about 15 minutes. Stir in the stock and wine, bring to a boil, and lower the heat. Partially cover and simmer, stirring occasionally and scraping the bottom of the pan with a spoon, for 40 minutes. Pour the liquid through a strainer set over a bowl. Press hard on the solids to extract as much liquid as possible. Discard the solids.

Position a rack in the middle of the oven and preheat the oven to 350° F.

Return the veal to the pot, add the garlic, and cover with the stock. Set the pan over medium heat and bring to a simmer. Cover and bake, turning the meat occasionally, until the veal is very tender, 1½ to 2 hours. In a small bowl combine the minced parsley and orange zest.

Transfer the veal shanks to a plate and keep warm. Press the braising liquid and garlic through a sieve set over a bowl; there should be about 1½ cups. In a saucepan over low heat, bring the braising liquid to a simmer; adjust the seasoning. Whisk in the butter 1 tablespoon at a time; the sauce will thicken and become glossy.

Set the veal shanks on plates beside the polenta (recipe follows). Spoon the sauce over the shanks, dividing it evenly. Sprinkle each shank with the parsley-orange mixture and serve immediately.

●

polenta with the last of the basil

serves 4

Nowadays, in many markets there is no "last" of the basil; the fragrant green stuff is as readily available on Christmas Eve as it is on the Fourth of July. Still, when frost is imminent, we can at least imagine that we are facing six months without this fundamental herb, and so can celebrate its theoretical farewell here, sprinkled abundantly over a mound of steaming polenta.

Polenta (recipe follows), hot
½ cup finely minced fresh basil
⅓ pound Parmesan cheese in one piece, at room temperature
Freshly ground black pepper

Spoon a generous dollop of polenta onto each of 4 plates. Sprinkle generously with basil and, with a swivel-bladed vegetable peeler, shave several large curls of Parmesan over each portion. Season generously with black pepper and serve immediately.

●

polenta

serves 6 to 8

6 cups water
1½ cups yellow cornmeal, preferably stone-ground

2½ teaspoons salt
1 bay leaf

In a heavy 4½- to 5-quart pot, gradually whisk the water into the cornmeal. Whisk in the salt; stir in the bay leaf. Set the pan over medium heat and bring to a boil, stirring once or twice. Lower the heat, partially cover, and simmer, stirring often, until the cornmeal is very thick, about 40 minutes. Remove from the heat; discard the bay leaf.

leftovers

If there is any remaining veal, remove the meat from the bone and mix it with any leftover sauce. Reheat, add cooked pasta, such as penne, and simmer just until heated through. Serve with grated Parmesan and a green salad. There will be leftover polenta. Pour it while hot onto a plate and spread it about ½ inch thick. Chill it, cut it into rounds, squares, or diamonds, and sauté or grill it until lightly browned. Serve with meats, poultry, or eggs. Any leftover tart will be good the next day, especially if drizzled with a bit of heavy cream.

●

peach and blush tomato tart

serves 8

A slight ripening of the tomatoes (to the point at which they blush partially pink) and the addition of juicy, fresh peaches tame the astringency found in the more typical green tomato pie, resulting in a delicious flavor marriage that will leave most diners confused—although delighted—as to the source. This tart is beautiful, too, topped with a crackly sugar crust and served, if you wish, with ice cream or sour cream and a "flower" composed of fresh raspberries and a sprig of mint.

DEEP TART CRUST

2¼ cups unbleached all-purpose flour
¼ teaspoon salt
1 stick (4 ounces) unsalted butter, well chilled and cut into small pieces
¼ cup solid vegetable shortening, well chilled and cut into small pieces
5 to 6 tablespoons ice water

FILLING

3 ripe large peaches (about 1½ pounds), pitted and sliced ¼ inch thick
2 large tomatoes (about 1 pound), barely beginning to ripen, trimmed and sliced ¼ inch thick
¾ cup packed light brown sugar
⅓ cup unbleached all-purpose flour
2 tablespoons amaretto liqueur

kitchen-counter carrot cake with
cream cheese icing

makes 1 two-layer cake, serving 10 to 12

This recipe, in an earlier version, was handed to me surreptitiously and was said to be the Commissary's carrot cake. When that popular Philadelphia restaurant finally published the official recipe for its legendary carrot cake, it resembled not at all the one I had baked and boasted about for years. So much for insider trading. Here's what I now think of as *my* Carrot Cake, and it's said to be delicious.

1½ cups unbleached all-purpose flour
½ cup whole-wheat flour
1 teaspoon ground cinnamon
1 teaspoon baking soda
1 teaspoon salt
1 cup granulated sugar
½ cup packed light brown sugar
1¼ cups corn oil
4 large eggs
1 pound carrots, peeled and coarsely shredded
1 cup (about 4 ounces) walnuts, coarsely chopped
1 cup (about 5 ounces) dried tart cherries (see Cook's and Gardener's Sources)
Cream Cheese Icing (recipe follows)
3 tablespoons confectioners' sugar

Butter and flour two 9-inch round cake pans; tap out the excess flour. Position a rack in the middle of the oven and preheat the oven to 350° F.

In a medium bowl stir together the all-purpose flour, whole-wheat flour, cinnamon, soda, and salt.

In a large bowl combine the sugars. Whisk in the corn oil. Whisk in the eggs, one at a time. Stir in the carrots, walnuts, and dried cherries. Add the dry ingredients and stir until just combined; do not overmix.

STREUSEL TOPPING

7 tablespoons granulated sugar
¼ cup unbleached all-purpose flour
½ stick (4 tablespoons) unsalted butter, well chilled and cut into small pieces

Vanilla ice cream or sour cream, for serving
Fresh raspberries and fresh mint sprigs, for garnish

For the crust In a bowl or in a food processor combine 2 cups of the flour and the salt. Cut in the butter and shortening until mixture resembles coarse meal. Add the ice water, 1 tablespoon at a time, until a soft dough forms. Turn the dough out onto a work surface lightly dusted with 2 tablespoons flour. Gather the dough into a ball, flatten it into a disk, and wrap it well in plastic wrap. Refrigerate at least 1 hour. *The dough can be prepared up to 3 days ahead.*

Lightly dust a work surface with the remaining 2 tablespoons flour and roll the dough out into a round about ⅛ inch thick. Transfer the dough to a 10-inch fluted tart pan, 1¼ inches deep, with a removable bottom. Trim and finish the edge. Refrigerate the shell for at least 30 minutes. *The formed shell can be refrigerated, well wrapped, for up to 1 day.* (See Note for partially baking this tart shell.)

For the filling In a medium bowl combine the peaches, tomatoes, brown sugar, flour, and amaretto; let stand at room temperature for 30 minutes.

For the topping In a small bowl stir together the sugar and flour. Thoroughly cut in the butter until pieces the size of peas are formed. Refrigerate, covered, for 30 minutes.

Position a rack in the upper third of the oven and set a baking sheet on it. Preheat the oven to 450° F.

Spoon the filling into the chilled (unbaked) shell. Sprinkle the topping evenly over the filling, using it all. Set the tart on the baking sheet and bake 10 minutes. Lower the temperature to 350° F and bake another 30 to 40 minutes, until the topping is crisp, the crust is golden, and the filling is thick and bubbling. Cool completely on a rack before cutting.

Top each slice of tart with a scoop of ice cream or a dollop of sour cream. Arrange 2 or 3 raspberries and a sprig of mint to resemble a flower on each portion if desired, and serve immediately.

NOTE *For a partially baked Deep Tart Crust (required in some recipes), position a rack in the middle of the oven and set a heavy cookie sheet on the rack. Preheat the oven to 400° F.*

Line the tart shell with waxed paper or foil, fill the shell with dried beans or pie weights, and set it on the preheated baking sheet. Bake 10 minutes. Remove the beans and waxed paper. Pierce the shell lightly all over with a fork. Return it to the oven and bake another 10 to 12 minutes, until golden and crisp. Transfer to a rack and cool completely.

Divide the batter between the prepared pans and spread it evenly. Bake about 25 minutes, until a tester inserted into a cake layer comes out clean. Cook the cake layers in the pans on a rack for 10 minutes. Turn the layers out onto the rack and cool them completely.

Invert 1 layer onto a cake plate. Spread the top of the layer with about one-third of the icing. Invert the second layer atop the first. Spread the sides of the cake with the remaining icing. *The cake can be prepared up to 1 day ahead. Cover it and store at room temperature.*

Just before serving, transfer the confectioners' sugar to a small strainer and dust it lightly over the unfrosted top of the cake.

●

cream cheese icing

makes enough for a large layer cake

1 pound cream cheese, softened
3 tablespoons unsalted butter, softened
2 cups confectioners' sugar
2 tablespoons fresh lemon juice, strained
1 tablespoon finely minced lemon zest

In a large bowl cream together the cream cheese and butter. Slowly beat in the confectioners' sugar. Stir in the lemon juice and zest. *The icing can be prepared 1 day ahead and stored, covered, in the refrigerator. Let it come to room temperature before using.*

paper bags of cracker jacks and peanuts in the shell

ball-park hot dogs on

pepper-onion frankfurter rolls with

stadium chili, garlicky peppers and mushrooms,

and beer-braised sauerkraut with caraway seeds

tarragon mustard slaw (page 55)

new potato salad with bacon and mustard seeds

(page 106)

chocolate-dipped chocolate malted ice cream cones

The theme is baseball and the inspiration is that period in October when interest in the national pastime reaches its annual peak, but the menu is suitable for any number of other laid-back, autumn weekend occasions, especially the kind at which kids and hot dogs seem to belong.

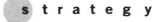 **s t r a t e g y**

Although there are many components here (homemade buns, three hot-dog toppings, two side dishes, and a dessert of some complexity), there are multiple do-ahead steps in every recipe, and if you take advantage of all of them, you'll find yourself with remarkably little last-minute fussing. Prepare a double batch of the slaw (omit the beets) and of the potato salad. Ice a washtub full of beers and sodas.

ball-park hot dogs

makes 24

Prepared with care, imagination, and quality ingredients, and served with classic condiments—catsup, mustards, relish—or with my more adventurous toppings below, even the prosaic wienie-on-a-bun that is the nutritional mainstay of American sports cuisine can make memorable eating.

24 good-quality frankfurters
Pepper-Onion Frankfurter Rolls (recipe follows), partially split
Catsup, mustards, and pickle relish, for serving
Optional toppings (recipes follow)

Preheat the broiler or a gas barbecue. Slash the frankfurters to prevent curling. Broil or grill on medium-high heat, turning occasionally, until browned and crisp, about 5 minutes. Transfer to a platter.

Place the rolls cut side up under the broiler or cut side down on the grill and cook until lightly browned and crisp, about 2 minutes. Transfer to plates. Place 1 frankfurter in each roll. Pass the condiments and toppings.

pepper-onion frankfurter rolls

makes 24

One of these deliciously peppery onion-topped rolls is the perfect utility player in a premium chili-, kraut-, or pepper-topped dog. They're a lot of fun to make—and they freeze beautifully—but if time gets short (or if your nostalgia for the authentic stadium frankfurter is overwhelming), don't hesitate to substitute store-bought buns.

1 stick (4 ounces) unsalted butter
2½ cups finely diced yellow onions
2½ cups milk
4 teaspoons sugar
4 teaspoons salt
1 package dry yeast
1 tablespoon freshly ground black pepper
5 cups (about) unbleached all-purpose flour

In a medium skillet over moderate heat, melt the butter. Add the onions and cook, stirring once or twice, until tender and golden, about 10 minutes. Transfer the onions and butter to a strainer set over a large mixing bowl. Press to extract most of the butter; transfer the onions to a small bowl and reserve.

In a small saucepan combine the milk, sugar, and salt. Set over medium heat and bring to a simmer, stirring to dissolve the sugar and salt. Pour the hot milk into the large bowl with the butter and let stand until cooled to lukewarm (110° F), about 5 minutes. Sprinkle the yeast over the milk; stir to dissolve. Let stand until foamy, about 5 minutes.

Stir in the pepper. Stir in enough flour (about 4 cups) to produce a soft, slightly sticky dough. Turn the dough onto a heavily floured surface and knead until smooth, about 5 minutes. The dough should remain soft and heavy. Turn the dough in a large greased bowl until well coated, cover with a kitchen towel, and let rise in a warm place until doubled in bulk, about 1½ hours.

Punch the dough down and divide it in half. On a lightly floured surface briefly knead each piece, then form each one into a ball. Grease 2 medium bowls and transfer each ball to a bowl, turning to coat them well. Cover and refrigerate 3 hours.

Grease one or two 12- by 17-inch jelly-roll pans. Flouring the work surface only if necessary, roll one ball of dough out to a rough rectangle about ¼ inch thick. Using a pizza cutter or a long sharp knife, cut the dough into twelve 5- by 2½-inch rectangles. Fold each rectangle of dough in half lengthwise and press the seam to seal. Trim the corners of each to round them slightly and transfer the rolls to the prepared jelly-roll pans, placing them about ½ inch apart and about ½ inch from the sides of the pan. Repeat with the second ball of dough. (Since the rolls will have the best shape if they are baked close together, try to fit them all in one pan.)

Cover the rolls with a towel and let them rise in a warm place for 1 hour, until they are light and puffy and touching slightly.

Position racks in the upper and lower thirds of the oven and preheat the oven to 400° F.

Scatter the reserved onions over the risen rolls. Bake on the upper rack about 20 minutes, until the rolls are crisp and golden and the onions lightly browned. If you have used 2 pans, exchange the position of the pans on the racks from top to bottom and from front to back at the halfway point. Cool in the pan on a rack for 5 minutes, then remove from the pan and cool completely on the rack. *The rolls can be baked up to 3 days ahead and refrigerated, or up to 1 month ahead and frozen.*

•

stadium chili

makes about 6 cups

The perfect hot-dog–topping chili is this one—beanless, relatively mild, and thick enough not to drip onto your Bermuda shorts. Encourage guests to further gussy up their chili dogs by setting out bowls of grated Cheddar cheese, diced onions, and chopped pickled jalapeños. This chili also tastes good in a bowl, of course. In that event you may want to stir in a generous quantity of good-quality canned dark red kidney beans that have been rinsed and drained.

3 tablespoons olive oil
3 cups finely chopped yellow onions
5 garlic cloves, peeled and minced
2 pounds ground beef
2 tablespoons mild powdered chiles (see Cook's and Gardener's Sources)
1 tablespoon ground cumin, preferably from toasted seeds (page 63)
1 tablespoon dried oregano, crumbled
2 teaspoons unsweetened cocoa powder
2 teaspoons salt
1 teaspoon celery seeds
1 teaspoon ground turmeric
1 teaspoon ground cinnamon
½ teaspoon crushed dried red pepper
2 cups tomato juice
2 cups canned beef broth
¼ cup yellow cornmeal

In a 5-quart heavy nonreactive pan warm the olive oil over medium heat. Add the onions and garlic and cook, uncovered, stirring once or twice, for 10 minutes. Add the ground beef and cook, stirring and breaking up the lumps, for about 8 minutes, until the meat is evenly crumbled and is no longer pink.

Stir in the powdered chiles, cumin, oregano, cocoa, salt, celery seeds, turmeric, cinnamon, and dried red pepper; cook another 3 minutes, stirring often. Stir in the tomato juice and beef broth and bring to a boil. Lower the heat and simmer, uncovered, stirring occasionally, until the chili is thick and reduced by one-third, about 1½ hours.

Stir in the cornmeal and adjust the seasoning. *The chili can be prepared ahead and refrigerated up to 3 days or frozen up to 1 month. Rewarm over medium-low heat, stirring often.*

●

garlicky peppers and mushrooms

There's more than one way to top a hot dog, and this sauté of mushrooms and many-colored peppers, zapped with plenty of garlic, is a tasty alternative to more traditional embellishments. For a completely different effect, try this on grilled Italian sausages, tucked into grill-toasted pepper-onion rolls (page 257) and topped with a bit of melted mozzarella.

⅓ cup olive oil

6 large, meaty sweet peppers of assorted colors, preferably Dutch, trimmed and cut into ¼-inch-wide strips

1¼ pounds fresh mushrooms, trimmed and sliced thick

8 garlic cloves, peeled and sliced

2½ teaspoons salt

1 teaspoon freshly ground black pepper

½ cup minced wide-leaf parsley

In a large skillet heat the oil over medium heat. Add the pepper strips, mushrooms, garlic, and salt; cook, covered, stirring once or twice, for 8 minutes, until the vegetables have rendered their juices and are becoming tender.

Raise the heat to high and cook, uncovered, stirring and tossing, until the juices have evaporated and the vegetables are sizzling, 5 to 7 minutes. Remove from the heat and stir in the pepper and parsley. *The recipe can be prepared several hours ahead. Warm the mixture over low heat just before serving.*

●

beer-braised sauerkraut with

caraway seeds

makes about 8 cups

Simmered with onions, beer, and chicken stock, tangy kraut becomes sweet, mellow, and user-friendly. Caraway provides welcome punctuation, and teamed with a juicy frank and good mustard, lowly cabbage hits a flavor home run. For the best flavor and texture, use fresh kraut (the kind that comes refrigerated in jars or plastic bags).

4 pounds sauerkraut
5 tablespoons unsalted butter
3 cups finely chopped yellow onions
1 carrot, peeled and finely chopped
2 teaspoons caraway seeds
3 cups Chicken Stock (page 90) or canned broth
1 cup lager beer

Drain the sauerkraut. In a colander rinse it briefly under cold running water. Drain well.

In a large nonreactive saucepan over low heat, melt the butter. Add the onions, carrot, and caraway seeds; cook, covered, stirring once or twice, until very tender, about 15 minutes. Mix in the sauerkraut, stock, and beer and bring to a boil. Lower the heat and simmer, uncovered, stirring occasionally, until the liquid is evaporated and the sauerkraut is tender and shiny, about 1 hour. *The recipe can be prepared 3 days ahead. Reheat until steaming before serving.*

●

chocolate-dipped chocolate malted
ice cream cones

<u>makes 12</u>

These confections may recall those hawked by vendors at the stadium, but the homemade version is immeasurably tastier. Bring them out during the seventh-inning stretch (or at any point at which your team is losing) to get the crowd on its feet and cheering again.

If you want the real taste of chocolate malt, you'll probably have to make your own ice cream, but if time is tight, purchased premium chocolate, coffee, or vanilla ice cream will work well too.

Chocolate Malted Ice Cream (recipe follows)
12 old-fashioned sugar cones
2 cups (about 8 ounces) finely chopped walnuts
8 ounces semisweet chocolate, chopped
2 tablespoons vegetable oil

Soften the ice cream slightly in the refrigerator if necessary for scooping. Gently pack some ice cream into the hollow part of each cone. Top each with a small rounded scoop of ice cream. As the cones are filled, set them, scoop end up, in short glasses and freeze until the ice cream is very firm, preferably overnight.

Place the walnuts on a large plate. Place the chocolate in a shallow metal bowl and set the bowl over a small saucepan of barely simmering water. Stir until the chocolate melts. Remove the bowl from the water and stir in the vegetable oil. Let the chocolate stand until cool but still liquid, about 5 minutes.

Dip the ice cream of 1 cone into the chocolate, rotating it to coat completely and tilting the bowl if necessary. Hold the cone until the chocolate is almost set, about 10 seconds. Immediately roll the bottom half of the dipped portion of ice cream into the nuts, pressing gently to make them adhere. Set the cone in a short glass and set the glass in the freezer. Repeat with the remaining cones, chocolate, and nuts. Freeze the cones until firm, about 1 hour. *Can be prepared 2 days ahead. Wrap solidly frozen cones individually in plastic wrap and store in the freezer.* Serve frozen.

chocolate malted ice cream

makes about 1½ quarts

The toasted taste of malt and chocolate combine in this ice cream to evoke sweet childhood nostalgia. Of course, this is delicious in the chocolate-coated cones above, but it is also worth making and eating for its own sake—try it in a tin roof sundae, topped with hot fudge sauce and a shower of Spanish peanuts.

4 egg yolks
¾ cup sugar
8 ounces semisweet chocolate, chopped
2 cups whipping cream
2 cups half-and-half
¾ cup plain malted milk powder
1 tablespoon Vanilla Rum (page 66) or vanilla extract

In a large bowl whisk together the egg yolks and sugar. In the top of a double boiler over simmering water, stir the chocolate until melted. Scrape into a large bowl.

Meanwhile, in a heavy saucepan over high heat, bring the whipping cream and half-and-half just to a boil. Gradually whisk the hot cream into the egg mixture. Return the mixture to the saucepan, set it over low heat, and cook, stirring constantly with a wooden spoon, until a finger drawn across the back of the spoon leaves a path, about 5 minutes; do not boil. Gradually whisk the hot custard into the chocolate. Whisk in the malted milk and vanilla rum (the custard may appear grainy). Press plastic wrap onto the surface of the custard and refrigerate until very cold, preferably overnight.

Pour the custard into the canister of an ice cream maker and churn according to the manufacturer's directions. Store the ice cream in the freezer. *Can be prepared 3 days ahead.*

leftovers

Extra buns can be refrigerated or frozen for use at another meal. Leftover toppings and salads can provide the basis for a substantial midnight snack or casual supper. The chili, in particular, holds up well. The cones can be stored an extra day or two in the freezer before they begin to get soggy and the ice cream begins to crystallize.

tomato bruschetta

herbed oven-roast of italian sausages,

potatoes, sweet peppers, and garlic

mixed green salad with red wine vinaigrette

christopher styler's tiramisù

What is it about Italian food? Ease of preparation, lusty seasoning, uncomplicated eating pleasure—these are my guesses, and when a lazy autumn weekend comes to an amiable conclusion, this feast for eight good friends, as often as not, is the menu to which I turn.

strategy

There is enough frequent fiddling with the menu's otherwise simple one-dish main course to suggest that this is a party-in-the-kitchen meal, with everyone pitching in or at least keeping the cook company. Prepare 20 cups of Basic Mixed Green Salad (page 23), dressing it with olive oil and red wine vinegar. For ease of serving, as well as for terrific eating, the roasted sausages with the vegetables and garlic should be served on the same plate with the salad. Mop up the mixed juices left on your plate with some good, crisp bread. The do-ahead dessert needs about 5 hours' refrigeration to be in optimum condition. An uncomplicated, hearty, slightly acidic red wine, such as Barbera d'Asti, cooled ever so slightly, is a great match for this menu's rich, simple flavors.

tomato bruschetta

serves 8

Crisp grilled slabs of good bread, smothered with a tangy, juicy tomato salad, is the most common form bruschetta takes. Although other toppings are possible, this is the most popular version, especially when the last crimson tomatoes of summer are at hand. If firing up the outdoor grill is an option, by all means do so, although excellent rough (preferably whole-wheat) Italian bread, toasted indoors by more conventional means, will make an equally satisfying starter.

4 large (about 2 pounds total) ripe red tomatoes
½ cup (about) olive oil
2 tablespoons balsamic vinegar
2 garlic cloves, peeled and crushed through a garlic press
1 teaspoon salt
8 thick (1 inch) slices crusty whole-wheat bread
Freshly ground black pepper
¼ cup minced fresh basil

Halve, seed, and juice the tomatoes; cut the flesh into ½-inch chunks. In a medium bowl combine the tomato chunks, ¼ cup of the olive oil, and the vinegar, garlic, and salt. Let stand 15 minutes.

Toast the bread. If using a grill, brush both sides of each slice of bread lightly with the remaining olive oil before grilling.

Season the tomato mixture with a generous grinding of fresh black pepper. Arrange the warm toasted bread on 8 plates. Spoon the tomatoes and the juices from the bowl over the bread. Sprinkle each serving with the basil and serve immediately.

●

herbed oven-roast of italian sausages, potatoes, sweet peppers, and garlic

serves 8

Sausages are sizzling. These assemblages of unmentionable pork bits—ground, seasoned, and stuffed into (let's face it) a previously owned intestine—are a newly respectable, newly chic comfort food from coast to coast. Fancifully flavored sausages are on the cutting edge, but succulent, fennel-scented, old-fashioned sweet Italian sausage, available in most supermarkets, is the star of this easygoing oven roast. The regular turning and rearranging of the ingredients in their roasting pan, although sweaty kitchen business, yields crisp, brown, and delectable results.

3 pounds (16 medium links) sweet Italian sausage with fennel seeds
½ cup olive oil
3 pounds medium red-skinned potatoes, well scrubbed and cut into eighths
6 large, meaty sweet peppers (red, yellow, and/or orange), preferably Dutch, trimmed and
    cut into eighths
24 large garlic cloves, unpeeled
⅔ cup minced wide-leaf parsley
2 tablespoons minced fresh thyme, oregano, or marjoram
1 teaspoon coarse (kosher) salt
Freshly ground black pepper

Position a rack in the upper third of the oven and preheat the oven to 400° F.

With the tip of a sharp knife, prick each sausage several times. In a large, shallow baking dish just large enough to hold the sausages and potatoes in a single layer, toss the sausages with 2 tablespoons of the olive oil. Bake 15 minutes. Add the potatoes to the dish and drizzle them with ¼ cup of the olive oil. Turn the sausages and bake 30 minutes.

Add the peppers and garlic and drizzle them with the remaining 2 tablespoons oil. Turn the sausages and potatoes, releasing them carefully from the bottom of the pan with a spatula if necessary. Bake 15 minutes. Turn the sausages and potatoes again and toss the peppers and garlic cloves. Bake another 15 minutes (for a total baking time of 1¼ hours), until all ingredients are well browned and the potatoes and garlic are tender. Sprinkle with parsley, thyme, salt, and pepper, toss, and serve immediately.

christopher styler's tiramisù

serves 8

Tiramisù is a wildly popular Italian dessert, created in Venice. Simultaneously sophisticated (but then even the roughest Italian food seems sophisticated) and comforting, it is sweet, simple, and rich. There are countless versions (some, in fact, downright eccentric), but this one, from chef and author Christopher Styler (*Primi Piatti*, HarperCollins), is easy to assemble, requiring little actual cooking, and scrumptious. Mascarpone, the rich Italian cheese that is the basis for this puddinglike confection, can be made at home (page 35) or purchased, along with the requisite *savoiardi* (crisp ladyfingers) by mail (see Cook's and Gardener's Sources).

½ cup water
1 cup sugar
⅔ cup whipping cream
1 pound mascarpone, homemade (page 35) or purchased, at room temperature
⅔ cup brewed espresso, cooled to room temperature
⅓ cup dark rum
24 *savoiardi* (one 7-ounce package)
Crème Anglaise (recipe follows)
Unsweetened cocoa powder, for garnish

In a small saucepan over medium heat, combine the water and ⅓ cup of the sugar. Bring just to a boil, stirring to dissolve. Cool to room temperature.

Whip the cream to soft peaks. In a medium bowl whisk together the mascarpone and remaining ⅔ cup sugar. Do not overmix or the mascarpone will separate. Fold in the whipped cream.

In a wide, shallow dish combine the sugar syrup, espresso, and rum. Working quickly, dip half the *savoiardi*, one at a time, into the espresso mixture and quickly transfer them to a shallow dish, such as a 9- by 13-inch oval gratin, arranging them evenly. Spoon about half the mascarpone mixture over the soaked *savoiardi*. Repeat the soaking process with the remaining *savoiardi*, arranging them evenly over the mascarpone layer. Top the *savoiardi* with the remaining mascarpone mixture, spreading it evenly to the edges of the dish. Cover with plastic wrap and refrigerate for 5 hours. Let the tiramisù stand at room temperature for 30 minutes before serving.

Spoon the tiramisù onto 8 dessert plates. Spoon the crème anglaise around each portion, dividing it evenly and using it all. Generously sift cocoa through a sieve over each portion. Serve immediately.

crème anglaise

makes about 2 ½ cups

⅓ cup sugar
5 large egg yolks
2 cups half-and-half
1 tablespoon Vanilla Rum (page 66) or vanilla extract

In a medium bowl gradually whisk the sugar into the egg yolks.

In a heavy medium saucepan over moderate heat, bring the half-and-half just to a boil. Continue whisking the egg mixture while slowly dribbling in the hot half-and-half.

Return the mixture to the saucepan and set over medium heat. Cook, stirring constantly with a wooden spoon, until the mixture is steaming and the bubbles have disappeared from the surface, 3 to 4 minutes. An instant-reading thermometer will register between 165° and 170° F, and a finger drawn across the back of the spoon will leave a track.

Remove from the heat and transfer immediately to a small bowl. Stir often while cooling the crème to room temperature. Stir in the vanilla rum. Cover the crème with plastic wrap, pressing it onto the surface to keep a skin from forming. Refrigerate until cold, at least 2 hours. *The crème anglaise can be prepared up to 3 days ahead.*

l e f t  v e r s

The bruschetta is not successful as a leftover. Any remaining sausages and vegetables can be reheated (a bit of tomato sauce and mozzarella will help out if things seem dry). The tiramisù will become very soft and even more puddinglike, but the flavor will remain good for 48 hours. Enjoy some after a hard day.

bourbon fruitcakes

Despite what Johnny Carson and Calvin Trillin have alleged, there *are* edible, even delicious, fruitcakes out there, and for many people it wouldn't be the holidays without one. This recipe makes just such a cake, combining the maximum of fruit (none of it from the artificial, Day-Glo fruit factory) with the minimum of batter, plus a slug of good bourbon for moisture and flavor. This isn't the buried-in-powdered-sugar-in-a-closet-for-three-years sort of fruitcake; it should be consumed within a week to ten days of baking.

1½ pounds dried apricots, quartered
1½ pounds pitted dates, quartered
1½ pounds pecans, coarsely chopped
1 cup (4 ounces) dried tart cherries (see Cook's and Gardener's Sources)
2 cups unbleached all-purpose flour
2½ teaspoons baking powder
½ teaspoon salt
6 eggs, at room temperature
¾ cup granulated sugar
¾ cup packed light brown sugar
¾ stick (6 tablespoons) unsalted butter, melted
⅓ cup bourbon
2 tablespoons Vanilla Rum (page 66) or vanilla extract

Position a rack in the middle of the oven and preheat the oven to 325° F. Generously butter six 3½- by 6-inch (2-cup) loaf pans. Line the bottoms with waxed paper; butter the paper.

In a very large bowl combine the apricots, dates, pecans, and dried cherries. Add ½ cup of the flour and toss thoroughly, carefully separating any pieces of fruit that are stuck together.

In a medium bowl sift together the remaining 1½ cups flour, the baking powder, and salt.

Separate the eggs, transferring the whites to a medium bowl and the yolks to a large bowl. Whisk the sugars into the yolks and beat until fluffy. Whisk in the butter, bourbon, and vanilla rum, and then the flour mixture.

Beat the whites until stiff peaks form. Stir one-third of the beaten whites into the egg mixture to lighten it. Fold in the remaining egg whites; do not overmix. Pour the batter over the fruit in the large bowl and stir until all the fruit is lightly coated with batter. Divide the batter among the prepared pans, pressing it firmly into each pan with a flattened palm.

Bake for 50 to 60 minutes, until the cakes have risen and are lightly browned and a tester inserted into the center comes out clean.

Cool the cakes in the pans on a rack for 10 minutes, then turn the cakes out of the pans and cool to room temperature on a rack. Wrap each fruitcake tightly in plastic wrap. Store in a cool place and use within 10 days.

le petit robert's stuffed cabbage casseroles

mixed green salad

with red wine vinaigrette and roquefort

walnut whole-wheat bread (page 148)

deep-dish cranberry apple pie

Here is a menu for a wintry day, one happily spent cooking and puttering in an oven-warmed kitchen, perhaps as snow quietly falls outside the frosty window. The reward for so much industry is the meal itself, featuring a casserole of savory pork-and-bacon–stuffed cabbage leaves, a hearty salad, and a spectacular-looking and -tasting deep-dish pie of apples, cranberries, and raisins.

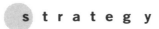 **s   t   r   a   t   e   g   y**

Although there are two long cooking stages, the stuffed cabbage casseroles are not technically demanding—in fact, the hardest part is finding six individual covered casseroles attractive enough to present at the table. It's an effort worth making (try restaurant supply houses)—the effect as each diner uncovers his or her own steaming little pot is unbeatable—but lidless casseroles can be covered with foil and made to do. Prepare 15 cups of Basic Mixed Green Salad (page 23), dress it with red wine vinegar and olive oil, and sprinkle 8 ounces coarsely crumbled imported Roquefort over the salads. The walnut bread is the ideal accompaniment to the cheese-spangled salads, but any good crusty bread can be substituted. The pie should be baked before the casseroles go into the oven but can be gently reheated during the meal if you want to serve it warm. Drink a lightly chilled young red from Cahors in southwest France, one with a good balance of fruit and acid.

●

le petit robert's stuffed cabbage
casseroles

serves 6

This individual casserole approach to serving stuffed cabbage is obviously suited to restaurant use, and this recipe is adapted from one served at a much beloved but long defunct Greenwich Village bistro called Le Petit Robert. Robert's version is simple but highly satisfying, sauced with tomato-tinged wine, Calvados, and aromatic vegetables (*mirepoix*).

STUFFING

6 slices dry white sandwich bread, torn into pieces
1½ cups milk
1½ pounds coarsely ground pork, not too lean
4 ounces smoked slab bacon, finely diced
½ cup minced wide-leaf parsley
2 garlic cloves, peeled and minced
2 shallots, peeled and minced
1 tablespoon minced fresh thyme
2 teaspoons salt
1 teaspoon freshly ground black pepper

MIREPOIX

⅓ cup olive oil
2 cups coarsely chopped yellow onions
1½ pounds carrots, peeled and sliced ¼ inch thick
2 bay leaves
3 cups Chicken Stock (page 90) or canned broth
½ cup dry white wine
3 ounces tomato paste (half of a 6-ounce can)

TO ASSEMBLE

1 large head Savoy cabbage (about 1½ pounds)
18 whole juniper berries
6 tablespoons Calvados (unsweetened French apple brandy)
12 tablespoons dry white wine

For the stuffing In a bowl combine the bread and milk and let stand 5 minutes. With your hands, squeeze the soaked bread to extract as much milk as possible.

In a mixing bowl, using a table fork, lightly combine the soaked bread, ground pork, bacon, parsley, garlic, shallots, thyme, salt, and pepper. Cover and let stand at room temperature while preparing the *mirepoix* and cabbage leaves.

For the *mirepoix* In a deep skillet over medium heat, warm the olive oil. Add the onions, carrots, and bay leaves; cook, uncovered, stirring once or twice, for 20 minutes, until the vegetables are browned. Stir in the chicken stock, wine, and tomato paste; simmer, uncovered, stirring occasionally, for 1 hour, or until reduced by half. Discard the bay leaves.

To assemble Meanwhile, core the cabbage and separate the leaves. Bring a large pot of water to a simmer. Working in batches, blanch the cabbage leaves, cooking the hard outer leaves for about 2½ minutes and the more tender inner leaves for about 1½ minutes. As you proceed, transfer the leaves to a large bowl of cold water. When all the cabbage leaves are blanched, drain them well. Cut out and discard the tough ribs from the outer leaves.

Position a rack in the middle of the oven and preheat the oven to 400° F.

Line six 2½- to 3-cup ceramic casseroles (with lids if possible) with the large cabbage leaves, leaving enough overhanging leaf to later enclose the stuffing. Distribute the smaller cabbage leaves in the bottoms of the lined casseroles. Divide the stuffing evenly between the casseroles, mounding it slightly in each. Lightly press 3 juniper berries into the stuffing in each casserole. Spoon 1 tablespoon Calvados and 2 tablespoons wine over the stuffing in each casserole. Wrap the overhanging leaves over the stuffing to enclose it completely. Ladle the *mirepoix* generously over the cabbage. Cover with the lids (or foil) and set the casseroles in a shallow baking pan just large enough to accommodate them comfortably. Add hot tap water to the pan to come halfway up the sides of the casseroles.

Bake the casseroles for 1 hour. Raise the oven temperature to 450° F, remove the lids from the casseroles, and bake another 10 to 15 minutes, until the tops are lightly browned. Put the lids, if you have them, back on the casseroles for maximum impact at the table, and serve immediately.

●

deep-dish cranberry apple pie

serves 8

This pie began as an improvisation, when I stirred some leftover raw cranberry sauce into an apple pie in the making. The results were colorful and good, and I now do it on purpose. Over succeeding cranberry seasons, the pie has evolved into a deep-dish affair, always baked in a brown, oval English stoneware casserole that seems made for it. I often serve the pie at Thanksgiving, frequently accompanied by scoops of Häagen-Dazs orange sorbet/vanilla ice cream swirl. The crust is thick but tender—a perfect foil to the tart, juicy filling.

CRUST

2¾ cups unbleached all-purpose flour

½ teaspoon salt

¾ stick (6 tablespoons) unsalted butter, well chilled and cut into small pieces

½ cup solid vegetable shortening, well chilled and cut into small pieces

½ cup (about) ice water

FILLING

2½ pounds (5 large) tart apples, such as Granny Smith, cored, peeled, and very thinly sliced

⅓ cup unbleached all-purpose flour

1½ cups cranberries, picked over and rinsed

1 cup sugar

Finely minced zest of 2 large oranges

1 cup golden raisins

½ cup fresh orange juice, strained

1 egg, beaten

1 tablespoon sugar

For the crust In a food processor or a large bowl, combine 2½ cups of the flour and the salt. Cut in the butter and shortening until the mixture resembles coarse meal. Mix in enough ice water, 1 tablespoon at a time, to form a soft dough. Sprinkle the work surface with 2 tablespoons of the remaining flour. Turn the dough onto the floured surface. Gather it into a ball, flatten into a disk, and wrap tightly in plastic wrap. Refrigerate at least 45 minutes. *The dough can be prepared 1 day ahead.*

For the filling In a large bowl stir together the apples and flour. In a food processor combine the cranberries, sugar, and orange zest; process until finely chopped. Stir the cranberry mixture, the raisins, and the orange juice into the apples and let stand, stirring once or twice, for 30 minutes.

Position a rack in the middle of the oven and preheat the oven to 400° F.

Spoon the filling into a deep 10-cup soufflé dish or casserole. Flour the work surface with the remaining 2 tablespoons flour. Roll out the chilled pastry slightly larger than the circumference of the dish you have selected. Place the dough atop the dish and trim the overhang to ½ inch. Crimp the edges decoratively, pressing the dough to the dish. Pierce the dough in several places with a knife.

Bake the pie for 15 minutes. Lower the temperature to 375° F. Brush the crust with the beaten egg, sprinkle it evenly with the sugar, and bake another 40 to 45 minutes, until the top is a deep golden brown. Cool on a rack. Serve warm, reheating the pie if necessary.

l e f t o v e r s

Any remaining stuffed cabbage can be gently reheated in a 325° F oven the next day. Cold leftover fruit pie has always been one of my favorite breakfasts, and this one is no exception.

black olives with orange and basil (page 73)

sausage, mushroom, and polenta gratin

mixed green salad with balsamic vinaigrette

amaretto-and-wine-poached dried fruit compote (page 43)

hazelnut biscotti (page 44)

"Casserole for supper" sometimes means mystery meat under a blanket of canned soup, and sometimes it can mean this—a lasagna-like layered gratin of cooked corn-meal, gooey cheese, and a slightly spicy sausage and mushroom sauce. Slowly baked to crusty excellence and served up with green salad and an easy fruit dessert, it's a happy way to face the end of the weekend.

strategy

This is the perfect supper menu for a busy day. Every dish, including the desserts, can be done well in advance, and while the gratin bakes, there is time to set the table, pour the wine (a tomato-compatible Italian red, like Barbera d'Alba, for example), nibble some good olives, and prepare 15 cups of Basic Mixed Green Salad (page 23), dressing it with olive oil and balsamic vinegar. Any good, crusty plain bread will be fine here, although garlic bread (page 243) would be a nice touch.

sausage, mushroom, and polenta gratin

serves 6

Spooned out of the bubbling dish, the gratin reveals two layers of hot tender polenta enclosing a sausage, mushroom, and tomato filling. The layers lead some to describe this as lasagna. While it's not, technically speaking, it's just as much fun to make and it's just as good to eat.

SAUSAGE-MUSHROOM FILLING

1 pound sweet Italian sausage with fennel seeds, removed from the casings and crumbled
5 tablespoons olive oil
12 ounces fresh white or brown (cremini) mushrooms, wiped clean, trimmed, and sliced
    thick
Salt
½ cup dry red wine
1 cup finely diced yellow onion
4 garlic cloves, peeled and minced
1½ teaspoons dried basil, crumbled
¾ teaspoon dried marjoram, crumbled
½ teaspoon crushed dried red pepper
2 bay leaves
1 can (28 ounces) Italian plum tomatoes, crushed (with the fingers) with their juices

TO ASSEMBLE

1 tablespoon olive oil
Polenta (page 252), hot
2 tablespoons grated Parmesan cheese
8 ounces grated melting cheese, such as Monterey Jack, Fontina, or processed Provolone

For the sausage-mushroom filling In a large skillet over medium heat, cook the sausage, stirring occasionally, until it is lightly browned, about 10 minutes. Drain on paper towels; discard any rendered fat but do not clean the skillet.

Set the skillet over medium-high heat. Add 2 tablespoons of the olive oil. When the oil is hot, add the mushrooms and toss to coat. Cook over high heat, tossing and stirring, for 2 minutes. Stir in ½ teaspoon salt, cover, lower the heat, and cook, stirring once or twice and scraping browned bits from the bottom of the pan, until the mushrooms have rendered their juices and are tender, 3 to 4 minutes. Uncover the skillet. Raise the heat to high, stir in the red wine, and cook, stirring once or twice, until the pan juices are reduced to a glaze that just coats the mushrooms. Transfer to a bowl. Do not clean the skillet.

Set the skillet over medium-low heat. Add the remaining 3 tablespoons olive oil and stir in the onion, garlic, basil, marjoram, dried red pepper, and bay leaves. Cover and cook, stirring once or twice, until the onion is tender, about 10 minutes.

Stir in the tomatoes and their juices and ½ teaspoon salt. Bring to a boil, then lower the heat slightly and simmer briskly, uncovered, stirring once or twice, until thickened, about 30 minutes. Stir in the sausage and the mushrooms with any juices in the bowl and continue to simmer, stirring occasionally, until very thick, 10 to 15 minutes. Remove from the heat, discard the bay leaves, and cool. *The filling can be prepared 3 days ahead; cover and refrigerate. Return to room temperature before use.*

To assemble Grease a 9- by 13-inch oval gratin dish with the oil. Pour one-third of the hot polenta into the prepared dish, spreading it into an even layer about ½ inch thick. Spoon the sausage-mushroom filling evenly over the polenta. Sprinkle the sausage mixture with the Parmesan and the melting cheese. Pour the remaining polenta over the cheese layer, spreading it evenly to the edge of the dish. Cool to room temperature, cover, and refrigerate until firm, preferably overnight. *The gratin can be prepared to this point 2 days ahead; return to room temperature before proceeding.*

Position a rack in the upper third of the oven and preheat the oven to 400° F.

With a knife, cut a shallow crosshatched diamond pattern into the upper polenta layer. Bake the casserole, uncovered, until the top is crisp and golden and the filling is bubbling, about 40 minutes. Let stand on a rack 15 minutes before cutting. Serve on the same plate with the salad.

l e f t o v e r s

Any remaining gratin can be stored in the refrigerator and reheated, covered with foil, in a 375° F oven. It may even taste better after two bakings than it did after one.

millie's sweet-mustard—glazed pork and ham loaf

buttered sugar snap peas

carrot and potato gratin (page 141)

peppered pear pie

bourbon brown-sugar ice cream

Meat loaves are either relished or rejected, depending, I think, on the success or failure of those we ate growing up. This old-fashioned Sunday supper (pie à la mode for dessert!) is thus to me a magnificent feast and features my grandmother Millie's absolutely delicious ham loaf.

s t r a t e g y

This is such a simple and straightforward meat, veg, and potato menu that a strategy hardly seems necessary. To lessen last-minute kitchen business, start the ice cream two days ahead, freeze it one day ahead, and bake the pie the morning of the meal. The peas can be blanched one day ahead and reheated just before serving time. Drink a cold beer with the meal and a big cup of coffee with dessert.

millie's sweet-mustard–glazed

pork and ham loaf

serves 8

This meat loaf comes pretty much unaltered from my grandmother Millie's handwritten recipe book. The simple list of ingredients says to me that it's a Depression-era dish. It's also the prodigal meal, the one my mother prepares for my first dinner when I'm visiting home in Wray, Colorado. It's a popular dish there, and the local markets make up their own versions of the ground-meat mixture (often including a bit of beef along with the ham and pork). Elsewhere I advise you to order the ground pork from the butcher and to chop the ham yourself in the food processor.

1 pound baked smoked ham, trimmed of any fat and rind and cut into chunks
1½ pounds ground pork, not too lean
1 cup (about 2½ ounces) finely crushed saltine crackers
1 cup milk
2 eggs, beaten
1 teaspoon freshly ground black pepper
Sweet Mustard Glaze (recipe follows)

Position a rack in the lower third of the oven and preheat the oven to 350° F.

In a food processor finely chop the ham. In a large bowl stir together the ham and pork. Add the cracker crumbs, milk, eggs, and pepper; mix thoroughly (hands work best). Transfer the meat mixture to a shallow baking dish, such as a 9- by 13-inch oval gratin, and form it into a flat loaf. With the back of a knife, press a crosshatched diamond pattern about ½ inch deep into the upper surface of the loaf.

Bake 30 minutes. Spread one-third of the mustard glaze over the loaf and bake 15 minutes. Spread half the remaining glaze over the loaf and bake 15 minutes. Spread the last of the glaze over the loaf and bake another 15 to 20 minutes, until the loaf is glazed and brown and a meat thermometer inserted in the center reads 165° F.

Cool 5 minutes and transfer the loaf to a serving platter. Let stand another 5 minutes before cutting.

●

sweet mustard glaze

makes about 1 cup

1 cup packed light brown sugar
⅓ cup cider vinegar
⅓ cup water
¼ cup Dijon-style mustard

In a small nonreactive saucepan over low heat, whisk together the sugar, vinegar, water, and mustard. Bring to a boil, lower the heat, and simmer uncovered, stirring once or twice, for 20 minutes. Cool to room temperature. *The glaze can be prepared several days ahead. Store it, covered, at room temperature.*

●

buttered sugar snap peas

serves 8

Green beans or fresh green peas can be substituted.

2 pounds sugar snap peas (see Cook's and Gardener's Sources)
Salt
5 tablespoons unsalted butter
Freshly ground black pepper

Tip the sugar snaps, string them if necessary, and cut them in half on an angle. Bring a pot of water to a boil. Stir in 1 tablespoon salt and the peas; cook, stirring once or twice, until just tender, about 4 minutes. Drain and immediately transfer to a bowl of iced water. Cool completely and drain thoroughly. *The peas can be prepared 1 day ahead. Wrap well and refrigerate.*

In a large skillet heat the butter over medium heat. Add the peas, season with ½ teaspoon salt and a generous grinding of black pepper, and cook, stirring and tossing often, until just heated through, 3 to 4 minutes. Adjust the seasoning and serve immediately.

peppered pear pie

makes one 10-inch pie, serving 8

Teamed with ginger and lemon, black pepper makes this an altogether warming and delicious pie. For best results, the pears should be slightly underripe. Serve each slice with a generous scoop of Bourbon Brown-Sugar Ice Cream.

Deep Tart Crust (page 252), shaped into a disk and chilled
3 tablespoons fresh lemon juice, strained
3 pounds (about 7 medium) Bartlett pears, slightly underripe
½ cup golden raisins
½ cup sugar
¼ cup unbleached all-purpose flour
1 tablespoon finely minced lemon zest
1 teaspoon ground ginger
1 teaspoon freshly ground black pepper
Streusel Topping (page 252), chilled

Lightly flour a work surface. Roll out the chilled pastry to a round about ¼ inch thick. Transfer the dough to a regular 10-inch pie pan. Trim the edge to ½ inch and crimp it decoratively. Cover and refrigerate for at least 30 minutes. *The pie shell can be formed up to 1 day ahead.*

Fill a medium bowl with cold water and stir in the lemon juice. Core and peel the pears, adding them to the acidulated water as you do so. Drain the pears, pat them dry, and thinly slice. In a medium bowl combine the pears, raisins, sugar, flour, lemon zest, ginger, and pepper. Let the filling stand at room temperature for 30 minutes.

Position a rack in the upper third of the oven and set a heavy baking sheet on it. Preheat the oven to 450° F.

Spoon the filling into the chilled shell. Sprinkle the streusel evenly over the filling. Set the pie on the heated baking sheet and bake 10 minutes. Lower the oven temperature to 350° F and bake the pie another 30 to 40 minutes, until the topping and crust are golden and the filling is thick and bubbly. Cool completely on a rack before cutting.

●

bourbon brown-sugar ice cream

makes about 1½ quarts

The alcohol makes the ice cream slightly resistant to quick freezing. Be certain to use the full amount of the ice and salt called for in your ice cream maker's directions and churn it for the longest possible time.

4 egg yolks
1 cup packed light brown sugar
2 cups whipping cream
2 cups half-and-half
⅓ cup bourbon
1 tablespoon Vanilla Rum (page 66) or vanilla extract

In a large bowl whisk the egg yolks and brown sugar until thick.

In a medium, heavy pan over moderate heat, combine the whipping cream, half-and-half, and bourbon. Bring slowly just to a boil, stirring occasionally. Whisking constantly, dribble the hot cream into the egg mixture. Return this mixture to the pan and set the pan over low heat. Cook, stirring constantly with a wooden spoon, until the custard has thickened slightly and leaves a heavy track on the back of the spoon when a finger is drawn across it, about 4 minutes. Do not let the custard boil.

Remove the custard from the heat and immediately transfer to a bowl. Cool to room temperature and stir in the vanilla rum. Cover with plastic wrap, pressing the wrap onto the surface of the custard to keep a skin from forming. Refrigerate until very cold, at least 5 hours but preferably overnight.

Strain the custard into the canister of an ice cream maker and churn according to the manufacturer's directions. Store the ice cream in the freezer. *The ice cream can be prepared up to 2 days ahead.* Soften the ice cream slightly in the refrigerator if necessary for scooping.

l e f t o v e r s

The ham loaf makes great sandwiches, or it can be wrapped in foil and reheated. This pie's zesty seasoning makes it less than successful for breakfast, but it makes a great sweet snack, accompanied by a glass of cold milk. The ice cream will keep in the freezer for several days before becoming too hard and grainy to enjoy.

green goddess chicken salad

herbed sourdough toast

chewy granola thins

fresh strawberries

During the fine days of spring, chicken salad is my lunchtime solution to the twin problems of hunger and the reborn urge to entertain. Chicken's compatibility with a wide range of lusty seasonings means the meal, though light, won't be dull; a garnish of seasonal vegetables rounds out a generous plateful of springtime satisfaction.

s t r a t e g y

This is an easy menu, and while I don't think chicken salad ever tastes as wonderful after refrigeration, you could, in a pinch, make it a day in advance. Certainly the mayonnaise can—and should—be completed ahead, in order for its flavors to fully develop. The herbed butter also keeps well in the refrigerator for several days or in the freezer for months. The cookies can be baked a day ahead, and if you don't have your own homemade granola, a good-quality health food store variety can be used with great success. Fancy, long-stemmed strawberries are particularly attactive, but if you can't find them, choose the best (reddest, most ripe) regular berries and set them out in a cool, white bowl. Drink a light, uncomplicated white wine with a good balance of fruit and acidity—a Gewürztraminer or Riesling, for example.

●

green goddess chicken salad

serves 6 to 8

Named after a play that starred the actor George Arliss, the cool, green tarragon-and-anchovy-scented dressing was apparently created in the mid-1920s in San Francisco and soon became an American favorite. While the dressing seems a little heavy over leafy greens, it is perfect on this meaty, main-course summer salad. (A good alternative is the Caesar Dressing on page 49.) The chicken will be at its moist, tender best if cooked shortly before serving time.

3 pounds skinless, boneless chicken breasts
Salt
1 cup thinly sliced celery
Green Goddess Mayonnaise (recipe follows)
Leaf lettuce (such as romaine), sliced cucumbers, and red and yellow cherry tomatoes, for garnish

In a large skillet arrange the chicken breasts in a single layer. Add enough lightly salted cold water to cover the chicken and set over medium heat. Bring slowly to a simmer, turning the breasts once. Simmer for 5 minutes. Check the chicken for doneness. Remove the skillet from the heat and cool the chicken to room temperature in the poaching liquid. Drain and pat dry.

Trim any fat and cartilage from the chicken and tear the meat into bite-sized pieces. In a bowl combine the chicken and celery with 2 cups of the dressing. Adjust the seasoning. On plates arrange the lettuce leaves, cucumbers, and tomatoes. Spoon the chicken salad onto the plates, drizzle the lettuce and vegetables with some of the remaining dressing, and serve.

●

green goddess mayonnaise

makes about 2½ cups

½ cup finely chopped wide-leaf parsley
2 eggs, at room temperature
3 green onions, trimmed and sliced
¼ cup white wine tarragon vinegar
2 tablespoons Dijon-style tarragon mustard
4 oil-packed anchovy fillets, chopped

1½ teaspoons dried tarragon, crumbled
1½ teaspoons salt
½ teaspoon freshly ground black pepper
1 cup corn oil
¾ cup olive oil

In a food processor combine the parsley, eggs, green onions, vinegar, mustard, anchovies, tarragon, salt, and pepper. Process until smooth. With the machine running, add the oils in a slow, steady stream; the dressing will thicken. Transfer the mayonnaise to a storage container, cover, and refrigerate for at least 24 hours to allow the flavors to develop. *The mayonnaise can be prepared up to 3 days ahead. Return it to room temperature before using.*

●

herbed sourdough toast

serves 6 to 8

The San Francisco origins of the main-course salad suggested the use of sourdough to me, but any good, crusty bread can be substituted. My recommended herbs, too, can be replaced by whatever your garden or market supplies—just be sure they are thoroughly patted or spun dry after washing, or they'll be difficult to purée into the butter. Serve the toast in a napkin-lined basket and pass the butter in a crock or ramekin.

1 bunch chives, coarsely chopped (about ⅓ cup)
½ cup coarsely chopped wide-leaf parsley
1 stick (4 ounces) unsalted butter, softened
Pinch of salt
Freshly ground black pepper
4 thick slices sourdough or other country-style bread, cut from the center of a day-old loaf

In a small food processor combine the chives and parsley and chop fine. Add the butter, the salt, and a generous grinding of black pepper and process until almost smooth. Transfer the butter to a small crock or ramekin and cover. *The butter can be refrigerated for several days or frozen up to 1 month. Return to room temperature before using.*

Cut the slices of bread in half. In a toaster or under the broiler, toast the bread until golden brown. Serve immediately, accompanied by the butter.

chewy granola thins

A big jar well stocked with almost any cookie is a useful weekend resource, providing dessert for casual lunches, snacks for hungry kids, and sweet treats for all hands. When the cookies are these granola-crunchy little thins, the reasons for baking up a batch are even more compelling. I like them best with my own homemade granola (page 287), but you can substitute a good-quality purchased brand.

2 cups plus 2 tablespoons unbleached all-purpose flour
1 teaspoon baking soda
1 teaspoon salt
2 sticks (8 ounces) unsalted butter, softened
¾ cup granulated sugar
¾ cup packed light brown sugar
2 eggs
3 cups granola, preferably Cherry-Almond Granola (page 287)

Position racks in the upper and lower thirds of the oven and preheat the oven to 375° F.

In a medium bowl thoroughly stir together the flour, soda, and salt. In a large bowl cream together the butter and both sugars. Whisk in the eggs one at a time. Stir in the flour mixture, and when it is almost incorporated, stir in the granola.

Drop the dough onto ungreased baking sheets by rounded tablespoonfuls, spacing them about 1½ inches apart. Bake until the cookies are lightly colored but still rather soft, about 13 minutes; exchange the position of the pans from upper to lower and from front to back halfway through the baking.

With a pancake turner, carefully transfer the soft cookies to parchment paper to cool. Repeat with the remaining cookie dough, allowing the baking sheets to cool completely before reuse.

Store the cookies in an airtight container at room temperature.

l e f t o v e r s

Although the chicken salad won't be at its best the next day (liquid from the celery thins the dressing), it can still brighten a brown bag lunch. Store the salad separately from any leftover garnishing vegetables. Leftover mayonnaise can be spread on a sandwich (try crab cakes or roast turkey breast), served as a dip for crudités, or brushed over chicken or fish before baking. Don't keep it more than 4 days in the refrigerator. Stored airtight, the cookies will keep up to 4 days, although they gradually will lose their chewy quality.

cherry-almond granola

A jar full of this cherry-almond treat is a reassuring weekend staple and a healthful, high-fiber alternative to the candy bars that masquerade under the same name. It can't be beat for munching out of hand or tossing onto a bowl of yogurt or into a batch of cookies (where, somehow, it *belongs*). Kids can help put it together, and then earn as their reward the ultimate between-meal snack—a crisp wedge of Granny Smith apple, spread with peanut butter and topped with a hearty sprinkle of fresh, homemade granola. This recipe is equally good made with golden raisins in place of the cherries.

½ cup packed light brown sugar
¼ cup unsulphured molasses
¼ cup honey
¼ cup cold water
3 tablespoons vegetable oil
3 cups old-fashioned rolled oats
1 cup dried tart or sweet cherries (see Cook's and Gardener's Sources)
1 cup coarsely chopped unblanched almonds
½ cup raw pumpkin seeds (available at health food stores)
⅓ cup dried flaked unsweetened coconut (available at health food stores)
⅓ cup raw sunflower seeds (available at health food stores)
¼ cup wheat germ
2 tablespoons sesame seeds, preferably unhulled (available at health food stores)

Position a rack in the middle of the oven and preheat the oven to 325° F.

In a small heavy saucepan over medium heat, combine the brown sugar, molasses, honey, water, and vegetable oil and bring just to a boil.

Meanwhile, in a medium roasting pan combine the remaining ingredients. Slowly pour the hot syrup over the oat mixture, stirring to moisten evenly. Bake, stirring occasionally, about 40 minutes, until the granola is lightly browned and slightly crunchy (it will become crunchier as it cools). Cool completely and store in an airtight container at room temperature.

confetti deviled eggs (page 103)

shrimp, leek, and dill spread

cool-as-a-cucumber, potato, and mint soup

chicken, tomato, and arugula sandwiches

smoked salmon sandwiches with caper-mustard butter

long-stemmed strawberries with

sour cream and brown sugar

fragrant iced tea

Here is a tennis and croquet menu with a British theme, one that is perfect for a warm spring afternoon or evening, giving everyone the first excuse of the season to wear white linen, seersucker, and silk.

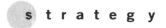

strategy

This is an indoor or outdoor picnic, one that can be as formal or as casual as you like. The deviled eggs are optional but a nice addition to a menu that consists, more or less, of cool finger food. Half the menu (the shrimp spread and the soup) can be done well in advance, while the sandwiches necessarily require last-minute assembly. Serve the strawberries with separate bowls of sour cream and brown sugar and let guests dip as they please.

●

shrimp, leek, and dill spread

makes 3 cups

Serve this rich version of potted shrimp in a cool heavy crock and let guests spread it on very plain crisp crackers, such as Carr's Water Biscuits or Bath Olivers.

7 tablespoons unsalted butter
3 medium leeks (white part only), well cleaned and finely chopped
¼ cup minced shallots
1½ pounds medium shrimp, peeled and deveined
½ cup sour cream
2 teaspoons salt
½ teaspoon freshly ground black pepper
2 tablespoons minced fresh dill
Fresh dill sprigs and lemon slices, for garnish
Plain crackers, for serving

In a medium skillet over low heat, melt 3 tablespoons of the butter. Add the leeks and shallots, cover, and cook, stirring often, until tender, 10 to 12 minutes. Transfer the mixture to a food processor.

In a large skillet melt the remaining 4 tablespoons butter over medium heat. Add the shrimp and cook, stirring and tossing, until the shrimp are pink, curled, and just cooked through, 4 to 6 minutes. With a slotted spoon remove about one-third of the shrimp and reserve them. Transfer the remaining shrimp with their buttery juices to the food processor containing the leek mixture.

Add the sour cream, salt, and pepper; process until smooth. Transfer to a bowl. With a knife, coarsely chop the reserved shrimp and stir them, along with the minced dill, into the puréed mixture. Transfer to a 3-cup crock or bowl and smooth the top. Cover and refrigerate until very cold, preferably overnight. *The spread can be prepared up to 2 days in advance.*

Garnish with the dill sprigs and lemon slices and serve accompanied by plain crackers.

●

cool-as-a-cucumber, potato, and mint soup

<u>serves 8</u>

Pass the soup in mugs, along with the sandwiches, or use bowls for a more formal seated party. In another menu, add poached shrimp to the soup just before serving— a perfect late-spring main course.

3 tablespoons unsalted butter
2 cups dried yellow onion
4 large cucumbers (about 2¾ pounds), peeled, seeded, and chopped
1 pound (2 medium) boiling potatoes, peeled and chopped
4 cups Chicken Stock (page 90) or canned broth
Salt
½ cup half-and-half
¼ cup minced fresh mint, plus fresh mint sprigs for garnish
3 tablespoons red wine vinegar
½ teaspoon freshly ground white pepper

In a 4-quart soup pot over medium heat, melt the butter. Add the onion, cover, and cook, stirring once or twice, until tender, about 15 minutes.

Add the cucumbers, potatoes, stock, and 2 teaspoons salt; bring to a boil. Lower the heat, partially cover, and simmer the soup until the cucumbers and potatoes are very tender, about 40 minutes.

Cool slightly. In a food processor or a food mill fitted with the medium blade, purée the soup until smooth in batches. If using the food processor, pour the puréed soup through a sieve over a large bowl, mashing any remaining lumps of potato through the sieve. Cover and refrigerate until very cold, at least 5 hours. *The soup can be prepared to this point up to 2 days ahead.*

Stir in the half-and-half, mint, vinegar, and white pepper. Adjust the seasoning. Serve in chilled mugs or bowls, garnished with sprigs of mint.

chicken, tomato, and arugula sandwiches

makes 6 sandwiches (12 halves)

Too generously filled for teatime but too graceful to be considered really two-fisted, these chicken sandwiches and the salmon ones that follow are the perfect compromise for civilized but satisfying spring entertaining. Kitchen assistance, in the form of a modest assembly line of one or two volunteers, will make putting them together a relative snap.

3 whole boneless, skinless chicken breasts (about 1¼ pounds total)
Salt
12 slices white sandwich bread, toasted on one side
Lemony Mayonnaise (recipe follows)
Freshly ground black pepper
2 ripe medium tomatoes, cut into 12 thin slices
About ½ bunch arugula leaves, rinsed, spun dry, and stems trimmed

Arrange the chicken breasts in a single layer in a large skillet. Cover with lightly salted cold water and set over medium heat. Bring slowly to a simmer, turning the breasts once. Simmer until just cooked through, about 5 minutes. Remove the skillet from the heat and cool the chicken to room temperature in the poaching liquid. Drain and pat dry.

Trim any fat or cartilage from the chicken breasts and thinly slice across the grain and on a slight angle. Arrange the bread slices, toasted side down, on the work surface, and spread generously with the mayonnaise, leaving a border since you'll be trimming the crusts. Arrange the sliced chicken over the mayonnaise on 6 of the bread slices, dividing it evenly and using it all. Season with salt and pepper to taste. Top each chicken portion with 2 tomato slices. Invert the 6 remaining bread slices, mayonnaise side down, onto the sandwiches. Flatten the sandwiches slightly with your palm, then trim away the crusts. Cut the sandwiches in half diagonally, then cover loosely with plastic wrap until serving time. *The sandwiches can be prepared up to 45 minutes in advance. Drape the plastic-wrapped sandwiches with a dampened clean kitchen towel.*

Just before serving, tuck one or two arugula leaves into each sandwich half so that the stem ends are hidden and the ruffled leaf is visible. Secure the sandwiches with a pick if desired.

•

lemony mayonnaise

makes 3 cups

2 egg yolks, at room temperature

2 tablespoons (about) fresh lemon juice, strained

2 teaspoons finely minced lemon zest

1 teaspoon Dijon-style mustard

½ teaspoon salt

¼ teaspoon freshly ground black pepper

¾ cup corn oil

¼ cup olive oil

In a medium bowl whisk together the egg yolks, 2 teaspoons of the lemon juice, and the lemon zest, mustard, salt, and pepper. Continue to whisk while adding the corn and olive oils drop by drop; the mayonnaise will thicken. Adjust the seasoning, adding more lemon juice to taste. The mayonnaise should be tart. Cover and refrigerate until ready to use. *The mayonnaise can be prepared up to 2 days ahead.*

●

smoked salmon sandwiches with
caper-mustard butter

makes 6 sandwiches (12 halves)

The better the salmon, the better these simple sandwiches will be; it's worth springing for the best smoked fish you can. A health food store is a good place to locate good-quality whole-wheat bread.

12 thin slices firm-textured whole-wheat sandwich bread
Caper-Mustard Butter (recipe follows), softened
12 ounces smoked salmon, thinly sliced (see Cook's and Gardener's Sources)
12 large watercress sprigs, rinsed, spun dry, and tough stems trimmed
12 small Belgian endive leaves, rinsed and spun dry

Spread 1 side of each slice of bread generously with caper-mustard butter, leaving a border since you'll be trimming the crusts. Lay the slices, butter side up, on a work surface. Arrange the salmon over the butter on 6 of the slices. Invert the remaining slices of bread, butter side down, over the salmon.

Trim the crusts. Cut the sandwiches in half and cover the sandwiches loosely with plastic wrap until serving time. *The sandwiches can be prepared up to 45 minutes in advance. Drape the plastic-wrapped sandwiches with a dampened clean kitchen towel.*

Just before serving tuck a sprig of watercress and a leaf of endive into each sandwich half so that the stem ends are hidden and the tops are showing. Secure the sandwiches with a pick if desired.

●

caper-mustard butter

makes about ¾ cup

1 stick (4 ounces) unsalted butter, softened
1 tablespoon coarse-grained mustard
1 tablespoon Dijon-style mustard

1 tablespoon small (nonpareil) capers, drained
1 tablespoon fresh lemon juice, strained
¼ teaspoon freshly ground black pepper

In a small bowl mash together the butter, both mustards, and the capers, lemon juice, and pepper until well combined. Cover and refrigerate until ready to use. *The butter can be prepared and refrigerated up to 3 days or frozen up to 1 month.*

fragrant iced tea

makes 3 quarts

Other flavored teas, such as mango or black currant, can be substituted. Prevent cloudy tea by adding warm (not cold) water to the infusion and by serving the tea shortly after it is brewed, without refrigeration. The modest touch of sugar, by the way, brings out the fruit flavors of the tea and is, in my opinion, essential.

¼ cup Earl Grey tea leaves
¼ cup blackberry-flavored tea leaves
3 tablespoons orange pekoe tea leaves
4 quarts water
2 bay leaves
⅓ cup sugar

Combine the tea leaves. Bring 1 quart of the water to a full rolling boil. Stir in the tea mixture and bay leaves, remove from the heat, and cover. Let stand 5 minutes.

Strain the tea, discarding the leaves, into a heatproof gallon container. Stir in 3 quarts warm water and the sugar. Cool to room temperature. Serve in tall glasses over ice.

leftovers

The shrimp spread can be refrigerated to be enjoyed as an hors d'oeuvre at another meal (if you're scraping the bottom of the crock, spread it on crackers in the kitchen and garnish each with a sprig of dill before serving). It can also be used as a premium sandwich filling. Refrigerated mayonnaise will keep several days for use in the usual mayo ways—this one is particularly good in tuna salad. The caper butter can be kept refrigerated or frozen to be melted over a piece of broiled fish or chicken for wonderful flavor and gloss.

asparagus with crab mayonnaise

madeira-glazed country ham

creamed baby carrots, new potatoes,

and sugar snap peas with mint

buttermilk biscuits

strawberry-rhubarb crumble

A grand Sunday dinner, with a glistening country ham and an array of seasonable vegetables in the middle of the table and a crowd of family and friends around, is among the most agreeable of ways to celebrate spring.

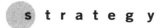

strategy

The soaking and simmering of the country ham should be started a day or two ahead, but the actual baking and glazing is relatively simple. Asparagus, sugar snaps, new potatoes, and baby carrots all can be blanched a day ahead. Bake the dessert early in the day, and pop the biscuits into the oven when the ham comes out (they'll bake while the ham is resting and then being carved). Serve this meal family-style, passing the bowls, platters, and baskets around the table. (For a completely different menu with just one significant change, replace the ham with the Roast Leg of Lamb with Caramelized Shallots, page 158.) A light, well-balanced Chardonnay or a Riesling is a good wine choice for the smoky, salty, and slightly nutty-tasting ham.

●

asparagus with crab mayonnaise

serves 8

A lush, pink mayonnaise chock-full of lump crabmeat is the extravagant dressing for these cool green spears of asparagus. Much like the classic caviar-topped baked potatoes, this combination is a wonderful pairing of the rare and expensive with the abundant and affordable—a state of affairs that usually leads to the increased appreciation of both elements.

2 egg yolks, at room temperature
3 tablespoons lemon juice, strained
1 tablespoon tomato paste
1 teaspoon Dijon-style mustard
Salt
½ teaspoon freshly ground black pepper
1¼ cups corn oil
2 pounds medium asparagus, trimmed and peeled (page 74)
1 pound fresh jumbo lump crabmeat, picked over
1 tablespoon finely minced shallot

In a medium bowl whisk together the egg yolks, the lemon juice, the tomato paste, the mustard, 1 teaspoon salt, and the pepper. Gradually whisk in the oil; the mayonnaise will thicken. Adjust the seasoning. *The mayonnaise can be prepared up to 2 days ahead; cover tightly and refrigerate. Return to room temperature before using.*

Bring a large pot of water to a boil. Stir in 1 tablespoon salt. Add the asparagus and cook 4 to 5 minutes, until just barely tender. Transfer immediately to a bowl of ice water. Cool completely, drain well, and pat dry. *The asparagus can be cooked up to 1 day ahead; wrap well and refrigerate. Return to room temperature before using.*

Fold the crabmeat and shallot into the mayonnaise and adjust the seasoning. Arrange the asparagus on 8 appetizer plates. Spoon the crab mayonnaise over the center of each portion of asparagus, dividing it evenly and using it all. Serve, passing a peppermill at the table.

madeira-glazed country ham

serves 8, with generous leftovers

The ham will provide plenty of leftovers. Freeze it for use on another weekend or enjoy it in sandwiches, omelets, salads, hors d'oeuvres, and so on.

1 Smithfield-type country ham (about 12 pounds), soaked and simmered (page 166)
1 cup medium-dry Madeira, such as Rainwater
⅓ cup packed dark brown sugar

Position a rack in the lower third of the oven and preheat the oven to 350° F. Cut away all but ⅛ inch of the fat covering the upper surface of the ham and set the ham, fat side up, in a shallow baking pan. Bake the ham 30 minutes. In a small bowl stir together the Madeira and brown sugar and baste the ham with half the mixture. Bake another 10 minutes, then baste with the remaining Madeira mixture. Bake 25 minutes more, basting every 5 minutes with the accumulated pan juices. Remove from the oven and let rest at room temperature for 30 minutes, basting often. To serve, thinly slice the ham and arrange the slices on a platter. Serve hot, warm, or cold.

buttermilk biscuits

makes about 15 large biscuits

Here is my basic buttermilk biscuit recipe—perfect alongside a country ham and essential for many a weekend meal. These biscuits can't be prepared in advance, but with practice they'll go together with ease.

4 cups bleached all-purpose flour (measure by stirring it with a fork, spooning it into dry-
     measure cups and sweeping the tops level)
2 tablespoons baking powder
1¼ teaspoons salt
¾ stick (6 tablespoons) unsalted butter, well chilled and cut into small pieces
⅓ cup solid vegetable shortening, well chilled and cut into small pieces
1½ cups buttermilk, chilled

Position a rack in the upper third of the oven and preheat the oven to 450° F.
    In a large bowl stir together 3¾ cups of the flour, the baking powder, and the salt. Cut in the butter and shortening until the mixture forms bits the size of peas. Stir in

the buttermilk until a rough dough forms. Turn the dough onto a surface floured with the remaining ¼ cup flour and knead about 20 seconds, until the dough just holds together. Roll out the dough ½ inch thick. With a 2½-inch round cutter, form the biscuits. Transfer them to an ungreased baking sheet, spacing them well apart. Gather the scraps into a ball and roll again. Cut out the remaining biscuits and transfer them to the sheet.

Bake the biscuits about 12 minutes, until puffed, crisp, and golden. Serve hot or warm.

•

creamed baby carrots, new potatoes, and sugar snap peas with mint

serves 8

This single side dish takes care of all three of the menu's vegetables in one easy skillet. The potatoes, carrots, and sugar snaps all can be cooked one day ahead. Peeled baby carrots are increasingly available in better produce sections or can even be ordered by mail if you're the determined sort, but regular carrots that have been peeled and cut into ½-inch slices can be substituted.

3 pounds (about 24) small red-skinned potatoes, well scrubbed
Salt
2 pounds baby carrots, trimmed and peeled (see Cook's and Gardener's Sources)
2 pounds sugar snap peas, tipped, stringed if necessary, and cut in half on an angle
3 tablespoons unsalted butter, softened
3 tablespoons unbleached all-purpose flour
1¾ cups Chicken Stock (page 90) or canned broth
1¾ cups whipping cream
Freshly ground white or black pepper
½ cup minced fresh mint

With a vegetable peeler remove a ½-inch-wide band of peel from around the middle of each potato. In a heavy pot cover the potatoes with cold water, stir in 1 tablespoon salt, and set over medium heat. Bring to a boil, then lower the heat and simmer briskly until the potatoes are just tender, about 7 minutes. With a slotted spoon transfer the potatoes to a bowl of ice water. Cool completely and drain thoroughly.

Return the water to a boil. Add the baby carrots and cook, stirring once or twice, until the carrots are just tender, about 4 minutes. With a slotted spoon, transfer the carrots to a bowl of ice water. Cool completely and drain thoroughly.

Return the water to a boil. Add the sugar snaps and cook, stirring once or twice, until they are just tender, about 4 minutes. Drain and transfer immediately to a bowl of ice water. Cool completely and drain thoroughly. *The vegetables can be prepared to this point 1 day ahead. Wrap separately and refrigerate.*

In a small bowl thoroughly mash together the butter and flour. In a wide, deep skillet over low heat, combine the potatoes, the chicken stock, the cream, and ½ teaspoon salt. Bring to a simmer. Add the carrots and sugar snaps and simmer another 1 to 2 minutes, until heated through. Whisk in the butter mixture and a generous grinding of pepper and simmer until thick, 1 to 2 minutes. Adjust the seasoning, remove from the heat, and stir in the mint. Let stand, covered, for 1 minute before serving.

●

strawberry-rhubarb crumble

serves 8

A classic pairing of seasonal red fruits, baked under a buttery crunch of brown sugar, almonds, and oats, this juicy crumble is the perfect conclusion to a big spring dinner. Serve it slightly warm, drizzled with a bit of heavy cream.

TOPPING

1 cup unbleached all-purpose flour
⅓ cup (about 3 ounces) unblanched whole almonds
½ cup old-fashioned rolled oats
1 teaspoon ground allspice
1½ sticks (6 ounces) unsalted butter, well chilled and cut into small pieces

FILLING

3 pints strawberries, rinsed if necessary, hulled and halved
6 cups diced (¼ inch) rhubarb
1½ cups sugar
⅔ cup unbleached all-purpose flour
2 teaspoons ground allspice
1 tablespoon Vanilla Rum (page 66) or vanilla extract

Whipping cream, for serving

For the topping   In a food processor, in the order listed, combine the flour, almonds, oats, allspice, and butter. Process about 45 seconds, until a lumpy dough forms. Transfer the topping to a bowl, cover, and refrigerate. *The topping can be prepared up to 1 day ahead.*

For the filling   In a large bowl combine the strawberries, rhubarb, sugar, flour, allspice, and vanilla rum; let stand at room temperature until juicy, about 30 minutes.

Position a rack in the middle of the oven and preheat the oven to 375° F.

Spoon the filling evenly into a shallow baking dish, such as a 9- by 13-inch oval gratin. With a fork, coarsely crumble the chilled topping and sprinkle it evenly over the filling. Set the pan on the rack and bake until the topping is browned and the filling is bubbling, about 40 minutes. Serve hot or warm, accompanied by whipping cream if desired.

l e f t  v e r s

The crab mayonnaise can be used as a very rich sandwich filling, should there be any left. The country ham will provide the basis for many meals, both as a main course or used as an ingredient in appetizers, salads, pastas, and so on. The creamed vegetables will reheat to provide a homey side dish for a lunch or supper. The crumble is delicious cold, for breakfast or whenever. Try it topped with a dollop of plain yogurt.

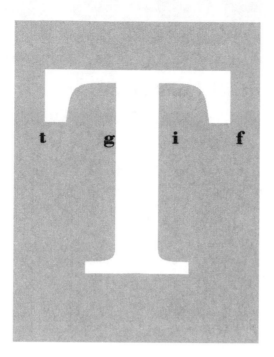

●

bow ties with sausage, tomatoes, and cream

serves 4

Penne, rotelle, or medium-sized pasta shells will also be good in this recipe. The nubbly pink sauce is rich but enlivened by a generous dose of dried red pepper. Minced fresh basil, should you have it, is a colorful and tasty substitution for the parsley.

2 tablespoons olive oil
1 pound sweet Italian sausage with fennel seed, casings removed, crumbled
½ teaspoon crushed dried red pepper
½ cup diced yellow onions
3 medium garlic cloves, peeled and minced
1 can (28 ounces) Italian-style plum tomatoes, drained and chopped
1½ cups whipping, or heavy, cream
Salt
12 ounces dried semolina pasta bow ties (*farfalle*), preferably imported
¼ cup minced wide-leaf parsley
Freshly grated Parmesan cheese, for serving

In a large skillet heat the oil over medium heat. Add the sausage and red pepper; cook, breaking the meat up with a spoon, until it is no longer pink, about 7 minutes. Add the onions and garlic, and cook, stirring occasionally, until the onion is tender and the sausage is lightly browned, about 7 minutes. Add the tomatoes, the cream, and ½ teaspoon salt. Lower the heat slightly and simmer until the mixture thickens, about 4 minutes. *The recipe can be prepared to this point 1 day ahead and refrigerated. Reheat just until simmering before proceeding.*

Bring a large pot of water to a boil. Stir in the pasta and 1 tablespoon salt. Cook, uncovered, stirring occasionally, until the pasta is just tender, 8 to 10 minutes. Drain well.

Stir the pasta into the sauce and cook, stirring once or twice, until the pasta is heated through and has absorbed some of the sauce, about 2 minutes. Stir in the parsley and serve, passing the grated cheese at the table.

country pâté and lentil salad
with basil dressing

serves 6

This salad combines basil-and-garlic–zapped lentils with chunks of rich and flavorful country terrine, served up with prime tomatoes on a bed of assorted greenery. Good—even excellent—commercial pâtés are widely available, and you should not hesitate to take advantage of their convenience (cubed smoked turkey breast can be substituted). Note that the lentils require no soaking and cook in about 20 minutes. Crusty bread, a cool pink or white wine, and fresh fruit will complete this Friday-night feast.

1 pound dried brown lentils, picked over
Salt
2 cups packed fresh basil leaves, plus fresh basil sprigs for garnish
3 medium garlic cloves, peeled
⅓ cup red wine vinegar
⅔ cup olive oil
½ cup diced red onions
Freshly ground black pepper
1 pound *pâté de campagne,* well chilled, fat trimmed, cut into 1-inch cubes
2 medium bunches watercress, tough stems trimmed, rinsed, spun dry, and torn into bite-sized pieces
1 large bunch arugula, tough stems trimmed, rinsed, spun dry, and torn into bite-sized pieces
3 ripe large tomatoes, cut into wedges

Rinse the lentils under running water. Over high heat bring a medium saucepan of water to a boil. Stir in the lentils and 2 teaspoons salt. Lower the heat and simmer, partially covered, until the lentils are just tender, about 20 minutes. Drain.

Meanwhile, in a food processor combine the basil leaves, the garlic, the vinegar, the oil, and 2 teaspoons salt. Process until smooth.

Transfer the hot lentils to a large bowl. Immediately pour the dressing over the lentils and toss well; cool to room temperature. Stir in the onions and season generously with pepper. *The salad can be prepared to this point 1 day ahead; refrigerate, covered. Return it to room temperature before proceeding.*

Gently fold the chilled cubes of pâté into the lentils. Adjust the seasoning. Line 6 plates with the watercress and arugula. Mound the salad on the plates and top with the tomato wedges. Garnish with basil sprigs and serve immediately.

grilled vegetable salad with mozzarella

<u>serves 6</u>

This recipe is here to refute my reputation as the "pork chop king." I do love red meat, but it's not all I eat, and when I'm taking a break from pork chops this light, beautiful, and very satisfying grilled vegetable and fresh mozzarella salad, napped with a smoked jalapeño vinaigrette, is often on the menu.

2 cups aromatic wood smoking chips, such as mesquite or hickory (see Cook's and Gardener's Sources)

18 small red-skinned potatoes (about 2 pounds), well scrubbed

1 tablespoon salt

3 large, meaty sweet red peppers, preferably Dutch, trimmed and quartered

3 medium zucchini, scrubbed, trimmed, and quartered lengthwise

3 medium yellow squash, scrubbed, trimmed, and quartered lengthwise

18 large green onions, trimmed

½ cup olive oil

Coarse (kosher) salt

6 thick slices crusty country-style bread

1½ pounds fresh mozzarella, sliced thick, at room temperature (see Cook's and Gardener's Sources)

Chipotle Vinaigrette (recipe follows)

Soak the wood chips in water for 30 minutes. In a pan cover the potatoes with cold water. Stir in 1 tablespoon salt, set over medium heat, and bring to a boil. Lower the heat slightly and cook until the potatoes are just tender, about 9 minutes. Drain.

Prepare a charcoal fire and let it burn until the coals are evenly white, or preheat a gas grill (medium-high heat). Drain the wood chips and scatter them over the coals or grill stones. Position the grill rack about 6 inches above the heat source. Brush the potatoes, peppers, zucchini, squash, and green onions with half of the olive oil. When the wood chips are smoking, arrange the vegetables on the grill rack, cover, and cook, turning them once, until they are lightly browned and just tender, 3 to 4 minutes per side. Transfer the vegetables to a platter and season to taste with coarse salt. Brush the bread slices with the remaining olive oil and grill, turning them once, until crisp and lightly browned, 3 to 4 minutes per side.

Arrange the mozzarella, grilled vegetables, and grilled bread on serving plates. Nap the salads with some of the chipotle vinaigrette and serve immediately, passing the remaining vinaigrette at the table.

chipotle vinaigrette

makes about 1 cup

Use the Embassa brand of canned chipotles (see Cook's and Gardener's Sources) if you can. The fiery adobo, or thick paste, in which they are packed is very flavorful and will help to thicken the vinaigrette.

3 tablespoons white wine vinegar
2 canned chipotles, stemmed and minced, plus 1 to 2 tablespoons of the adobo in which
    they are packed
2 egg yolks, at room temperature
1 tablespoon Dijon-style mustard
½ teaspoon salt
1 cup olive oil

In a medium bowl whisk together the vinegar, the chipotles, their adobo, the egg yolks, the mustard, and the salt. Continue to whisk while slowly dribbling in the olive oil; the dressing will thicken. Adjust the seasoning. *The dressing can be prepared up to 1 hour ahead. Rewhisk if necessary before serving.*

•

orecchiette baked with olives, vegetables, and mozzarella

serves 4

Orecchiette—ear-shaped pasta—are fun to eat, but this simple, colorful main-course pasta can also be prepared using ziti, rigatoni, or short fusilli. Francine the Caterer, a remarkably carnivorous person, adds to this dish one pound of sweet Italian sausage that has been crumbled and browned in a skillet. Serve the pasta on the same plate with 10 cups Basic Mixed Green Salad (page 23), including romaine and arugula and dressed with olive oil and balsamic vinegar.

3 tablespoons olive oil
2 medium zucchini, scrubbed, trimmed, and cut into ½-inch cubes
Salt
Freshly ground black pepper
8 ounces dried semolina *orecchiette* pasta, preferably imported
1 cup imported brine-cured black olives, such as Kalamata, pitted and chopped
4 firm, ripe plum tomatoes, halved and diced
1 cup grated Parmesan cheese
8 ounces whole-milk mozzarella, preferably fresh (see Cook's and Gardener's Sources), cut into ½-inch dice, at room temperature

In a large skillet, preferably nonstick, heat the olive oil over medium-high heat. Add the zucchini and cook, stirring occasionally, until lightly browned, about 5 minutes. Season with ½ teaspoon salt and ¼ teaspoon pepper. Using a slotted spoon, transfer the zucchini to a large bowl.

Bring a large pot of water to a boil. Stir in 1 tablespoon salt and the pasta; cook, stirring once or twice, until the pasta is tender but firm, about 10 minutes. Drain well and transfer to the bowl with the zucchini.

Position a rack in the upper third of the oven and preheat the oven to 375° F. Lightly oil a shallow baking dish, such as a 9- by 13-inch oval gratin. Stir the olives, the tomatoes, and ½ cup of the Parmesan cheese into the zucchini-pasta mixture. Season generously with freshly ground black pepper and spoon the mixture into the prepared pan. Scatter the mozzarella evenly over the pasta.

Bake until the cheese is melted and the pasta is heated through, 10 to 12 minutes. Serve immediately and pass the remaining ½ cup Parmesan cheese at the table.

orecchiette with mushrooms, gorgonzola, watercress, and walnuts

serves 4

What began as an improvisational clean-out-the-fridge supper (the kind that is frequently more filling than inspired) turned out to be a happy plate of food so good I repeat it often—and not just on Friday. This pasta does not require the addition of grated Parmesan cheese.

10 ounces *orecchiette* or other disk-shaped dried semolina pasta, preferably imported
Salt
½ stick (4 tablespoons) unsalted butter
¼ cup minced shallots
10 to 12 ounces cremini, porcini, or shiitake mushrooms, wiped clean, trimmed, and quartered (shiitake stems discarded)
⅓ pound Gorgonzola *dolcelatte,* rind trimmed, cheese cut into small pieces
1 bunch watercress, rinsed, spun dry, tough stems trimmed, and coarsely chopped (about 4 loosely packed cups)
⅓ cup chopped walnuts

Bring a large pot of water to a boil. Stir in the pasta and 1 tablespoon salt. Cook, uncovered, stirring occasionally, until the pasta is just tender, 8 to 10 minutes. Drain well.

Meanwhile, in a large skillet over low heat, melt the butter. Add the shallots, cover, and cook, stirring once or twice, for 5 minutes. Stir in the mushrooms, season with ½ teaspoon salt, and cook, covered, stirring once or twice, until the mushrooms have rendered their juices and are just tender, about 10 minutes. Remove from the heat and stir in the Gorgonzola.

Add the pasta and watercress to the mushroom mixture; toss gently. Cover and let stand for 1 minute. Divide the pasta among plates and sprinkle with walnuts. Serve immediately and pass the peppermill at the table.

•

tortellini with peas and prosciutto

serves 4

Tortellini—like chocolate—is a word that signals instant comfort and bliss. Home-made tortellini are a culinary wonder; the store-bought kind are wonderful in another way—as the convenient conclusion to a busy day. Wonderful tortellini is never more wonderful than when sauced with this classic amalgam of cream, Parmesan cheese, prosciutto, and peas.

1 pound fresh cheese tortellini
Salt
1½ cups whipping cream
Pinch of freshly grated nutmeg
6 tablespoons freshly grated Parmesan cheese
¾ cup frozen tiny peas, thawed and drained
1½ ounces sliced prosciutto, fat trimmed, julienned
Freshly ground black pepper

Bring a large pot of water to a boil. Stir in the pasta and 1 tablespoon salt. Cook, uncovered, stirring occasionally, until the pasta is barely tender, 8 to 10 minutes (it will cook further in the sauce). Drain well.

Meanwhile, in a small heavy saucepan over medium heat, bring the whipping cream to a boil. Lower the heat, stir in the nutmeg, and simmer briskly, uncovered, until slightly thickened, 8 to 10 minutes. Remove from the heat and whisk in the Parmesan cheese.

Return the tortellini to the pasta pot. Add the warm cream mixture, the peas, and the prosciutto, set over low heat, and simmer, stirring gently once or twice, until the tortellini are tender, about 4 minutes. Season generously with fresh pepper and add salt if necessary. Serve immediately.

linguine puttanesca

serves 4

Who were the ladies of easy virtue who gave title to this Italian classic? Prostitutes possibly, stirring up a quick meal before rushing off to more urgent business? Or were they respectable housewives, hurrying home from their afternoon liaisons, and anxious to offer a dish so flavorful their husbands would think it had been simmering, well attended, all day?

I honor them all, for the dish is both urgently quick and remarkably flavorful, and indeed tastes as if hours of work had gone into it. Only you will know the truth. The sauce is—naturally—spicy; adjust the amount of crushed red pepper to suit your palate.

¼ cup olive oil
½ cup diced yellow onions
4 garlic cloves, peeled and sliced
½ teaspoon crushed dried red pepper
2 cups canned crushed tomatoes
Salt
10 ounces dried semolina linguine, preferably imported
10 imported brine-cured black olives, such as Kalamata, pitted and coarsely chopped
6 oil-packed anchovy fillets, drained and coarsely chopped
2 tablespoons small (nonpareil) capers, drained
Grated Parmesan cheese, for serving

In a large skillet warm the olive oil over medium heat. Add the onions, garlic, and dried pepper; cook, uncovered, stirring once or twice, until the garlic is lightly colored, about 5 minutes. Add the tomatoes and ½ teaspoon salt, cover the skillet, and simmer, stirring once or twice, for 15 minutes.

Meanwhile, bring a large pot of water to a boil. Stir in 1 tablespoon salt, add the linguine, and cook until just tender, about 10 minutes. Drain thoroughly.

Stir the olives, anchovies, and capers into the sauce and raise the heat to medium-high. Add the linguine and simmer, tossing and stirring, until the pasta has absorbed most of the sauce, 2 to 3 minutes. Serve immediately and pass the grated cheese at the table.

spaghettini with seafood, sun-dried tomatoes, and lemon

serves 4

One reason restaurants like serving pasta dishes (aside from the splendid markups possible) is the speed with which many of them come together. While customer turnover is probably not a priority at your house, speed can still be a useful thing when there are hungry people needing to eat in a hurry. Enjoy this seafood pasta as an Italian would, without adding any Parmesan cheese.

12 ounces dried semolina spaghettini, preferably imported
Salt
4 tablespoons olive oil
3 tablespoons unsalted butter
5 medium garlic cloves, peeled and minced
⅔ pound medium shrimp, shelled and deveined
⅔ pound sea scallops
1 cup Fish Stock (page 91)
½ cup diced oil-packed sun-dried tomatoes, homemade (page 46) or purchased (see Cook's and Gardener's Sources)
⅓ cup minced wide-leaf parsley
Zest of 2 lemons, finely julienned
Freshly ground black pepper

Bring a large pot of water to a boil. Add the pasta and 1 tablespoon salt and cook, uncovered, stirring once or twice, until the pasta is barely tender, about 6 minutes. Drain well; toss with 1 tablespoon of the olive oil.

In a large skillet melt the butter with the remaining 3 tablespoons olive oil over low heat. Add the garlic and cook, stirring once or twice, for 3 minutes. Raise the heat to medium-high, add the shrimp and scallops, and cook, tossing and stirring, until the shrimp are pink, curled, and almost cooked through, 3 or 4 minutes.

Stir in the fish stock and pasta. Raise the heat to high and cook, tossing and stirring, until the pasta has absorbed most of the liquid and all of the ingredients are heated through, about 3 minutes. Add the sun-dried tomatoes, parsley, and lemon zest, season generously to taste with pepper, add additional salt to taste, and toss thoroughly. Serve immediately.

moist-baked halibut with smoked-salmon—
dill butter

serves 4

Halibut is a glorious fish that comes into its own in late spring, when on both the West and East coasts good weather signals the beginning of the abundant harvest. Oven poaching the fish surrounded by a bit of liquid keeps it tender and moist; a delicate topping of pink-and-green salmon-dill butter adds gloss, color, and flavor. Serve the halibut with tender asparagus and steamed new potatoes.

DILL BUTTER

1 stick (4 ounces) unsalted butter, softened
1½ ounces good-quality smoked salmon, minced
3 tablespoons minced fresh dill
Freshly ground black pepper

4 thick (1 inch) halibut steaks (1½ to 2 pounds)
½ cup dry white wine
Salt
Freshly ground black pepper

In a small bowl cream together the butter, the salmon, the dill, and ¼ teaspoon pepper. Taste and adjust the seasoning. *The butter can be prepared ahead and refrigerated up to 3 days or frozen up to 1 month. Return the butter to room temperature before using.*

Position a rack in the lower third of the oven and preheat the oven to 400° F.

Arrange the halibut steaks in a shallow nonreactive baking dish just large enough to hold them in a single layer. Pour the wine over the fish and add enough water to bring the level of liquid halfway up the sides of the fish. Sprinkle lightly with salt and pepper and bake 8 to 10 minutes, until the fish just begins to flake.

Transfer the halibut to plates and top each steak with a generous dollop of the smoked-salmon butter. Serve immediately.

●

grilled swordfish steaks with mixed
tomato salad

serves 4

Thick and smoky steaks of grilled fish make one of the speediest end-of-the-week suppers I know. Round out the menu with some good goat's-milk or sheep's-milk cheese, crusty bread for swabbing up the last of the tomato juices, a green salad, and fresh fruit, with or without a little heavy cream as you see fit.

Tomatoes grow in a rainbow of colors—red, yellow, orange, white, miltihued, striped, even green when fully ripe (look for Evergreen or Green Grape varieties; see Cook's and Gardener's Sources). While the salad looks and tastes best when the widest variety of tomato colors and shapes is used, a single type—as long as it is perfectly ripe—will also make great eating. Tuna or shark can be substituted for the swordfish.

About 2 pounds assorted tomatoes, such as cherry, yellow plum, Italian plum, beefsteak, and/or ripe green
3 tablespoons balsamic vinegar
6 tablespoons olive oil
2 garlic cloves, peeled and crushed through a garlic press
1½ cups aromatic wood smoking chips, such as mesquite or applewood (see Cook's and Gardener's Sources)
½ cup minced fresh basil, plus fresh basil sprigs for garnish
½ teaspoon salt
½ teaspoon freshly ground black pepper
4 thick (1 inch) swordfish steaks (1½ to 2 pounds)

Rinse and trim the tomatoes, then cut them into 1-inch chunks. There should be about 5 cups. In a bowl combine the tomatoes, the vinegar, 3 tablespoons of the olive oil, and the garlic. Cover and let stand at room temperature for about 1 hour. Soak the wood chips in water for 30 minutes.

Prepare a charcoal fire and let it burn down until the coals are evenly white or preheat a gas grill (medium-high heat).

Stir the basil, salt, and pepper into the tomato salad. Drain the wood chips and scatter them over the coals or grill stones. Position the grill rack about 6 inches above the heat source. Brush the swordfish steaks with the remaining 3 tablespoons olive oil and when the wood chips are smoking, lay the steaks on the grill. Cover and cook, turning once, until just done, 3 to 4 minutes per side.

Transfer the steaks to plates. Divide the tomato salad and its juices evenly over the swordfish, garnish with basil sprigs if desired, and serve immediately.

pork scaloppine with rosemary, lemon, and olives

serves 4

The scaloppine are cut from the tenderloin and flattened with a meat pounder or the flat bottom of a small, heavy pan. Like veal scaloppine, they are elegant and ready in mere minutes, and you may sauce them with any number of flavorful possibilities. The recipe suggests fresh rosemary, but you may substitute fresh (but not dried) thyme, oregano, marjoram, or basil, and you could replace the lemon zest with orange zest. Accompany the scaloppine with plain buttered pasta and follow with a green salad.

2 pork tenderloins (about 1½ pounds total)
⅓ cup unbleached all-purpose flour
½ teaspoon salt
¼ teaspoon freshly ground black pepper
4 tablespoons (about) olive oil
3 garlic cloves, peeled and minced
1 tablespoon minced fresh rosemary
¼ cup dry white wine
½ cup Chicken Stock (page 90) or canned broth
3 ripe plum tomatoes, trimmed, seeded, and cut into ¼-inch dice
16 Niçoise olives, rinsed and drained
Zest of 1 medium lemon, removed in strips with a citrus zester

Beginning at the thick end, cut each tenderloin crosswise into six ½-inch slices (reserve the tapered ends for another use). Between sheets of waxed paper, flatten each slice of tenderloin into a 3-inch oval about ¼ inch thick.

On a plate mix together the flour, salt, and pepper. In a large skillet warm 2 tablespoons of the oil over medium-high heat. Coat the pork with the seasoned flour and shake off the excess. Add half of the pork to the hot oil and cook, turning once, until lightly colored, about 4 minutes per side. Transfer the browned scaloppine to a plate and keep warm. Repeat with the remaining scaloppine, adding additional oil to the pan between batches if necessary to prevent sticking.

Turn the heat under the skillet to low. Add the garlic and rosemary and cook, stirring often to keep the garlic from browning, for 3 minutes. Stir in the wine and raise the heat to high. Cook, stirring and scraping the pan well, until the wine has evaporated, about 1 minute.

Stir in the stock, raise the heat to high, and bring to a boil. Cook, stirring, until the stock is reduced by half, about 2 minutes. Stir in the tomatoes, olives, and lemon zest, bring to a boil, and cook until heated through, about 30 seconds. Taste and adjust the seasoning.

Arrange the scaloppine on plates and spoon the sauce over them. Serve immediately.

●

pork chops with peppery bourbon-maple pan gravy

serves 4

OK—*one* pork chop recipe. A heavy skillet with a tight-fitting lid is the key to successful top-of-the-stove pork chop cookery. Order super-thick (1½-inch) chops and slow-simmer them with a bit of flavorful moisture. The maple-pepper pairing was suggested by the cure used on a country ham I once enjoyed. Bourbon was in the air at the time, and in my glass (though not actually in the ham itself), and so in the dish below I've used all three elements with tasty results. Serve the chops with Mashed Sweets (page 128) and blanched Brussels sprouts that have been glazed with hot butter.

4 thick (1½-inch) pork loin chops (about 10 ounces each)
Salt
⅓ cup unbleached all-purpose flour
2 tablespoons corn oil
¾ cup Chicken Stock (page 90) or canned broth
6 tablespoons bourbon
4½ tablespoons genuine maple syrup (see Cook's and Gardener's Sources)
1 cup crème fraîche, homemade (page 217) or purchased, or whipping cream
1 teaspoon freshly ground black pepper

Season the chops lightly on both sides with salt. Put the flour in a shallow dish (like a pie plate) and coat the chops in the flour, shaking off the excess.

In a large heavy skillet warm the oil over medium-high heat. Add the chops and brown well, turning them once, about 4 minutes per side. Transfer the chops to a plate. Discard the oil but do not clean the skillet.

Add the stock, bourbon, and maple syrup to the skillet. Set it over medium heat and bring the liquid to a boil, scraping any browned bits from the bottom of the pan. Return the chops to the skillet, lower the heat, and cover tightly. Simmer the chops, turning them once, until just cooked through, about 20 minutes.

Transfer the chops to a platter and keep warm. Set the skillet over high heat, bring to a boil, and cook until the pan juices are syrupy, about 4 minutes. Whisk in the crème fraîche and pepper and bring to a boil. Cook, stirring, until the gravy thickens, about 4 minutes. Adjust the seasoning, spoon the gravy over the chops, and serve immediately.

grilled veal chops smothered with tomato, mint, and watercress salad

serves 4

A smoky, juicy grilled veal chop, hidden under a mound of cool, tart green salad, is a Manhattan trattoria staple. Teachers of authentic Italian cooking grouse about this dish, saying there is no such practice in Italy, but in Manhattan (virtually an island off the coast of Italy these days) it's wildly popular no matter what its provenance. Accompany the chops with good bread (toasted on the grill or not, as you wish) and pour a decent Barbera d'Alba. Dessert, if you're sticking with the Manhattan trattoria theme, should be Tiramisù (page 267). Offer grappa and espresso afterward. The recipe can also be prepared with thick pork chops, arugula can be added to the salad along with the watercress, and basil can be substituted for the mint.

½ cup olive oil
4 tablespoons red wine vinegar
5 garlic cloves, peeled and minced
4 thick (1½-inch) veal loin or rib chops (about 10 ounces each)
1½ cups aromatic wood smoking chips, such as mesquite or grapevine (see Cook's and Gardener's Sources)
1 large bunch watercress, tough stems trimmed, rinsed, and spun dry
2 ripe medium tomatoes, seeded and coarsely chopped
⅓ cup minced fresh mint
Salt
Freshly ground black pepper

In a small bowl whisk together ¼ cup of the olive oil, 2 tablespoons of the vinegar, and half the garlic. In a shallow nonreactive dish pour the marinade over the veal chops and let stand at room temperature, covered, turning occasionally, for 1 hour. Soak the wood chips in water for 30 minutes.

Light a charcoal fire and let it burn until the coals are evenly white or preheat a gas grill (medium-high heat). Drain the wood chips and scatter them over the coals or grill stones. Position a rack about 6 inches above the heat source. Remove the chops from the marinade, and when the wood chips are smoking, lay the chops on the grill. Cover and cook, turning the chops once, until browned and almost cooked through but still pink and juicy at the center, about 8 minutes per side.

Meanwhile, in a large bowl toss together the watercress, tomatoes, and mint. In a small bowl whisk together the remaining ¼ cup olive oil, 2 tablespoons vinegar, and the garlic. Whisk in ½ teaspoon each salt and pepper.

Transfer the chops to plates and season with a sprinkle of salt and a grind of pepper. Pour the dressing over the salad and toss. Spoon the salad and any dressing or juices in the bowl evenly over the chops and serve immediately.

●

pan-grilled lamb steaks with sun-dried tomato and green olive butter

serves 4

I store a triple batch of the colorful compound butter in the freezer and often melt a thick pat of it over grilled or poached chicken or fish as well as the lamb steaks below. The steaks are center-cut sections from a leg of lamb and are sometimes offered as a special or can be ordered from the butcher. I use a heavy ridged cast-iron grill pan that sits over two burners, but the steaks also can be cooked under the broiler or grilled outdoors. Serve the lamb with buttered orzo (rice-shaped pasta) and a green salad or a steamed green vegetable, such as broccoli.

½ stick (4 tablespoons) unsalted butter, softened
4 large oil-packed sun-dried tomato halves, homemade (page 46) or purchased (see Cook's and Gardener's Sources), chopped
3 large green olives, preferably imported, pitted and chopped
½ teaspoon freshly ground black pepper
2 center-cut lamb leg steaks (1½ inches thick and 1 pound each), at room temperature
3 tablespoons olive oil
¼ teaspoon salt

In a small bowl mash together the butter, sun-dried tomatoes, olives, and pepper. Form the butter into a cylinder about 2 inches long and wrap it in plastic wrap. *The wrapped butter can be refrigerated up to 1 week or frozen up to 3 months. Return to room temperature before use.*

Set a ridged metal grill pan or heavy cast-iron skillet over high heat. Brush both sides of the lamb steaks with the olive oil. Lay the steaks on the grill pan. Sear the steaks on each side for 3 minutes, then lower the heat and cook another 4 minutes per side for medium-rare.

Transfer the steaks to a cutting board. Cut the steaks in half, discarding the center bone. Season with the salt. Top each steak with a pat of the compound butter and serve immediately.

cook's

and

gardener's

sources

The following sources are recommended for some of the more difficult to locate but still essential ingredients, vegetable seeds, and equipment called for in this book. In addition to the various catalogues and other specialty suppliers, one source—Dean & DeLuca—offers personal shopping, whereby virtually anything in the store, in any amount (half pound of this, jar of that), is available—for a price, of course. Express shipping allows even the most perishable of goods to arrive in excellent condition.

1. Dean & DeLuca
560 Broadway
New York, NY 10012
800-221-7714
In New York State,
212-431-1691

2. Balducci's
11-02 Queens Plaza South
Long Island City, NY 11101-4908
800-225-3822
212-673-2600

3. Williams-Sonoma
P.O. Box 7456
San Francisco. CA 94120-7456
800-541-2233

4. Sunnyland Farms, Inc.
P.O. Box 8200
Albany, GA 31706-8200
912-883-3985

5. Earthy Delights
618 N. Seymour Street
Lansing, MI 48933
800-367-4709
In Michigan,
517-371-2411

6. The Mozzarella Company
2944 Elm Street
Dallas, TX 75226
800-798-2954 or
214-741-4072

7. Santa Cruz Chile and Spice Co.
P.O. Box 177
Tumacacori, AZ 85640
602-398-2591

8. Embassa Foods
1048 Burgrove Road
Carson, CA 90746
213-537-1200

9. D'Artagnan, Inc.
399-419 St. Paul Avenue
Jersey City, NJ 07306
800-327-8246
In New Jersey,
201-792-0748

10. Burger's Smokehouse
RFD 3 Box 126
Highway 87 South
California, MO 65018-9903
314-796-4111

11. Early's Honey Stand
P.O. Box K
Spring Hill, TN 37174-0911
800-523-2105

12. Aidell's Sausage Company
1575 Minnesota Street
San Francisco, CA 94107
415-285-6660

13. Neuske-Hillcrest Farm Meats
Highways 29 and 45
Wittenberg, WI 54499
800-382-2266

14. Boyajian, Inc.
33 Belmont Street
Cambridge, MA 02138
617-876-5400

15. Chukar Cherry Company
306 Wine Country Road
P.O. Box 510
Prosser, WA 99350
800-624-9544
In Washington State,
509-786-2055

16. Community Kitchens
P.O. Box 2311
Baton Rouge, LA 70821-2311
800-535-9901

17. New England Cheesemaking
Supply Company
85 Main Street
Ashfield, MA 01330
413-628-3808

18. Lawrence Curry
P.O. Box 5721
Burlington, VT 05402-5721

19. Hoppin' John's
30 Pinckney Street
Charleston, SC 29401

20. McNulty's Tea & Coffee, Inc.
109 Christopher Street
New York, NY 10014
800-356-5200
In New York State,
212-242-5351

21. Starbucks Coffee Company
2203 Airport Way South
Seattle, WA 98134

22. The Coffee Connection
342 Western Avenue
Brighton, MA 02135

23. The Grill Lover's Catalog
P.O. Box 1300
Columbus, GA 31993-2499
800-252-8248

24. The Cook's Garden
P.O. Box 65
Londonderry, VT 05148
800-824-3400

25. Shepherd's Garden Seeds
30 Irene Street
Torrington, CT 06790
203-482-3638 or
408-335-6910

26. Seeds Blum
Idaho City Stage
Boise, ID 83706
208-342-0858

27. Le Marche Seeds International
Box 190
Dixon, CA 95620
916-678-9244

28. Crowley Cheese
Healdville Road
Healdville, VT
802-259-2340

29. The Charcoal Companion
7955 Edgewater Drive
Oakland, CA 94621
800-521-0505
In California,
510-632-2100

30. Broadway Panhandler
520 Broadway
New York, NY 10012
212-966-3434

31. Chef's Catalog
3215 Commercial Avenue
Northbrook, IL 60062-1900
800-338-3232

32. Bridge Kitchenware
214 E. 52nd Street
New York, NY 10022
212-688-4220

ingredients, vegetable seeds,

and equipment

COOK'S
AND
GARDENER'S
SOURCES

•

321

(Numbers following items indicate the mail order sources, above, that carry that product.)

Andouille sausage   1, 2, 12, 16
Arborio rice   1, 2
Black walnuts   2, 4
Bocconcini   2
Bread- or pizza-baking stones   3
Butter muslin   17
Caviar   1, 2, 14
Champagne vinegar   1, 2
Chipotle chiles   1, 8
Coeur à la crème molds   1, 17
Coffee   1, 2, 16, 20, 21
Colby cheese   28
Country ham   1, 2, 10, 11, 19
Crystallized ginger   1, 2
Curry powder   1, 2, 18
Dried cherries, cranberries, and other fruit   1, 2, 15
Electric water smokers   3
Fiddlehead ferns   1, 2, 5
Fromage blanc starter   17
Hazelnut oil   1, 2
Irish oatmeal   1, 2, 3
Key lime juice   1, 2, 3
Magret   1, 2, 9
Maple syrup   1, 2, 3
Mascarpone   1, 2
Old Bay Seasoning   1, 2
Omelet pans   3, 30, 31
Pizza- or bread-baking stones   3, 30, 31
Poblano chiles   1, 2
Porcini mushrooms, dried   1, 2
Potato curler   16
Powdered chiles   7
Pudding mold   1, 3
Pumate (sun-dried tomato) oil   1

Rabbit   *1, 2, 9*

Römertopf clay baker   *3, 31*

Rose flower water   *1, 2, 3*

Salad spinner, rotary   *3, 16*

Savoiardi   *1, 2*

Scrapers, heat-resistant, for omelet making   *1, 16*

Seeds for tomatoes and salad greens   *23, 24, 25, 26*

Smoked salmon   *1, 2, 14*

Smokehouse bacon   *1, 2, 3, 10, 11, 13, 16*

Square flan form   *32*

Sun-dried tomatoes (pumate)   *1*

Tapenade (olivada)   *1, 2*

Wood chips for smoking and grilling   *2, 3, 22, 29*

index

Adobo, Honey-Orange, 241
Aioli, Green, 77
Almond-Cherry Granola, 287
Amaretto-and-Wine-Poached Dried Fruit
 Compote, 43
Antipasto Platter, Al Forno-style, 72
Appetizers and first courses:
 Antipasto Platter, Al Forno–style, 72
 Asparagus with Crab Mayonnaise, 296
 Black Olives with Orange and Basil, 73
 Confetti Deviled Eggs, 103
 Country Ham, Sweet Potato, and Green
  Onion Beignets, 118
 Crab-and-Prosciutto-Stuffed Mushrooms,
  249
 Creamed Fiddlehead Ferns and Mushrooms
  on Toast, 161
 Deep-Fried Ravioli with Red Pepper May-
  onnaise, 111
 Florence Fabricant's Crostini with Two
  Spreads, 125
 Mixed Seafood Fry with Green Aioli, 133
 Oven-baked Asparagus with Green Sauce,
  157
 Shrimp, Leek, and Dill Spread, 289
 Tomato Bruschetta, 265
 see also Salads, first-course
Apple:
 Cranberry Deep-Dish Pie, 273
 Cranberry, and Sour Cream Cake with
  Black Walnuts, 56
 Orange, and Cranberry Compote, 207
 Scrapple, 184
Applewood-Smoked Turkey Breast, 38
Asparagus:
 Bacon, and Ricotta Tart, 219
 with Crab Mayonnaise, 296
 Oven-Baked, with Green Sauce, 157
 Risotto with Porcini, Basil and, 73

Baja Breezes, 199
Ball-Park Hot Dogs, 257
Barbecue Vinaigrette, 229
Barley, Corn, and Bacon Casserole, 235
Basil:
 Blackberry Vinegar, 238
 Buttermilk Fried Chicken, 104
 Green Sauce, 157
 Polenta with Last of the, 251

Bean(s):
 Black, Corn, Tomato, and Poblano Chile
  Salad, 242
 Black, Spicy Sausage, and Pepper Cal-
  zones, 58
 Pinto, Fritters with Goat-Cheese Cream and
  Salsa, 200
 soaking, 33
 Tiny Green, with Dill Vinaigrette, 177
 see also White Bean(s)
Béchamel, Parslied Garlic, 115
Beef:
 Braised Chile, Tacos with Corn and Olives,
  62
 Stadium Chili, 259
Beer-Braised Sauerkraut with Caraway Seeds,
 261
Beets:
 Salad with Cucumbers, Feta, Dill and, 112
 Tarragon Mustard Slaw, 55
Beignets, Country Ham, Sweet Potato, and
 Green Onion, 118
Berry Picker's Pie à la Mode, 107
Beverages:
 Baja Breezes, 199
 Cappuccino Coolers, 171
 Coffee, 173–74
 Fragrant Iced Tea, 294
 Fresh Limeade Plus!, 64
 Kir Royale, 222
 Lemon Bloody Marys, 211
 Lemon Vodka, 213
 Rum-Spiced Cider, 184
Biscotti, Hazelnut, 44
Biscuits, Buttermilk, 297
Black Bean:
 Corn, Tomato, and Poblano Chile Salad,
  242
 Spicy Sausage, and Pepper Calzones, 58
Blackberry:
 Basil Vinegar, 238
 Corn-Muffin Cake, Kitchen-Counter, 109
 Sauce, 96
Black-eyed Pea Salad with Cilantro-Orange
 Dressing, 63
Bloody Marys, Lemon, 211
Blueberry(ies):
 Lime Sauce, Peaches and Ice Cream with,
  22

Blueberry(ies) (*cont.*)
    Red, White and, 231
    Three-B Flapjacks, 181
Bocconcini, Green Salad with Prosciutto-
        Wrapped Pears and, 40
Bourbon:
    Black-Walnut Cake, Lemon-Glazed, 196
    Brown-Sugar Ice Cream, 282
    Fruitcakes, 269
Bow Ties with Sausage, Tomatoes, and
        Cream, 302
Bran Muffins with Honey Butter, Santa Fe,
        201
Breads:
    Buttermilk Biscuits, 297
    Cheddar-Dill Scones with Honey Mustard
        Butter, 27
    Double-Corn Muffins with Sour Cream and
        Chives, 178
    Focaccia, 32
    Garlic Pizza Crisps, 41
    Grill-Warmed Tortillas with Garlic Butter,
        243
    Herbed Sourdough Toast, 285
    Parmesan Planks, 43
    Pepper-Onion Frankfurter Rolls, 257
    Santa Fe Bran Muffins with Honey Butter,
        201
    Sprouted Wheat Berry and Walnut, 189
    Walnut Whole-Wheat, 148
Breakfast and brunch dishes, *see* Main
        dishes, breakfast or brunch; Muffins
Brine-Cured Breast of Duck on Bed of Cab-
        bage, Apples, and Leeks, 146
Broccoli, Pasta, and Chickpea Salad with
        Sun-Dried Tomatoes, 32
Brownies, Raspberry, 88
Bruschetta, Tomato, 265
Burritos with Avocado and Tomato, Breakfast,
        199
Buttermilk Biscuits, 297
Butters:
    Caper-Mustard, 293
    Garlic, 243
    Honey, 202
    Honey Mustard, 28
    Smoked-Salmon—Dill, 311

Cabbage:
    Beer-Braised Sauerkraut with Caraway
        Seeds, 261
    Old Bay Slaw, 69
    Sauté, 146
    Stuffed, Casseroles, Le Petit Robert's, 272
    Tarragon Mustard Slaw, 55
Caesar Dressing, 49
Cajun Catsup, 155

Cake(s) (savory):
    Crab, Sandwiches, 68
    Grits, Country Ham, and Sweet Pepper,
        with Poached Eggs, 205
Cakes (dessert):
    Apple, Cranberry, and Sour Cream, with
        Black Walnuts, 56
    Bourbon Fruitcakes, 269
    Kitchen-Counter Blackberry Corn-Muffin,
        109
    Kitchen-Counter Carrot, with Cream
        Cheese Icing, 254
    Lemon-Glazed Bourbon Black-Walnut, 196
    Marmalade Gingerbread, 149
    Orange-Glazed Raspberry Loaf, 237
California Club Sandwiches, 48
Calzones, Spicy Sausage, Pepper, and Black
        Bean, 58
Campfire Trout with Hazelnut Sauce, 215
Caper-Mustard Butter, 293
Cappuccino Coolers, 171
Caramel:
    Crème Café, 143
    Oranges in Tequila Liqueur, 50
Carrot(s):
    Baby, New Potatoes, and Sugar Snap Peas
        with Mint, Creamed, 298
    Cake with Cream Cheese Icing, Kitchen-
        Counter, 254
    and Lentil Gratin, 135
    and Potato Gratin, 141
    and Potato Pancakes, 216
Catsup, Cajun, 155
Caviar, in Eggs and Eggs in Crisp Potato
        Skins, 211
Cheddar-Dill Scones with Honey Mustard
        Butter, 27
Cheese course, 150–51
Cherry-Almond Granola, 287
Chewy Granola Thins, 286
Chicken(s):
    Basil Buttermilk Fried, 104
    Clay-Baker Tarragon, with Potatoes and
        Carrots, 162
    Dijon Ragout of Vegetables and, 119
    Hash, Sherried, 194
    Pamela Morgan's Grill-Smoked, 234
    Roasted, with Basil-Garlic Sauce, 140
    Salad, Green Goddess, 284
    Stock, 90
    Tomato, and Arugula Sandwiches, 291
    Warm Barbecued, Salad, 229
Chicken Liver Spread, 125
Chickpea, Pasta, and Broccoli Salad with
        Sun-Dried Tomatoes, 32
Chili, Stadium, 259
Chipotle Vinaigrette, 305

Chocolate:
  -Dipped Chocolate Malted Ice Cream
    Cones, 262
  Malted Ice Cream, 263
  Raspberry Brownies, 88
  Shortbreads, Mexican, 245
  Walnut Fudge, Adrienne Welch's, 136
  Walnut Steamed Pudding, 122
Chopped Romaine and Spinach Salad with
    Caesar Dressing, 49
Chowder, Jasper White's Lobster and Corn,
    26
Chutney, End-of-Summer, 246
Cider:
  Doughnuts with Maple-Cream Icing, 191
  Rum-Spiced, 184
Cilantro Vinaigrette, 242
Clams, in Mixed Grill of Shellfish, 240
Clay-Baker Tarragon Chicken with Potatoes
    and Carrots, 162
Club Sandwiches, California, 48
Coeurs à la Crème with Mango Sauce and
    Strawberries, 78
Coffee, 173–74
  Cappuccino Coolers, 171
  Crème Café Caramel, 143
Cognac-and-Wine-Poached Dried Fruit Com-
    pote, 43
Cohen, Gerry, 51
Compotes:
  Amaretto-and-Wine-Poached Dried Fruit,
    43
  Apple, Orange, and Cranberry, 207
  Strawberry, Pineapple, and Mango, 220
Condiments:
  Aunt Adrienne's Concord Grape Jelly, 182
  Blackberry-Basil Vinegar, 238
  Crème Fraîche, 217
  End-of-Summer Chutney, 246
  Gerry Cohen's Horseradish Mustard, 51
  Savory Oil, 232
  Spiced Cranberry Jam, 203
  Vanilla Rum, 66
  see also Butters; Dessert sauces; Salad
    dressings; Sauces; Vinaigrettes
Confetti Deviled Eggs, 103
Cookies:
  Chewy Granola Thins, 286
  Hazelnut Biscotti, 44
  Mexican Chocolate Shortbreads, 245
  Orange-Cornmeal Butter, 97
Cook's sources, 317–22
Cool-as-a-Cucumber, Potato, and Mint Soup,
    290
Corn:
  Barley, and Bacon Casserole, 235
  Black Bean, Tomato, and Poblano Chile

Salad, 242
Double-, Muffins with Sour Cream and
  Chives, 178
and Lobster Chowder, Jasper White's, 26
Muffin Cake, Kitchen-Counter Blackberry,
  109
Summer Spaghetti "alla Carbonara," 21
Zucchini, and Roasted Sweet Pepper Salad,
  Curried, 105
Cornmeal:
  Apple Scrapple, 184
  Orange Butter Cookies, 97
  Polenta, 252
Country Pâté and Lentil Salad with Basil
    Dressing, 303
Crab(s):
  Cake Sandwiches, 68
  Mayonnaise, Asparagus with, 296
  and-Prosciutto-Stuffed Mushrooms, 249
  Sautéed Softshell, with Pecans, 153
Cranberry:
  Apple, and Orange Compote, 207
  Apple Pie, Deep-Dish, 273
  Apple, and Sour Cream Cake with Black
    Walnuts, 56
  Jam, Spiced, 203
  and Pear Trifle, Gingered, 120
Cream Cheese Icing, 255
Creamed:
  Baby Carrots, New Potatoes, and Sugar
    Snap Peas with Mint, 298
  Fiddlehead Ferns and Mushrooms on Toast,
    161
Crème Anglaise, 268
Crème Café Caramel, 143
Crème Fraîche, 217
Crostini with Two Spreads, Florence Fabri-
    cant's, 125
Crusts, 107, 274
  Deep Tart, 252
  Pecan, 128
Cucumber(s):
  Cool-as-a-, Potato, and Mint Soup, 290
  Salad with Beets, Feta, Dill and, 112
Cumin seeds, toasting, 63
Curried Corn, Zucchini, and Roasted Sweet
    Pepper Salad, 105
Curry powders, 106
Custard(s):
  Crème Café Caramel, 143
  Sauce, 120

Desserts:
  Adrienne Welch's Chocolate-Walnut
    Fudge, 136
  Amaretto-and-Wine-Poached Dried Fruit
    Compote, 43

Desserts (*cont.*)

Caramel Oranges in Tequila Liqueur, 50

Christopher Styler's Tiramisù, 267

Coeurs à la Crème with Mango Sauce and Strawberries, 78

Crème Café Caramel, 143

Fresh Figs with Lemon Mascarpone and Raspberry Sauce, 34

Gingered Pear and Cranberry Trifle, 120

Raspberry Brownies, 88

Raspberry Brown-Rice Pudding, 224

Raspberry Key-Lime Squares, 69

Red, White, and Blueberries, 231

Red Fruit Sorbet, 244

Steamed Chocolate-Walnut Pudding, 122

Strawberry-Rhubarb Crumble, 299

see also Cakes; Cookies; Ice Cream; Pies; Tarts

Dessert sauces:

Blackberry, 96

Blueberry-Lime, 22

Custard, 120

Lemon Glaze, 196

Mango, 79

Raspberry, 34

Dijon Ragout of Chicken and Vegetables, 119

Dill Dressing, 112

Double-Corn Muffins with Sour Cream and Chives, 178

Doughnuts, Cider, with Maple-Cream Icing, 191

Dressings, *see* Salad dressings; Vinaigrettes

Duck:

Brine-Cured Breast of, on Bed of Cabbage, Apples, and Leeks, 146

Grilled Honey-Thyme *Magret* of, with Peaches, 86

Eggplant, Moussaka with Zucchini, Potatoes and, 113

Eggs:

Asparagus, Bacon, and Ricotta Tart, 219

Breakfast Burritos with Avocado and Tomato, 199

Confetti Deviled, 103

and Eggs in Crisp Potato Skins, 211

Poached, 206

Rich Scrambled, 212

Scrambled with Toast, 186

Tomato and Farmstead Goat-Cheese Omelets, 176

Ekus, Lisa, 182

Endive with Toasted Hazelnuts and Roquefort, 117

End-of-Summer Chutney, 246

Fabricant, Florence, 125

Fiddlehead Ferns, Creamed Mushrooms and, on Toast, 161

Figs, Fresh, with Lemon Mascarpone and Raspberry Sauce, 34

Finn, Molly, 230

First courses, *see* Appetizers and first courses; Salads, first-course

Fish:

Campfire Trout with Hazelnut Sauce, 215

Grilled Swordfish Steaks with Mixed Tomato Salad, 312

Moist-baked Halibut with Smoked-Salmon—Dill Butter, 311

Poached Monkfish and Green Bean Salad with Green Aioli and Potato Croutons, 76

Sautéed Salmon with Asparagus, New Potatoes, and Minted Hollandaise Sauce, 222

Smoked Salmon Sandwiches with Caper-Mustard Butter, 293

Stock, 91

see also Shellfish

Five-Grain Porridge, 188

Flapjacks, Three-B, 181

Focaccia, 32

Sandwiches, 31

Fragrant Iced Tea, 294

Frankfurter Rolls, Pepper-Onion, 257

Freeling, Nicholas, 13

French dishes:

Carrot and Potato Gratin, 141

Crème Café Caramel, 143

Frisée and Bacon Salad with Mustard-Anchovy Dressing, 139

Le Petit Robert's Stuffed Cabbage Casseroles, 272

Mixed Mushrooms with Shallot Persillade, 142

Patricia Wells's Provençal Baked Tomatoes, 127

Roasted Chickens with Basil-Garlic Sauce, 140

Frisée and Bacon Salad with Mustard-Anchovy Dressing, 139

Fritters:

Country Ham, Sweet Potato, and Green Onion Beignets, 118

Pinto Bean, with Goat-Cheese Cream and Salsa, 200

Fromage Blanc, New England Cheesemaking Company's, 80

Fruitcakes, Bourbon, 269

Fudge, Adrienne Welch's Chocolate-Walnut, 136

Gardener's sources, 317–22

Garlic:

Butter, 243

Parslied Béchamel, 115

Peppers and Mushrooms with, 260

Pizza Crisps, 41

Sauce, Greek, 93

Vinaigrette, 60

Ginger(ed):

Pear and Cranberry Trifle, 120

Sesame Rack of Lamb, 134

Gingerbread, Marmalade, 149

Glazes:

Chocolate, 88

Lemon, 196

Orange, 109, 237

Sweet Mustard, 280

Goat Cheese:

Cream, Pinto Bean Fritters with Salsa and, 200

and Tomato Omelets, 176

Grain:

Five-, Porridge, 188

Lentil, and Mushroom Salad with Basil, 87

Granola:

Cherry-Almond, 287

Thins, Chewy, 286

Grape Jelly, Aunt Adrienne's Concord, 182

Gratins:

Carrot and Lentil, 135

Carrot and Potato, 141

Sausage, Mushroom, and Polenta, 276

Greek dishes:

Grilled Lemon-Herb Rabbit on Bed of Artichoke, Red Pepper, and Black Olive Pasta, 94

Moussaka with Zucchini, Eggplant, and Potatoes, 113

White Beans with Garlic Sauce and Mixed Green Salad, 93

Green Aioli, 77

Green Beans, Tiny, with Dill Vinaigrette, 177

Green Goddess:

Chicken Salad, 284

Mayonnaise, 284

Greens:

cleaning and storing, 23–24

see also Salads, first-course; Salads, side-dish

Green Sauce, 157

Grill(ed):

Honey-Thyme *Magret* of Duck with Peaches, 86

Lemon-Herb Rabbit on Bed of Artichoke, Red Pepper, and Black Olive Pasta, 94

Mixed Shellfish, 240

Swordfish Steaks with Mixed Tomato Salad, 312

Veal Chops Smothered with Tomato, Mint, and Watercress Salad, 315

Vegetable Salad with Mozzarella, 304

Grilling, 99–101

Grill-Warmed Tortillas with Garlic Butter, 243

Grits, Country Ham, and Sweet Pepper Cakes with Poached Eggs, 205

Halberg, Franz, 16

Halibut, Moist-Baked, with Smoked-Salmon—Dill Butter, 311

Ham:

Pear, and Watercress Sandwiches with Horseradish Mayonnaise, 53

and Pork Loaf, Millie's Sweet-Mustard—Glazed, 279

see also Prosciutto

Ham, country, 165–66

Grits, and Sweet Pepper Cakes with Poached Eggs, 205

Madeira-Glazed, 297

Sweet Potato, and Green Onion Beignets, 118

Hash, Sherried Chicken, 194

Hazelnut(s):

Biscotti, 44

Toasted, Endive with Roquefort and, 117

Herbed:

Oven-Roast of Italian Sausages, Potatoes, Sweet Peppers, and Garlic, 266

Sourdough Toast, 285

Turkey Sausage Cakes, 180

Hollandaise Sauce, Minted, 223

Honey:

Butter, 202

Mustard Butter, 28

Mustard Dressing, 37

Oat Waffles with Raspberries and Ricotta, 171

Orange Adobo, 241

Honstein, Michael, 62

Horseradish Mustard, Gerry Cohen's, 51

Hot Dogs, Ball-Park, 257

Ice Cream:

Bourbon Brown-Sugar, 282

Chocolate Malted, 263

Cones, Chocolate-Dipped Chocolate Malted, 262

and Peaches with Blueberry-Lime Sauce, 22

Sundaes, Texas Legend, 64

Vanilla Rose, with Blackberry Sauce, 96

Icing:

Cream Cheese, 255

Maple-Cream, 191

Italian dishes:

Christopher Styler's Tiramisù, 267

Florence Fabricant's Crostini with Two Spreads, 125

Italian dishes (cont.)
  Focaccia, 32
  Focaccia Sandwiches, 31
  Hazelnut Biscotti, 44
  Herbed Oven-Roast of Sausages, Potatoes,
    Sweet Peppers, and Garlic, 266
  Nick Malgieri's Mascarpone, 35
  Risotto with Asparagus, Porcini, and Basil,
    73
  Spicy Sausage, Pepper, and Black Bean
    Calzones, 58
  Tomato Bruschetta, 265
  see also Pasta

Jam, Spiced Cranberry, 203
Jelly, Aunt Adrienne's Concord Grape, 182

Kerr, Park, 232
Kir Royale, 222

LaGasse, Emeril, 205
Lamb:
  Ginger-Sesame Rack of, 134
  Moussaka with Zucchini, Eggplant, and
    Potatoes, 113
  Roast Leg of, with Caramelized Shallots,
    158
  Steaks, Pan-Grilled, with Sun-Dried
    Tomato and Green Olive Butter, 316
Lemon:
  Bloody Marys, 211
  Glaze, 196
  Mayonnaise, 292
  Pie, Shaker, 28
  Strawberry Tart, 163
  Vodka, 213
Lentil:
  and Carrot Gratin, 135
  and Country Pâté Salad with Basil Dress-
    ing, 303
  Grain, and Mushroom Salad with Basil, 87
Le Petit Robert's Stuffed Cabbage Casseroles,
  272
Lime:
  Blueberry Sauce, Peaches and Ice Cream
    with, 22
  Key-, Raspberry Squares, 69
Limeade Plus!, Fresh, 64
Linguine Puttanesca, 309
Lobster:
  and Corn Chowder, Jasper White's, 26
  Mixed Grill of Shellfish, 240

Madeira-Glazed Country Ham, 297
Main dishes, breakfast or brunch:
  Apple Scrapple, 184
  Asparagus, Bacon, and Ricotta Tart, 219
  Burritos with Avocado and Tomato, 199

Campfire Trout with Hazelnut Sauce, 215
  Crab Cake Sandwiches, 68
  Eggs and Eggs in Crisp Potato Skins, 211
  Eggs Scrambled with Toast, 186
  Five-Grain Porridge, 188
  Grits, Country Ham, and Sweet Pepper
    Cakes with Poached Eggs, 205
  Herbed Turkey Sausage Cakes, 180
  Honey-Oat Waffles with Raspberries and
    Ricotta, 171
  Maple-Walnut Sticky Buns, 208
  Pinto Bean Fritters with Goat-Cheese
    Cream and Salsa, 200
  Rich Scrambled Eggs, 212
  Sautéed Salmon with Asparagus, New Pota-
    toes, and Minted Hollandaise Sauce, 222
  Sherried Chicken Hash, 194
  Three-B Flapjacks, 181
  Tomato and Farmstead Goat-Cheese Ome-
    lets, 176
Main dishes, for company dinner:
  Basil Buttermilk Fried Chicken, 104
  Brine-Cured Breast of Duck on Bed of
    Cabbage, Apples, and Leeks, 146
  Clay-Baker Tarragon Chicken with Potatoes
    and Carrots, 162
  Dijon Ragout of Chicken and Vegetables,
    119
  Ginger-Sesame Rack of Lamb, 134
  Grilled Honey-Thyme Magret of Duck with
    Peaches, 86
  Grilled Lemon-Herb Rabbit on Bed of Arti-
    choke, Red Pepper, and Black Olive
    Pasta, 94
  Moussaka with Zucchini, Eggplant, and
    Potatoes, 113
  Roasted Chickens with Basil-Garlic Sauce,
    140
  Roast Leg of Lamb with Caramelized Shal-
    lots, 158
  Roast Pork Loin with Madeira Mushroom
    Gravy, 126
  Sautéed Softshell Crabs with Pecans, 153
Main dishes, lunch or supper:
  Ball-Park Hot Dogs, 257
  Braised Chile Beef Tacos with Corn and
    Olives, 62
  Grilled Swordfish Steaks with Mixed To-
    mato Salad, 312
  Grilled Veal Chops Smothered with To-
    mato, Mint, and Watercress Salad, 315
  Herbed Oven-Roast of Italian Sausages, Po-
    tatoes, Sweet Peppers, and Garlic, 266
  Jasper White's Lobster and Corn Chowder,
    26
  Le Petit Robert's Stuffed Cabbage Casser-
    oles, 272
  Madeira-Glazed Country Ham, 297

Millie's Sweet-Mustard—Glazed Pork and Ham Loaf, 279
Mixed Grill of Shellfish, 240
Pamela Morgan's Grill-Smoked Chicken, 234
Pan-Grilled Lamb Steaks with Sun-Dried Tomato and Green Olive Butter, 316
Pasta and White Bean Soup with Sun-Dried Tomatoes, 40
Pork Chops with Peppery Bourbon-Maple Pan Gravy, 314
Pork Scaloppine with Rosemary, Lemon, and Olives, 313
Risotto with Asparagus, Porcini, and Basil, 73
Sausage, Mushroom, and Polenta Gratin, 276
Sautéed Salmon with Asparagus, New Potatoes, and Minted Hollandaise Sauce, 222
Spicy Sausage, Pepper, and Black Bean Calzones, 58
Veal Shanks Braised in Red Wine with Garlic and Orange, 250
see also Pasta; Salads, main-dish; Sandwiches
Malgieri, Nick, 35
Mango:
  Sauce, 79
  Strawberry, and Pineapple Compote, 220
Maple:
  Cream Icing, 191
  Walnut Sticky Buns, 208
Marmalade Gingerbread, 149
Mascarpone:
  Lemon, Fresh Figs with Raspberry Sauce and, 34
  Nick Malgieri's, 35
Mashed Sweets, 128
Mayonnaise:
  Crab, Asparagus with, 296
  Green Aioli, 77
  Green Goddess, 284
  Lemony, 292
Mexican dishes:
  Chocolate Shortbreads, 245
  see also Southwestern dishes
Minted Hollandaise Sauce, 223
Mirepoix, 272
Monkfish, Poached, and Green Bean Salad with Green Aioli and Potato Croutons, 76
Morgan, Pamela, 233, 234, 235, 236
Moussaka with Zucchini, Eggplant, and Potatoes, 113
Mozzarella, Grilled Vegetable Salad with, 304
Muffins:
  Double-Corn, with Sour Cream and Chives, 178

Santa Fe Bran, with Honey Butter, 201
Mushroom(s):
  Crab-and-Prosciutto-Stuffed, 249
  Creamed Fiddlehead Ferns and, on Toast, 161
  Garlicky Peppers and, 260
  Lentil, and Grain Salad with Basil, 87
  Mixed, with Shallot Persillade, 142
  Orecchiette with Gorgonzola, Watercress, Walnuts and, 307
  Sausage, and Polenta Gratin, 276
Mustard:
  Caper Butter, 293
  Glaze, Sweet, 280
  Honey Butter, 28
  Honey Dressing, 37
  Horseradish, Gerry Cohen's, 51

New England Cheesemaking Company's Fromage Blanc, 80

Oat-Honey Waffles with Raspberries and Ricotta, 171
Oil, Savory, 232
Old Bay Slaw, 69
Olive(s):
  Black, Cream, 85
  Black, with Orange and Basil, 73
  Orecchiette Baked with Vegetables, Mozzarella and, 306
Omelets, Tomato and Farmstead Goat-Cheese, 176
Orange(s):
  Apple, and Cranberry Compote, 207
  Caramel, in Tequila Liqueur, 50
  Cornmeal Butter Cookies, 97
  -Glazed Raspberry Loaf Cake, 237
  Honey Adobo, 241
Orecchiette:
  Baked with Olives, Vegetables, and Mozzarella, 306
  with Mushrooms, Gorgonzola, Watercress, and Walnuts, 307

Pancakes:
  Carrot and Potato, 216
  Three-B Flapjacks, 181
Parmesan Planks, 43
Parsley:
  Garlic Béchamel, 115
  Green Aioli, 77
  Green Sauce, 157
Pasta:
  Artichoke, Red Pepper, and Black Olive, Grilled Lemon-Herb Rabbit on Bed of, 94
  Bow Ties with Sausage, Tomatoes, and Cream, 302

Pasta (*cont.*)
Chickpea, and Broccoli Salad with Sun-
Dried Tomatoes, 32
Deep-Fried Ravioli with Red Pepper May-
onnaise, 111
Linguine Puttanesca, 309
Orecchiette Baked with Olives, Vegetables,
and Mozzarella, 306
Orecchiette with Mushrooms, Gorgonzola,
Watercress, and Walnuts, 307
Spaghettini with Seafood, Sun-Dried Toma-
toes, and Lemon, 310
Summer Spaghetti "alla Carbonara," 21
Tortellini with Peas and Prosciutto, 308
and White Bean Soup with Sun-Dried To-
matoes, 40
Pâté, Country, and Lentil Salad with Basil
Dressing, 303
Peach(es):
and Blush Tomato Tart, 252
and Ice Cream with Blueberry-Lime Sauce,
22
Pear(s):
and Cranberry Trifle, Gingered, 120
Pie, Peppered, 281
Prosciutto-Wrapped, Green Salad with *Boc-
concini* and, 40
Peas:
Tortellini with Prosciutto and, 308
see also Sugar Snap Pea(s)
Pecan Butter-Rum Tart, 128
Pepper(s):
Garlicky Mushrooms and, 260
Onion Frankfurter Rolls, 257
Red, Spread, 125
Roasted Sweet, Corn, and Zucchini Salad,
Curried, 105
Peppered:
Curly Fries, 154
Pear Pie, 281
Periyali (New York), 93
Pies:
Berry Picker's, à la Mode, 107
Deep-Dish Cranberry Apple, 273
Peppered Pear, 281
Shaker Lemon, 28
Pineapple, Strawberry, and Mango Compote, 220
Pinto Bean Fritters with Goat-Cheese Cream
and Salsa, 200
Pizza Crisps, Garlic, 41
Plums, in End-of-Summer Chutney, 246
Poached:
Eggs, 206
Monkfish and Green Bean Salad with Green
Aioli and Potato Croutons, 76
Polenta, 252
with the Last of the Basil, 251
Sausage, and Mushroom Gratin, 276

Pork:
Chops with Peppery Bourbon-Maple Pan
Gravy, 314
and Ham Loaf, Millie's Sweet-Mustard—
Glazed, 279
Le Petit Robert's Stuffed Cabbage Casser-
oles, 272
Loin, Roast, with Madeira Mushroom
Gravy, 126
Scaloppine with Rosemary, Lemon, and
Olives, 313
Spareribs with Honey-Orange Adobo,
241
see also Ham; Prosciutto; Sausage(s)
Porridge, Five-Grain, 188
Potato(es):
and Carrot Gratin, 141
and Carrot Pancakes, 216
Cool-as-a-Cucumber, and Mint Soup, 290
New, Baby Carrots, and Sugar Snap Peas
with Mint, Creamed, 298
New, Salad with Bacon and Mustard Seeds,
106
Peppered Curly Fries, 154
Skins, Eggs and Eggs in, 211
Tangy Mashed, Salad, 54
see also Sweet Potato(es)
Prosciutto:
Antipasto Platter, Al Forno-Style, 72
and-Crab-Stuffed Mushrooms, 249
Tortellini with Peas and, 308
-Wrapped Pears, Green Salad with *Boccon-
cini* and, 40
Provençal Baked Tomatoes, Patricia Wells's,
127
Puddings:
Coeurs à la Crème with Mango Sauce and
Strawberries, 78
Raspberry Brown-Rice, 224
Steamed Chocolate-Walnut, 122

Rabbit, Grilled Lemon-Herb, on Bed of Arti-
choke, Red Pepper, and Black Olive
Pasta, 94
Ragout of Chicken and Vegetables, Dijon,
119
Rainbow Tomato Salad with Caesar Dressing,
236
Raspberry(ies):
Brownies, 88
Brown-Rice Pudding, 224
Key-Lime Squares, 69
Loaf Cake, Orange-Glazed, 237
Red, White, and Blueberries, 231
Sauce, 34
Ravioli, Deep-Fried, with Red Pepper May-
onnaise, 111
Red, White, and Blueberries, 231

Red Fruit Sorbet, 244
Rhubarb-Strawberry Crumble, 299
Rice:
    Brown, and Raspberry Pudding, 224
    Risotto with Asparagus, Porcini, and Basil, 73
Roast:
    Chickens with Basil-Garlic Sauce, 140
    Ginger-Sesame Rack of Lamb, 134
    Leg of Lamb with Caramelized Shallots, 158
    Pork Loin with Madeira Mushroom Gravy, 126
Romaine:
    Spears with Garlic Vinaigrette, 60
    and Spinach Salad with Caesar Dressing, Chopped, 49
Roquefort, Endive with Toasted Hazelnuts and, 117
Rose Vanilla Ice Cream with Blackberry Sauce, 96
Rum:
    -Spiced Cider, 184
    Vanilla, 66

Salad dressings, 24
    Caesar, 49
    Dill, 112
    Green Goddess Mayonnaise, 284
    Honey-Mustard, 37
    see also Vinaigrettes
Salads, first-course:
    with Beets, Cucumbers, Feta, and Dill, 112
    Endive with Toasted Hazelnuts and Roquefort, 117
    Frisée and Bacon, with Mustard-Anchovy Dressing, 139
    Green, with Prosciutto-Wrapped Pears and Bocconcini, 40
Salads, main-dish:
    Country Pâté and Lentil, with Basil Dressing, 303
    Green Goddess Chicken, 284
    Grilled Vegetable, with Mozzarella, 304
    Poached Monkfish and Green Bean, with Green Aioli and Potato Croutons, 76
    Smoked Turkey, Brussels Sprouts, and Potato, with Honey-Mustard Dressing, 37
    Warm Barbecued Chicken, 229
Salads, side-dish:
    Black Bean, Corn, Tomato, and Poblano Chile, 242
    of Black-eyed Peas with Cilantro-Orange Dressing, 63
    Chopped Romaine and Spinach, with Caesar Dressing, 49

Curried Corn, Zucchini, and Roasted Sweet Pepper, 105
Lentil, Grain, and Mushroom, with Basil, 87
Mixed Tomato, 312
New Potato, with Bacon and Mustard Seeds, 106
Old Bay Slaw, 69
Pasta, Chickpea, and Broccoli, with Sun-Dried Tomatoes, 32
Rainbow Tomato, with Caesar Dressing, 236
Romaine Spears with Garlic Vinaigrette, 60
Succotash in Basil Vinaigrette, 230
Tangy Mashed Potato, 54
Tarragon Mustard Slaw, 55
Tomato, Sugar Snap Pea, and Watercress, 195
White Beans with Greek Garlic Sauce and Mixed Greens, 93
Salmon:
    Sautéed, with Asparagus, New Potatoes, and Minted Hollandaise Sauce, 222
    Smoked, Dill Butter, 311
    Smoked, Sandwiches with Caper-Mustard Butter, 293
Sandwiches:
    Ball-Park Hot Dogs, 257
    California Club, 48
    Chicken, Tomato, and Arugula, 291
    Crab Cake, 68
    Focaccia, 31
    Ham, Pear, and Watercress, with Horse-radish Mayonnaise, 53
    Smoked Salmon, with Caper-Mustard Butter, 293
Santa Fe Bran Muffins with Honey Butter, 201
Sauces:
    Black Olive Cream, 85
    Cajun Catsup, 155
    Greek Garlic, 93
    Green, 157
    Green Aioli, 77
    Honey-Orange Adobo, 241
    Lemony Mayonnaise, 292
    Minted Hollandaise, 223
    Parslied Garlic Béchamel, 115
    Velouté, 195
    see also Butters; Dessert sauces; Glazes; Salad dressings; Vinaigrettes
Sauerkraut, Beer-Braised, with Caraway Seeds, 261
Sausage(s):
    Apple Scrapple, 184
    Herbed Turkey, Cakes, 180
    Italian, Herbed Oven-Roast of Potatoes, Sweet Peppers, Garlic and, 266

INDEX

•

332

Sausage(s) (*cont.*)
  Mushroom, and Polenta Gratin, 276
  Spicy, Pepper, and Black Bean Calzones, 58
Savory Oil, 232
Scallops, in Mixed Seafood Fry with Green Aioli, 133
Scicolone, Michele, 46
Scones, Cheddar-Dill, with Honey Mustard Butter, 27
Scrapple, Apple, 184
Seafood, *see* Shellfish
Shaker Lemon Pie, 28
Shellfish:
  Jasper White's Lobster and Corn Chowder, 26
  Mixed Grill of, 240
  Mixed Seafood Fry with Green Aioli, 133
  Shrimp, Leek, and Dill Spread, 289
  see also Crab(s)
Sherried Chicken Hash, 194
Shortbreads, Mexican Chocolate, 245
Shrimp:
  Leek, and Dill Spread, 289
  Mixed Grill of Shellfish, 240
  Mixed Seafood Fry with Green Aioli, 133
Side dishes:
  Beer-Braised Sauerkraut with Caraway Seeds, 261
  Buttered Sugar Snap Peas, 280
  Carrot and Lentil Gratin, 135
  Carrot and Potato Gratin, 141
  Carrot and Potato Pancakes, 216
  Corn, Barley, and Bacon Casserole, 235
  Creamed Baby Carrots, New Potatoes, and Sugar Snap Peas with Mint, 298
  Garlicky Peppers and Mushrooms, 260
  Garlic Pizza Crisps, 41
  Mashed Sweets, 128
  Mixed Mushrooms with Shallot Persillade, 142
  Patricia Wells's Provençal Baked Tomatoes, 127
  Peppered Curly Fries, 154
  Polenta with the Last of the Basil, 251
  Sorrel and White Bean Purée, 159
  Tiny Green Beans with Dill Vinaigrette, 177
  see also Salads, side-dish
Slaws:
  Old Bay, 69
  Tarragon Mustard, 55
Smoked-Salmon—Dill Butter, 311
Smoked Turkey:
  Applewood-, Breast, 38
  Brussels Sprouts, and Potato Salad with Honey-Mustard Dressing, 37

Snacks:
  Cherry-Almond Granola, 287
  Cider Doughnuts with Maple-Cream Icing, 191
  see also Desserts
Sorbet, Red Fruit, 244
Sorrel and White Bean Purée, 159
Soups:
  Chilled Yellow Tomato, with Black Olive Cream, 85
  Cool-as-a-Cucumber, Potato, and Mint, 290
  Jasper White's Lobster and Corn Chowder, 26
  Pasta and White Bean, with Sun-Dried Tomatoes, 40
Sourdough Toast, Herbed, 285
Southwestern dishes:
  Baja Breezes, 199
  Black Bean, Corn, Tomato, and Poblano Chile Salad, 242
  Braised Chile Beef Tacos with Corn and Olives, 62
  Breakfast Burritos with Avocado and Tomato, 199
  Grill-Warmed Tortillas with Garlic Butter, 243
  Honey-Orange Adobo, 241
  Mixed Grill of Shellfish, 240
  Pinto Bean Fritters with Goat-Cheese Cream and Salsa, 200
  Santa Fe Bran Muffins with Honey Butter, 201
Spaghetti "alla Carbonara," Summer, 21
Spaghettini with Seafood, Sun-Dried Tomatoes and Lemon, 310
Spareribs with Honey-Orange Adobo, 241
Spiced Cranberry Jam, 203
Spinach and Romaine Salad with Caesar Dressing, Chopped, 49
Spreads:
  Chicken Liver, 125
  Red Pepper, 125
  Shrimp, Leek, and Dill, 289
Sprouted Wheat Berry and Walnut Bread, 189
Squid, in Mixed Seafood Fry with Green Aioli, 133
Stadium Chili, 259
Steamed Chocolate-Walnut Pudding, 122
Sticky Buns, Maple-Walnut, 208
Stocks:
  Chicken, 90
  Fish, 91
Strawberry:
  Lemon Tart, 163
  Pineapple, and Mango Compote, 220
  Rhubarb Crumble, 299

Streusel Topping, 252
Styler, Christopher, 267
Succotash in Basil Vinaigrette, 230
Sugar Snap Pea(s):
    Baby Carrots, and New Potatoes with Mint,
        Creamed, 298
    Buttered, 280
    Tomato, and Watercress Salad, 195
Summer Spaghetti "alla Carbonara," 21
Sundaes, Texas Legend Ice Cream, 64
Sweet Mustard Glaze, 280
Sweet Potato(es):
    Country Ham, and Green Onion Beignets,
        118
    Mashed, 128
Swordfish Steaks, Grilled, with Mixed Tomato
    Salad, 312

Tacos, Braised Chile Beef, with Corn and
    Olives, 62
Tangy Mashed Potato Salad, 54
Tarragon Mustard Slaw, 55
Tart (savory), Asparagus, Bacon, and Ricotta,
    219
Tarts (dessert):
    Peach and Blush Tomato, 252
    Pecan Butter-Rum, 128
    Strawberry-Lemon, 163
Tart Shell, 163
    see also Crusts
Tea, Fragrant Iced, 294
Tequila:
    Fresh Limeade Plus!, 64
    Liqueur, Caramel Oranges in, 50
Texas Legend Ice Cream Sundaes, 64
Thorne, John, 230
Three-B Flapjacks, 181
Tiramisù, Christopher Styler's, 267
Toast(s):
    Florence Fabricant's Crostini with Two
        Spreads, 125
    Herbed Sourdough, 285
    Tomato Bruschetta, 265
Tomato(es):
    Blush, and Peach Tart, 252
    Bruschetta, 265
    Chilled Yellow, Soup with Black Olive
        Cream, 85
    End-of-Summer Chutney, 246
    and Farmstead Goat-Cheese Omelets, 176
    Michele Scicolone's Marinated Dried, 46
    Patricia Wells's Provençal Baked, 127
    Rainbow, Salad with Caesar Dressing, 236
    Salad, Mixed, 312
    Sugar Snap Pea, and Watercress Salad,
        195

Tortellini with Peas and Prosciutto, 308
Tortillas, Grill-Warmed, with Garlic Butter,
    243
Trifle, Gingered Pear and Cranberry, 120
Trout with Hazelnut Sauce, Campfire, 215
Turkey:
    Breast, Applewood-Smoked, 38
    California Club Sandwiches, 48
    Sausage Cakes, Herbed, 180
    Smoked, Brussels Sprouts, and Potato
        Salad with Honey-Mustard Dressing, 37
Tzolis, Steve, 93

Vanilla:
    Rose Ice Cream with Blackberry Sauce,
        96
    Rum, 66
Veal:
    Chops, Grilled, Smothered with Tomato,
        Mint, and Watercress Salad, 315
    Shanks Braised in Red Wine with Garlic
        and Orange, 250
Velouté Sauce, 195
Vinaigrettes, 24
    Barbecue, 229
    Chipotle, 305
    Cilantro, 242
    Garlic, 60
Vinegar, Blackberry-Basil, 238
Vodka, Lemon, 213

Waffles, Honey-Oat, with Raspberries and
    Ricotta, 171
Walnut Whole-Wheat Bread, 148
Watercress, Tomato, and Sugar Snap Pea
    Salad, 195
Welch, Adrienne, 136
Wells, Patricia, 127
Wheat Berry, Sprouted, and Walnut Bread,
    189
White, Jasper, 26
White Bean(s):
    with Greek Garlic Sauce and Mixed Green
        Salad, 93
    and Pasta Soup with Sun-Dried Tomatoes,
        40
    and Sorrel Purée, 159
Whole-Wheat Bread, Walnut, 148
Wine, 130–31
    -and-Amaretto-Poached Dried Fruit Com-
        pote, 43
    with cheese course, 151

Zucchini, Corn, and Roasted Sweet Pepper
    Salad, Curried, 105

ABOUT THE AUTHOR

MICHAEL MCLAUGHLIN, a Colorado native, moved to New York City twelve years ago, his goal to become a food writer. A year later he was employed at an Upper West Side gourmet shop called The Silver Palate. One year after that *The Silver Palate Cookbook*, on which he collaborated with the shop's owners, was published to wide acclaim.

In 1984, he opened a restaurant dedicated to one of his favorite foods, chili (he has since sold his interest to his partners). The restaurant, called the Manhattan Chili Co. and located in Greenwich Village, soon became Manhattan's premier purveyor of top-notch chili as well as other imaginative Southwest-accented fare. The restaurant inspired Michael's next book, *The Manhattan Chili Co. Southwest American Cookbook*.

Following these outstanding successes, Michael turned his attention to writing about food and cooking full time. He wrote *The Back of the Box Gourmet*, which was published in 1991, and is a regular contributor to *Food & Wine* and *Bon Appétit*, as well as other national publications. Michael is now hard at work on another cookbook.